W9-CUH-646

"BEST OF
LOTUS"

REPRINT SERIES

LOTUS
Magazine

THE GOOD IDEAS BOOK

.

Tips and Techniques for Mastering *1-2-3* and *Symphony*

by
the staff and readers
of *LOTUS Magazine*

Series Editor: Steven E. Miller
LOTUS PUBLISHING CORPORATION

ADDISON-WESLEY PUBLISHING COMPANY, INC.
Reading, Massachusetts ▲▼ Menlo Park, California
New York · Don Mills, Ontario · Wokingham, England · Amsterdam · Bonn
Sydney · Singapore · Tokyo · Madrid · San Juan

RESEARCH LIBRARY
THE ANDREW JERGENS COMPANY
2535 Spring Grove Avenue
Cincinnati, Ohio 45214

Library of Congress Cataloging-in-Publication Data

Lotus magazine, the good ideas book : tips and techniques for
    mastering 1-2-3 and Symphony / by the staff and readers of Lotus
    magazine.
        p. cm. — ("Best of Lotus" reprint series)
    Includes index.
    ISBN 0-201-15664-4
    1. Lotus 1-2-3 (Computer program) 2. Symphony (Computer program)
3. Macro instructions (Electronic computers) 4. Business—Data
processing. I. Lotus magazine.
HF5548.4.L67L73   1988
005.36'9—dc19   88-10586 CIP

While every reasonable precaution has been taken in the preparation of this book,
the author and the publishers assume no responsibility for errors or omissions, or
for the uses made of the material contained herein or the decisions based on such
use. No warranties are made, express or implied, with regard to the contents of this
work, its merchantability, or fitness for a particular purpose. Neither the author nor
the publishers shall be liable for direct, indirect, special, incidental, or consequential
damages arising out of the use of or inability to use the contents of this book.

Under the copyright laws, this book may not be copied, photocopied, reproduced,
translated, modified, or reduced to any electronic medium or machine-readable
form, in whole or in part, without the prior written consent of Lotus Publishing
Corporation.

© Copyright 1988 by Lotus Publishing Corporation, One Broadway, Cambridge,
MA, 02142. All rights reserved. Printed in the United States, published simultaneously in Canada. Material reprinted from *LOTUS* magazine is copyrighted 1985,
1986, 1987 by Lotus Publishing and used with permission.

Many of the designations used by manufacturers and sellers to distinguish their
products are claimed as trademarks. Where those designations appear in this book,
and the author or publisher was aware of a trademark claim, the designations have
been printed in initial caps or all caps. Lotus, 1-2-3, and Symphony are registered
trademarks of Lotus Development Corporation, Inc. IBM is a registered trademark of
International Business Machines, Inc.

Book design by Elizabeth Van de Kerkhove. Cover illustration by Paul Meisel.

ISBN 0-201-15664-4
BCDEFGHIJ-HA-898
Second Printing, July 1988

ACKNOWLEDGMENTS

This book would not be possible without the staff of *LOTUS* magazine: Carolyn L. Adams, Suki Adams, Claudia Basso, Mary Ellen Bittel, Lisa Boyd, Chris Brown, Paula Dempsey, Cynthia G. Fitzgerald, Deborah Flynn-Hanrahan, Elisabeth Folsom, Rich Friedman, Daniel Gasteiger, Linda J. Gill, Christopher J. Gowland, Phyliss L. Greenberg, William H. Gregory, Ruth Hawryluk, Kathy Heaton, Robert Hildebrand, Elizabeth Jensen, Sue Ellen Kelly, Katherine Koerner, Alice H. Mangum, Subhadra Mattai, Eleanor M. McCarthy, Janet H. Meacham, Nancy E. Miller, Steven E. Miller, Kathy Minnix, Mary Jean Mockler, Christopher Morgan, Jeanne Nisbet, Madonna O'Brien, James R. Pierce, Stacy M. Pierce, Carol Recchino, Richard W. Ridington Jr., Phyllis A. Sharon, Jennifer Smith, Jan Souza, Carrie Thomas, Julie E. Tuton, Regina L. Twiss, Jill Winitzer.

In particular, the following staff members and freelance people edited reader contributions and wrote the responses published in the Good Ideas columns: William Dodson, Bill Gibson, Robert Hildebrand, Mary Kuppens, Steven E. Miller, and Dick Ridington. All the Q&As have been handled by Carrie Thomas. The Lotus Development Product Support staff was, as always, an invaluable resource.

The technical editors for this book have been invaluable in ensuring the accuracy of the material presented. Thanks to Carrie Thomas, Cynthia G. Fitzgerald, Mark Louis Salami, Stacie Manning, Scott I. Love, Jerry Mazziotta, and Bonnie Hauser Steinroeder.

Our Addison-Wesley editors have been a pleasure to work with: Julie Stillman and Steve Stancel, as well as Maeve Cullinane in production.

Finally, we acknowledge the staff of the Lotus Development Graphic Services department: Helen Betz, Andy Hollinger, Bonnie McCoy, Jennifer Nadeau, Diane Nicolai, Henry Nigro, Judy Riessle, Carrie Sherwood, Andrea Soule, and Gail Sweeney.

CONTENTS

Welcome to the

"BEST OF
LOTUS"

The job of *LOTUS* magazine is to give you access to the experts. We solicit the best authors and trainers. We present articles and technical advice from the people at Lotus Development Corporation. And we provide a forum for all of you to talk to each other in your efforts to apply computer skills to solving everyday business problems.

Monthly magazines are typically treated as disposable. You get them in the mail, scan the table of contents, read a bit, then throw them out. That's what we expected to happen to *LOTUS* magazine. But we were wrong.

From the earliest issues you let us know that you were saving your back copies and filling in gaps in your collection. (For those of you still wishing to do this, we have limited numbers of back issues at $5 each. Mail your check, address, and list of desired issues to *LOTUS*, P.O. BOX 9160, Cambridge, MA 02139-9160.)

It became obvious that you were archiving *LOTUS* to use as a reference source and a training tool. But as the pile of old issues climbed higher and higher, you began having problems finding the specific articles you dimly remembered reading sometime ago. Our semiannual indexes helped, but that wasn't enough.

As a way to meet this need and to make our old material available to new subscribers, we are offering a reprint series in book form. It will include *LOTUS* articles from all of our back issues and will be organized around such focused themes as macros, good ideas, worksheet skills, and business applications.

Our reasons for publishing *LOTUS* magazine are the same now as when we started. We believe *1-2-3* and *Symphony* users need straightforward, practical instruction on how to get the most from their computers and their software. Our research tells us that *1-2-3* and *Symphony* users are part of a special group of people who are using computers not only to automate manual tasks but also to create new ways of doing business. These people aren't computer experts. They occupy all levels of their organizations and hold all kinds of titles. What unites them is their desire to use the computer as an efficient tool.

Our ongoing challenge is to invent a new kind of magazine, suitable for both beginners and experts, written in ordinary language, that starts from the software you use and works through to the solutions you need. We are inspired by the growing network of local user groups, in which people come together to share their knowledge, listen to news announcements, attend a featured presentation, break up into special interest groups, and enjoy one another's company.

LOTUS, we believe, has to act and feel like a "user group in print." There has to be lots of room for reader feedback and contributions. In order to keep in front of such a rapidly changing industry, we have to stay in constant contact with our readers through mail-in cards, telephone surveys, focus groups, questionnaires, and direct phone calls. As it has turned out, we get hundreds of letters from you each month, and a good percentage of the material in every issue of *LOTUS* starts as a reader contribution.

We also know that *LOTUS* has to look good. We use high-quality paper, solicit illustrations from the best artists, and make sure our layout is clean, clear, and worth looking at. We feel we can't ask people to pay for something that looks second rate.

Finally, *LOTUS* can't be a textbook or a specifications sheet. This is not a techie magazine. Our readers are busy people who need to get their jobs done. Everything we publish has to immediately help someone accomplish something. Because you are busy people, our articles have to be relatively short, our illustrations instructive, our models effective.

Since the first issue of *LOTUS* reached readers in May 1985, the magazine's list of paid subscribers has grown faster than that of any other magazine in the history of United States publishing. We're very proud of that fact, primarily because it says we've stayed in touch with you, and are continuing to serve your needs. While we don't expect that growth rate to continue, we do intend to remain as closely connected to our readership as possible as the magazine continues to evolve and grow.

LOTUS was just the first venture of Lotus Publishing Corporation. We have worked with other publishers to create international editions of the magazine, the first appearing in the United Kingdom. We've published a special insert about engineering and scientific computing, called ESC. We've created a catalog sales operation called Lotus Selects. This reprint series signals our entrance into book publishing.

But in all our efforts, we know we will succeed only if we maintain an interactive relationship with our readers. Please let us know what you think of this book series and of our other endeavors. Our address is Lotus Publishing Corporation, P.O. Box 9160, Cambridge, MA 02139-9160.

Steven E. Miller
Series Editor
Director of New Product Development
Lotus Publishing Corporation

Introduction to
THE GOOD IDEAS BOOK

Having trouble figuring something out on your computer? Want to know a better way of doing some task? The first step most of us would take in either situation is to ask a friend.

But if two heads are better than one, how much better must one million heads be? That is the number of people who read each monthly issue of *LOTUS*. In fact, counting the inevitable readership turnover, we estimate that several million additional people have read *LOTUS* magazine since its inception in May, 1985. It is this massive membership in our "users group in print" that forms the basis for this book of good ideas.

As we've all learned, there is no better teacher than experience. And the success of *LOTUS* has rested on its ability to serve as a voice for the millions of *1-2-3* and *Symphony* users who wish to share their hard-earned expertise with each other. As people work their way up the learning curve, and discover new methods of using the software to solve their everyday business problems, they share their excitement and insights with each other by sending letters to *LOTUS*. Technical and editorial experts on the *LOTUS* staff consolidate this inpouring of ideas. The result is the monthly Good Ideas and Q&A columns, which are among the most popular parts of the entire magazine.

To create this book we have picked out the best of the best. We have gone back through every issue since *LOTUS* began and selected the most useful, elegant, and effective reader contributions from the Good Ideas and Q&A columns. Whenever possible we have included the name of the person who originally contributed the idea. In those cases where similar ideas were contributed by more than one reader or *LOTUS* staff member, we credited only the contributor of one version of the idea.

This book is a treasure chest of information. You can search through its contents in several ways. If you're a real glutton for punishment, you can start at the front and read it straight through. If you're trying to solve a problem, you can use either the table of contents or the extensive index to find items that might be relevant. If you're looking just for good tips, it might be easiest to start by scanning the table of contents for topics of particular interest. You can even randomly flip through the book; it won't take many turns of the page before you find some gem that makes the whole effort worthwhile.

Almost all of the material in this book is applicable for all versions of *1-2-3* and *Symphony*. We have indicated if a particular item is of interest only to users of a particular release or product.

This book does not cover every skill, command, or application you can use with *1-2-3* and *Symphony*. There are many aspects of the programs that are self-evident or that users readily pick up from the documentation and from helpful friends. There is no need to waste your time by telling you what you already know. Instead, this book gives you solutions to the hard-to-solve problems. It provides tips on how you can make your computer work more productively.

We are excited about this book. We think it is a unique concentration of the collective knowledge of millions of Lotus users. But it is only one part of a continuing process. If you have new questions you need answered or additional good ideas you want to share, please keep those letters coming! Even ideas that seem obvious to you may be a lifesaver to someone else. Send your letters to either the Good Ideas Editor or the Q&A Editor at *LOTUS* Magazine, P.O. BOX 9123, Cambridge, MA 02139-9123. We look forward to continuing our relationship with you.

"BEST OF *LOTUS*"

REPRINT SERIES

1

DOS AND DIRECTORIES

DOS stands for Disk Operating System, but it coordinates the monitor, keyboard, memory, and other peripherals as well as the floppy and hard disks. Many people never see the A> or C> DOS prompt. They go directly into their application software. If asked, many of these people would say they are running under *1-2-3*, not under the operating system. Some people even refer to their computer as their "Lotus machine."

But most of us run across DOS at least once in a while, if only to format new disks or deal with error messages, so we need to understand the basic DOS commands and functions. DOS can be intimidating to new users. You have to know the commands and their syntax before you enter the characters. There are no Lotus-style menus to simplify your selection. And DOS doesn't give you sufficient or clear feedback. Some of the good ideas in this section help you customize the DOS prompt so it provides more meaningful information while other tips warn you how to avoid common DOS errors.

The bulk of the tips concern creating and managing subdirectories. Without subdirectories, your hard disk is like a huge box into which someone has dumped hundreds of unlabeled pieces of paper. Subdirectories are like file drawers, each intended to hold material dealing with related topics. In other words, you can imagine your hard disk as a huge file cabinet, which is divided into drawers, called directories or subdirectories, and then further divided into folders, called files.

While subdirectories form the structure of a well-organized hard disk, paths are the way of finding your way from one place to another. A path is the route the computer must take, starting at the top level, or root directory, such as C:, through the various layers of subdirectories in order to get to a specific file. For example, the full path to your 1988 budget file location might be C:\123\FINANCE\88BUDG. A familiarity with both subdirectories and paths is important for more productive computing.

1

DOS

CUSTOMIZE THE DOS PROMPT

If you have the MS-DOS A> or C> prompt visible on your screen, entering the command *prompt <string>* makes *string* the new prompt. For example, entering *prompt Hi there!* replaces A> or C> with *Hi there!* If the string includes a dollar sign followed by one of the following characters, you can include special information in the prompt:

CHARACTER	RESULT
d	the current date
p	the full path name of the current directory
n	the current drive
t	the current time
v	DOS version number
g	greater-than sign (>)
l	less-than sign (<)
b	split vertical bar (¦)
q	equal sign (=)
e	an escape character
h	a backspace
$	dollar sign

Jean Stein
Berkeley, California

Try including prompt pg *in your autoexecuting startup file. Knowing your current directory can prevent many potentially disastrous accidents.*

MORE CUSTOMIZED DOS PROMPTS

I wanted my DOS prompt to display a great deal of information initially, but I didn't want the prompt to take up a lot of screen space. Within the DOS prompt command, I included an instruction that first displays the desired information and then backspaces over the displayed characters. For example, with the DOS prompt visible on your screen, entering *prompt $t------$hhhhhhhhhpg* temporarily

2

displays the current time but ends up with just the current directory visible. Include about 10 blanks or dashes after the initial text to allow time to see the text before the $h commands erase it, and use enough $h commands to erase the extra spaces as well as the initial prompt.

Cort Allen
San Jose, California

The characters appear and then disappear a little too fast for our taste, but readers might like to experiment with this technique.

AVOIDING FORMAT COMMAND DISASTER

I mainly use the DOS FORMAT command to prepare new floppy disks. On my IBM PC XT, the command is in the root directory of my hard disk. The proper way to invoke the command is to enter *format a:*. This formats the floppy disk that is in the A drive. The risk is that if I or anyone else forgets to include the *a:* as part of the command, the command will format the current disk, which is C — my hard disk. If this happens, my entire hard disk will be erased and reformatted. This is the stuff nightmares are made of.

To avoid this potential problem, I wrote a batch file that ensures that what I am formatting is a floppy disk. First, in the root directory of my hard disk, I used the DOS RENAME command to change FORMAT.COM to KILLDISK.COM. Then I created a batch file by entering at the DOS prompt:

```
copy con: format.bat
killdisk a:
^z
```

Produce the ^z character by holding the Control key and pressing z, or if you are using an IBM PC, press the F6 function key.

To format a disk, I still enter *format* at the DOS prompt, but I no longer worry about the drive designation. The batch file performs the rest of the work safely and automatically.

Gail Smith
Lake Oswego, Oregon

THE CHKDSK COMMAND

Please explain the DOS CHKDSK command.

William Finsch
Fort Collins, Colo.

The DOS CHKDSK command analyzes a floppy disk's or hard disk's directories and associated File Allocation Table (FAT) and gives you a status report on the drive that you specified and on the computer's memory. It is an external DOS command, which means that you must access a disk containing the CHKDSK.COM file or change your current directory to the subdirectory that contains CHKDSK.COM.

Exit to DOS (or select /System in 1-2-3 Release 2/2.01, SERVICES DOS in Symphony*) and enter* chkdsk x: *(where x stands for the drive). If you have a hard disk, enter* chkdsk c:. *If you specify a file name or a group of file names (*chkdsk c:\test.wr1 *or* chkdsk c:*.wr1*), CHKDSK will display the number of noncontiguous areas occupied by the file or files. In addition, CHKDSK gives you the following types of information.*

10592256	*bytes total disk space*
221184	*bytes in 14 hidden files*
40960	*bytes in 9 directories*
9187328	*bytes in 506 user files*
12288	*bytes in bad sectors*
1130496	*bytes available on disk*
655360	*bytes total memory*
310816	*bytes free*

In this example, CHKDSK was run on a 10-megabyte hard disk (there are 1,024 bytes in one kilobyte, K, thus 10592256/1024 = 10 megabytes). There are 14 hidden files (some are DOS hidden files, others are 1-2-3 and Symphony *hidden files). There are nine subdirectories and 506 data files. Unfortunately this hard disk has a small portion of bad sectors (12288/1024, or 12K). Bad sectors are sectioned off by DOS so that you can't store information on them. There is 1104K (1130496 bytes) available on the disk to store more files. Finally, this computer has 640K of RAM (655360/1024), and out of that RAM this computer currently has almost half free for working (*Symphony *has been loaded and the DOS add-in has been attached and invoked).*

The CHKDSK command will show problems in the File Allocation Table (FAT). DOS tries to save files in contiguous blocks on disk. If it can't store a file in contiguous blocks, it stores parts of the file in different tracks and sectors of the disk (noncontiguous). The FAT keeps track of the location of each segment of each stored file. Sometimes the FAT loses track of part of a file. That's when you get the error message Part of file is missing *when you try to retrieve a file in 1-2-3 or* Symphony. *Badly fragmented files can cause slower retrieval times. You can determine the number of noncontiguous files by entering* chkdsk x:*.*, *where x is the drive name.*

CHKDSK will not automatically correct errors found in a directory of FAT. However, in the CHKDSK/F command the /F parameter attempts to fix any part of the file that the FAT has lost. If CHKDSK finds lost pieces of a file (allocation units) on the disk, it will ask if you want to recover the lost data into files. If you answer Yes and the /F parameter was used, CHKDSK recovers each chain of lost allocation units into a file named FILEnnnn.CHK (where nnnn *is a sequential number starting with 0000). These files are stored on the root directory of the drive you specified. You can then use the DOS TYPE command to look at the files. Some files may be salvageable, others won't. Note that you will get the same message if you do not specify /F — but the program will not attempt to recover the lost chains even if you answer Yes.*

DOS WARNING!

Assume you are in DOS with the DOS prompt visible on your screen, and you attempt to copy a file from disk X in drive A to disk Y in drive B. And assume you mistakenly place an important program disk in drive B when you enter *copy a:file.ext b:*. But you're lucky — you left the write-protect tab on disk Y, so DOS gives you the error message:

> Write protect error writing B:
> Abort, Retry, Ignore?

What should you do? If you're like most people, you'd just take out the valuable disk from drive B, substitute another data disk, and press either R, for Retry, or I, for Ignore. But if you did this, you'd be in trouble.

It turns out that one of the first things DOS does when you issue the COPY command is to read and store the file-name directory of the target disk. In fact, DOS does this even before checking to see if the target disk is write-protected. Thus, if you remove the write-protected disk, insert the second data disk, and select either Retry, or Ignore, the COPY command continues where it left off. The directory from the removed disk is then placed on the newly inserted disk, which makes all the files previously on the inserted disk inaccessible (unless you use the DOS RECOVER command or a program like the Norton Utilities).

The solution is to select Abort, then change disks and try again.

DON'T USE THESE FILE NAMES!

IBM slipped a note into the DOS 2.1 manual that is also relevant to users of other versions of DOS stating that users shouldn't create files with names that DOS reserves for various devices. These names include CON, AUX, COM1, COM2, LPT1, PRN, LPT2, LPT3, and NUL. By using these names you will produce, at best, an error message and, at worst, a system crash with data loss.

Ronald A. Friedman
Damonics Computer Systems
Elmira, N.Y.

If you use an asterisk or a question mark in a file name, you will also destroy files. When 1-2-3 or Symphony saves a file, it first erases any existing files that have the same file name. If you use the asterisk or question-mark wildcard characters, the program will erase all files that meet the very broad wildcard matching criterion.

PARITY CHECKS 1 AND 2

What does the term *Parity Check 2* mean?

Marian Ereaux
Zortman & Landusky Mining
Zortman, Mont.

Parity Check 1 *refers to a problem involving the motherboard, the memory board that comes with the computer.* Parity Check 2 *refers to a problem involving add-on memory boards.*

Most parity check error messages result from a problem with a memory chip. If this is the case, you can usually identify the chip or chips causing the problem by using either the Diagnostics or Advanced Diagnostics disk. However, parity check errors can also result from something other than a bad chip.

In the case of the IBM PC, IBM distributes memory chips that run at either 200. 250, or 300 nanoseconds, (the higher number of nanoseconds, the slower the chip). A problem arises when you run a 300-nanosecond chip at a speed of 200 or 250 nanoseconds. Doing this may result in a parity check error message, and you can't locate the problem by running Diagnostics or Advanced Diagnostics: You have to look at the chips. Each chip is marked with a number (2, 2.5, or 3) indicating speed.

A parity check error message can also indicate memory malfunction as a result of an improperly installed microprocessor chip. The chip may have a poor connection with one of the chip leads. This problem tends to occur when you move the computer, which may loosen a chip, and will not turn up when you run Diagnostics.

One final consideration: Static electricity can cause parity-check errors. This can occur when you've left your work area and, on returning, touched your keyboard. A surge of static electricity may travel from your hand to the keyboard. You can get mats and sprays to relieve this annoying problem.

2

Directories and Paths

DIRECTORIES, SUBDIRECTORIES, AND PATHS

Your manuals use the terms *directory, subdirectory,* and *path.* What are they?

Robert Schirmer
Mamaroneck, New York

Every time you save a worksheet, you create a file on your floppy or hard disk. Certain files might contain budget information, while others might be memos or business plans. Most disk operating systems allow you to create directories that are like file drawers containing files with similar types of information. Just as a file drawer can have subsections, directories can have subdirectories, which can then have their own subdirectories. A formatted disk comes with one top-level directory called the root directory. You create the subdirectories. Even though you can create subdirectories on a floppy disk, they are most commonly used with hard-disk machines.

A diagram of the pathway between multiple subdirectories often looks like an upside-down tree, with the root directory at the top and subdirectories branching down. The flow from root to first-level subdirectory to second-level subdirectory to file is called a path.

You can store Symphony, 1-2-3, other programs, worksheets, and other data files in subdirectories.

If you are using DOS and wish to create a subdirectory on your hard disk, you must first have the DOS C> prompt visible on your screen. Type the command md *(make directory), then type a space and the name of the directory, for example, type* md budgets. *The newly created directory is subordinate to the directory you were in when you issued the command. For example, if you are in a subdirectory called PERSONAL and make a new subdirectory called MEMOS, you can gain access to MEMOS only via PERSONAL.*

You can also create a new, top-level subdirectory accessible from the root directory by including a backslash before the directory name: md\budgets.

To move from one subdirectory to another, enter cd *(change directory), and then type a backslash followed by the full path to the desired directory, for example,* cd\person\memos. *If you enter* cd\ *without a path, you will return to the root directory.*

Symphony *and* 1-2-3 *Release* 2/2.01 *fully support all directory-related DOS commands. File Manager and Disk Manager, found in the* 1-2-3 *Release 1A Access system, operate only on files in the current directory — the DOS PATH command does not work.*

LISTING SUBDIRECTORIES

Using DOS 2.0 or higher, you can get a listing at DOS level of your subdirectories by typing:

dir *.

Be sure to type the period after the asterisk. This is quite useful if you have lots of subdirectories and can't remember their exact names.

John Wilson
Goodyear Tire & Rubber Co.
Akron, Ohio

This command causes DOS to list every file in the current directory whose name has no extension. DOS considers subdirectories to be files when listing them. Since directories usually don't have extensions — although they can — and files usually do, the command generally gives you an accurate listing of the subdirectories in the current dirctory. To see all of the subdirectories on your hard disk, use the DOS command TREE. Since TREE is an external DOS command, TREE.COM must be on DOS's search path when you execute the command.

LONG DOS DIRECTORIES

When I am in DOS and display the directories of many of my data disks, the lists are too long to fit on the screen at one time. Is there any way to stop the scrolling or otherwise fit all the file names on the screen at one time?

Peg Cheney
Melrose, Mass.

You can view all large-directory files in two ways: (1) You can type dir/p (for "page") at a DOS prompt to display one screen of file names with the number of bytes in the file and the date you created the file. After presenting each screen of file names, the display pauses, and the message Strike a key when ready... *appears. You can press any key to display the next screenful of information. (2) You can type dir/w (for "wide") at a DOS prompt to view the file names without the number of bytes and the date you created the file. The file names fill the screen in a five-column format that allows you to include many file names in a single screen.*

PRINTING A DISK DIRECTORY

I have been unable to find a way to print a directory of a disk. I have tried using the PrintScreen key, but it doesn't print the screen contents. Help!

Theresa A. Levinski
St. John, Raham, & Weidmayar
Ann Arbor, Mich.

On some computers, such as the IBM PC, you can produce a printout of the screen while in DOS by holding down the Shift key and pressing the PrintScreen key. Check your computer manuals to make sure you are using the right keys.

You can also try holding down the Control key and pressing P. Thereafter, until you press Control-P again, DOS will print everything that displays on the screen while you work. You can also direct output of the DOS DIR command to your printer. If your printer is connected to the port defined as LPT1:, enter dir>lpt1: at the DOS prompt.

If your printer is connected to your computer by way of a serial cable/port, the printer may not be able to produce a printout of your screen (unless the DOS MODE command has been used to redirect the output). To find out if this is the case, start by checking the technical specifications in your printer manual to see what kind of interface your printer uses (parallel or serial).

If you use Symphony, *there's another solution. You can generate a directory listing by selecting SERVICES File Table and printing the result. This command places a table of file names, dates created, and file sizes in a worksheet.*

FILE MANAGER — I

Two people in our office share one IBM PC XT system and *1-2-3* Release 1A. To keep files separate, we created a subdirectory for each user. This situation works fine until someone tries to use the File Manager. Because the File Manager recognizes only drives A, B, and C, there is no way to sort files within a subdirectory. How can we access subdirectories through File Manager?

Donald Carter
Duplex Envelope Company
Richmond, VA.

File Manager, which is available only in Releases 1.0 and 1A of 1-2-3, *lets you use certain DOS commands by selecting choices from a menu. Release 1 recognizes only drives A and B; Release 1A recognizes drives A, B, and C. The DOS commands that File Manager accesses are COPY, ERASE, RENAME, ARCHIVE, and SORT. There is also a choice called Disk Drive, which lets you indicate which disk drive contains your source disk.*

The File Manager was not designed for use with hard-disk subdirectories. As a result, a copy of File Manager and the drivers installed in the 1-2-3 directory must be present in each subdirectory you want to use it in. To solve your problem, place a copy of the file called FILEMGR.COM and copies of the 1-2-3 drivers in each person's subdirectory. Then when someone wants to use File Manager, he or she must change to his or her subdirectory and type filemgr *at a DOS prompt.*

To copy your drivers from the 1-2-3 directory to your subdirectory called MYFILES, use the following command at the DOS C> prompt:

copy\123\??.drv\myfiles

FILEMGR.COM — II

In a previous Q&A item, you suggested that FILEMGR.COM could be used with subdirectories if the file exists in each subdirectory, along with the three or four driver (DRV) files.

Since I have nine subdirectories on my hard disk, the suggested approach would require disk space to store 45 files. Instead, I keep File Manager and the driver files in one subdirectory named *BIN*. To use the utility, I invoke a batch file created by entering the following text at the DOS prompt:

```
copy con:bucopy.bat
copy c:\bin\filemgr.com
copy c:\bin\??.drv
filemgr
del filemgr.com
del ??.drv
^z
```

Create the ^z sequence by holding down the Control key and pressing z. Once you've created this file, enter cd*subdirectory* (where *subdirectory* represents the subdirectory in which you want to use File Manager), then enter *bucopy*. When you exit from File Manager, DOS deletes the File Manager utility and driver files automatically.

Jim Butler
Playa Del Rey, Calif.

You're right, the method in the previous item isn't practical if you use many subdirectories. However, for your method to work, you still need to copy the file BUCOPY.BAT to each subdirectory in which you want to use File Manager, or use the PATH command in DOS to tell DOS where to find the new batch file. If you use the batch file in a directory containing your 1-2-3 Release 1A files, you'll wipe out your 1A installed driver set.

You can also shorten the second and third lines of your batch file by replacing them with these:

copy \bin\filemgr.com
copy \bin\??.drv

ACCESSING SUBDIRECTORIES WITH RELEASE 1A AND DOS 3

The Q&A section has pointed out that *1-2-3* Release 1A's File Manager cannot access subdirectories and that you must copy File Manager into every subdirectory you want to use with it. There is another solution if you are using DOS 3.0 or higher: the DOS SUBST (substitute) command. Using this command, you can assign to subdirectories single letters that represent separate drives. Applications programs, such as *1-2-3*, interpret these subdirectories as separate floppy drives.

The SUBST command lets you use letters from D to Z to assign up to 23 additional subdirectories as "drives." However, *1-2-3* Release 1A allows you to specify only disk drives named A through P, so you can assign only an additional 13 subdirectories as drives for *1-2-3*. Other applications programs may allow you to use the entire 23 letters.

To assign a drive name letter to a subdirectory, you must include a line in the CONFIG.SYS file located in your hard disk's root directory telling DOS the range of letters you are going to use (CONFIG.SYS is DOS's "configuration file"). Change your current directory to be the root directory of your hard disk. Check to see whether you have a CONFIG.SYS file. Type:

type config.sys

If the file exists, use any word processor or text editor that creates ASCII files to add the following line to the file:

lastdrive = z

If you don't currently have a CONFIG.SYS file, create one by typing, at the DOS prompt:

copy con:config.sys
lastdrive = z
^z

The ^z is created by pressing the F6 function key followed by the Return key which saves the file.

Then you must include an AUTOEXEC.BAT file in your hard disk's root directory that includes the SUBST statements that give a letter to selected subdirectories, such as:

c:\dos\subst o: c:\user1
c:\dos\subst p : c:\user2

You can place this information in the AUTOEXEC.BAT file in the same way that you added the line to the CONFIG.SYS file.

The above two lines assume that the DOS file SUBST.EXE is in the subdirectory DOS and that user1's files are in subdirectory *USER1,* while user2's files are in *USER2.* After these two lines are executed, DOS will treat C:\USER1 and C:\USER2 as two separate drives, O and P. Applications programs that you load later can access USER1 and USER2 simply by referring to the appropriate drive designation. For example, in *1-2-3*, change the file directory to O to access user1's files.

Chi Wang
Division of Capital Planning and Operations
Commonwealth of Massachusetts
Boston, Mass.

SECTION
2

STARTUP, INSTALL, AND DRIVER SETS

Getting a program up and running can be the most frustrating part of the entire learning process. Once the program is up, your efforts are directed toward actually using the software. But the startup phase doesn't even give you that satisfaction.

In general, each release of *1-2-3* and *Symphony* has been easier to install than its predecessors. But there are still lots of things that can go wrong. The first step, once you've broken open the shrink-wrap and read through the introductory booklets, is to install the software on your machine by transferring it from the floppy disks to your hard disk. Once that is finished you have to configure the program so that it knows exactly what kind of hardware you are using. The newer releases of Lotus Development products start off with a number of usually correct configuration assumptions, so it is possible to start using the program right away. Still, some of the assumptions may be wrong, and if you upgrade your hardware you will have to reconfigure the program. Configuration is a process most of us have to go through at least once.

The configuration process results in the creation of driver sets, collections of small programs that translate the program's output into the commands required by your hardware. You can create more than one driver set if you intend to use the program on different machines with different components or peripherals.

Even if you only use the software on one machine and never change your hardware, knowing how to speed your way through the startup process will make life a lot easier. And if you change machines or upgrade your current computer, these tips, and those contained in Section 3, can significantly shorten your down time.

1

Install and Startup

SCREEN SCROLLING

I am responsible for an IBM XT with a monochrome monitor and a Hercules graphics card. When I first installed *1-2-3* Release 2, all of our Lotus users noticed that the rate of screen scrolling was significantly slower than it was in Release 1A. I was able to increase the screen speed back to what people were accustomed to by reinstalling the graphics driver.

When you choose either the First-Time Installation or Change Selected Equipment options in the Install program, you are able to specify only the graphics-screen mode. This driver also commands the text-screen driver. If you select Hercules for graphics, the text-screen scroll speed automatically slows.

However, if you choose Advanced Options after going through the first-time installation process, select Modify Driver Set, Text Display, and IBM Monochrome Display. This returns your scroll speed to normal while maintaining the graphics capability.

J.P. Remes
Brunke & Silver
Cary, Ill.

REMINDER TO INSERT PROGRAM DISK

Our office staff often forgot to place the *1-2-3* System Disk in the A drive and were returned to the operating system. Since some of our users confused the System Disk with the similarly labeled Tutorial or Utilities disks, I created a batch file as follows to ensure that the System Disk is in drive A:

```
echo off
:test
cls
echo    Put the 1-2-3 System Disk in
echo    Drive A and press
echo    Return
```

```
pause
a:
if exist 123.EXE goto proceed
echo    The disk in drive A is not the
echo    1-2-3 System Disk
pause
c:
goto test
:proceed
c:
cd c:\123
lotus
cd\
```

The line *if exist 123.EXE goto proceed* tests to make sure that the disk in drive **A** is the System Disk (only the System Disk and Backup System Disk contain 123.EXE). If the file exists, the batch file will jump to the statement *:proceed* and load *1-2-3*. If not, the batch file will display an error message and begin again.

Gene Owens
Shrewsbury, Pa.

You can install the copy protection code for 1-2-3 *Release 2/2.01 and* Symphony *Release 1.2 directly on your hard disk so that you don't need to place a key disk in Drive A. However, if you do not install directly to the hard disk you can still use this technique. If you use* 1-2-3 *Release 2/2.01, change 123.EXE in the above batch file to 123.CMP. If you use* Symphony *Release 1.2, change it to SYMPHONY.CMP.* Symphony *Release 2 is not copy protected.*

SERVICES DOS AND /SYSTEM COMMANDS
Why do I lose memory every time I leave and reenter *1-2-3* Release 2/2.01 or *Symphony*?

Stephen Pepe
GCA Corp.
Andover, Mass.

You are probably using the /System command (1-2-3) *or SERVICES DOS command* (Symphony) *to leave the programs. If you want to leave and then reload either program without consuming additional memory, select /Quit* (1-2-3) *or SERVICES Exit* (Symphony).

When you turn your computer on, a copy of DOS is loaded into RAM. 1-2-3 *or* Symphony *is then loaded in the memory above the operating system (DOS). Later, if you select /System* (1-2-3 *Release 2/2.01) or SERVICES DOS* (Symphony), *the program and the worksheet you are working on are squeezed into the lower end of memory and another copy of DOS is loaded into the upper portion of memory. This*

allows you to use DOS commands or load another program that won't interfere with
1-2-3 or Symphony. *When you type* exit *at the DOS prompt and then press Return,*
the second copy of the operating system is erased from RAM and you are returned
to the worksheet you were working on.

If you then type 1-2-3, Lotus, Access *or* Symphony *at the DOS prompt, as if you*
were entering the program for the first time, and then press Return, you are really
loading the program into memory for the second time.

In Symphony, *you must use the SERVICES Application Attach command and*
select DOS.APP from the menu to attach DOS. The DOS.APP file resides on the Help
and Tutorial Disk. To automatically attach the DOS add-in whenever you load
Symphony, *select SERVICES Configuration Other Application Set, specify one of the*
numbers on the menu (1–8), select DOS.APP, and then select No.

DOS 3.0 INCOMPATIBILITY

Whenever I try to load *Symphony* Release 1, the disk-drive light goes on, but then the
screen goes blank except for a blinking cursor located in the top-left corner. I get
neither the date nor the time prompt. I had been using DOS 3.0, and the problem
emerged after I reinstalled DOS 2.1. I know this probably is not a problem with my
Symphony disks, but can you tell me what is going on?

Mike Michaud
Newark, New Jersey

An unusual incompatibility exists between DOS 3.0 and earlier versions of DOS.
When you use the SYS command to install DOS 3.0 on the Symphony *Program Disk*
and then replace it with DOS 2.0 or 2.1, the disk appears to work. The disk lights go
on, and the System Transferred *message appears. However, the old DOS has not*
been reinstalled on your disk. If you then try to load Symphony, *you get a blank*
screen. There is no way to go back to DOS 2.0 or 2.1; therefore, you must reinstall
DOS 3.0 on the disk.

This problem arises only with disks that were originally formatted with DOS 2.0
or 2.1 and were later upgraded to DOS 3.0. If you have a disk originally formatted
under DOS 1.1, you could install 2.0 or 2.1 after installing 3.0, and it will work.

EMPTY DRIVE B CAUSES PROBLEMS

Our company often transmits files from seven remote locations. The seven copies of
Symphony had been set up identically; each copy had a Communications Configuration file (CCF) that was automatically retrieved when *Symphony* was loaded
(SERVICES Configuration Communications). However, we experienced a frustrating
problem: From time to time, the communications settings were not the same. One
end of the communications had the default communications settings, not the ones
set in the configuration file. We had to break the connection, manually load the

configuration file, reconnect, and retransmit.

This problem occurred sporadically, and our remote users assured us that *Symphony* was being loaded properly. The problem seemed unsolvable. Luckily, we found the solution: The configuration file will not load automatically unless there is a disk in drive B when *Symphony* is first loaded. Sometimes our users neglected to put a data disk in drive B upon startup; that's when the problem arose. So be sure to have a disk in drive B when you invoke *Symphony*.

Jeff Honeycut
United Intermountain Telephone
Bristol, Tenn.

This problem occurs when you use Symphony *and the drive you have set as your default directory (SERVICES Configuration File) is empty.* Symphony *looks to that drive when loading. If the drive is empty, an error condition arises, in which case* Symphony *halts the loading process. When that happens, many of the settings on the Configuration settings sheet do not get read, including the specification for the configuration file, autoload add-ins, default window type, and document settings. When this happens,* Symphony *uses the settings that were shipped with the product and are stored internally, for example, no autoload Communications Configuration file, top and bottom document margins of two, and so on.*

The moral is, if you have set a floppy drive as the default directory, be sure it's not empty when you invoke the program, or you may be surprised at the settings.

STARTUP ERROR MESSAGE

When I try to load *Symphony* Release 1, a message appears stating *Symphony cannot start due to an error while reading the Symphony.CMP file.* Is something wrong with the disk?

Sylvia Payton
Salt Lake City, Utah

The disk may be damaged, but it is more likely that your computer does not have enough memory. Release 1 of Symphony *requires a minimum of 320K of RAM. To tell how much RAM is in your computer, place the DOS disk in drive A and with the DOS A> prompt visible, enter* chkdsk. *Below the display showing the status of your DOS disk are two more numbers. "Total memory" is the amount of RAM contained in your computer. The number for "bytes free" tells you how much memory is available for software programs or worksheets. If you are running any add-ins or background programs in addition to* Symphony, *they will take up memory.*

ONE DISK 1-2-3

Once you are comfortable with *1-2-3* Release 1A, you can erase the help file and copy *1-2-3*'s File Manager and PrintGraph files onto the System Disk for easy one-disk operation:

1. Delete 123.HLP and INSTALL.BAT from the *1-2-3* System Disk.

2. Copy FILEMGR.COM from the Utility Disk to the System Disk.

3. Copy GRAPH.EXE, GRAPH.CNF, LOTUS.DLB, and two fonts (I use both ROMAN1.FON and ROMAN2.FON) from the PrintGraph Disk to the System Disk. (Don't copy GRAPH.HLP, which uses a precious 20K of space.)

Now you can do all your *1-2-3* tasks, including printing graphs, using only one disk.

H.J.C. Weighell
Warwickshire, England

1-2-3 MAKES WORD PROCESSING LOCK UP

After using *1-2-3* Release 2 on my hard disk, I cannot load *Microsoft Word*. *1-2-3* seems to do something to my computer that makes it lock up. I find it cumbersome to turn off and then restart the computer to use *Microsoft Word*. Can anything be done about this?

Ted Wagner
Conographic Corp.
Irvine, Calif.

There is a problem with using 1-2-3 *Release 2 on a hard disk and then trying to access a word-processing package such as* Microsoft Word. *The problem was corrected in* 1-2-3 *Release 2.01. You should replace your* 1-2-3 *System Disk, Backup System Disk, and PrintGraph disk.*

If you have 1-2-3 *Release 2.01, be sure that you remove the* 1-2-3 *Release 2 copy protection with the COPYOFF or COPYHARD/U command found in* 1-2-3 *Release 2 before you installed* 1-2-3 *Release 2.01. If you have already done this and you are using* 1-2-3 Report Writer, *you should replace your* Report Writer *System Disk and Install and Tutorial disks.*

To replace these disks, send the original disks to the Information and Warranty Department, Lotus Development Corp., 55 Cambridge Pkwy., Cambridge, Mass., 02142. If you need additional information, call Information and Warranty at 617-623-6572.

ATTACHING APPLICATIONS

Is there a method for automatically attaching the Macro Library Manager whenever *Symphony* Release 1.1 or 1.2 is loaded? We have 25 files that are combined and extracted via macros. It seems like it would be more efficient to create macros in Hyperspace. However, we would like to avoid attaching the application each time we work.

Terrie R. Smith
St. Vincent Hospital & Health Care Center
Indianapolis, Ind.

If you are using a floppy disk, you must remove the write-protect tab prior to performing the next step. Select SERVICES Configuration Other Application Set, select 1 (or the first free choice if you already have applications such as DOS selected), then select MACROMGR.APP Yes Quit Update Quit. The menu choice Update saves the command to attach the Macro Library Manager in Symphony *'s configuration file (SYMPHONY.CNF) so that whenever you load* Symphony, *the Macro Library Manager will be automatically loaded.*

2

Drivers and Sets

DRIVER SET TOO BIG FOR FLOPPY DISK

I run *1-2-3* Release 2 from floppy disks. The COLOR.SET driver set I use is too large to fit on my System Disk, so I saved it onto another disk during installation. When I want to start *1-2-3*, I insert the System Disk into drive A and insert the disk containing the driver set into drive B. Then I type *123 B:COLOR*, which causes *1-2-3* to look to drive B for the driver set.

This technique works with *Symphony* as well and allows me to maintain as many driver sets as I want.

Joel McDaniels
Twin Forks, N.D.

You might find that your driver set fits on the System Disk if you eliminate your graphics printer driver — which can take a lot of space — from the driver set on that disk. You need a graphics printer driver only on the PrintGraph disk, which has more room. Use the Install program to eliminate particular drivers from an existing driver set.

BLINKING CURSOR IN RELEASE 2

I have an IBM PC with an IBM color monitor. When I try to load *1-2-3* Release 2, I get a blinking cursor at the top-left corner of my screen. What is happening?

Charles Wiener
Intel Corp.
Santa Clara, Calif.

You are using a driver that doesn't match the display card installed in your PC. Find out which graphics card (if any) you have and install the correct driver. For example, if you have a Hercules Color Graphics Card, select the IBM Color Graphics Adapter driver, not the Hercules driver. If you haven't installed a driver on the System Disk, for now, load 1-2-3 by using the System Disk. The default driver on the System Disk is the Universal Text display driver, and it should work no matter which graphics card you have installed. If it works, and you are able to use 1-2-3, go through the Install procedure and select the Universal Text Display driver, which assumes no graphics capability. If you have already installed drivers on the System Disk, rerun the First Time Installation procedure in the Install program and choose No in response to the question, Can your computer display graphs?

If you use an 8087 math coprocessor, the blinking cursor can also be caused by an incorrect DIP-switch setting. If you try the procedures already mentioned and these symptoms persist, check to see if the 8087 switch is set correctly. For an IBM PC or PC XT, Switch 2 on Switch Block 1 should be in the Off position if you have a *math coprocessor. Other computers may use different settings — consult your dealer for correct settings.*

WINDOW INCOMPATIBILITY IN DIFFERENT DRIVER SETS

I often interchange the driver sets in my IBM PC when I'm using *1-2-3* Release 2. I use a Hercules monochrome card for the denser 90-column-by-38-line screen display, and I use the IBM monochrome driver, which scrolls much faster than the Hercules.

But a problem arises when I use the IBM drivers: I retrieve worksheets that contain a window I'd saved using the Hercules 90-by-38 driver set. However, the window does not appear at the same position with the IBM driver as it does in the Hercules driver. Upper and left windows will show more rows and columns in the 90-by-38 setting than in the IBM 80-column-by-25-line display.

Also, when I save a file using the Hercules 90-by-38 driver set and the window is above line 7, the keyboard locks when I attempt to retrieve it with the IBM driver set. The vertical border of the worksheet scrolls across the screen for five minutes. When the scrolling stops, the file I'd retrieved appears, but without the window.

The best solution I've found is to clear the window before I save it with the Hercules 90-by-38 driver set. When I retrieve it with the IBM driver set, I reinsert the window where it was originally.

J.E. Kirkpatrick
Canyon Lake, Tex.

This solution will also work when you transfer files between different driver sets in 1-2-3 Release 2.01.

SECTION
3

MOVING BETWEEN RELEASES, PROGRAMS, AND MACHINES

Changing work environments always requires adjustment. The new environment may be a different release of the same product, or a different machine from the one you normally use, or an entirely different software program.

The transition from *1-2-3* Release 1A to Release 2 was rough. Hopefully, the transition to future releases will be smoother. Even so, it will always take some ingenuity to handle downward migration from a newer version of the product to an older version. This section helps relieve the upgrade blues.

The same need for ingenuity appears when you move data from one program to another, for example from *dBase* to *1-2-3*. This section contains some hints on the translation process.

Moving from one machine to another raises even trickier issues. Just because two computers run MS-DOS doesn't mean that their keyboards are identical or that their peripherals need the same commands. Unfortunately, hardware problems are even more of a moving target than software issues. *LOTUS* contains a monthly Hardware Hints page. But this material goes out of date almost as fast as we print it, because hardware manufacturers revise their products on an even more rapid timetable than do software developers. Nonetheless, we've included some hardware hints in this book.

Finally, although it's good news that Lotus is finally removing copy protection from its products, a lot of people still have older versions that include that cumbersome feature. So we've included a couple of tips on how to back up your hard disk without destroying the hidden protection files, and how to salvage the situation if you've already made a mistake.

23

1

Moving Between 1-2-3 Releases

USING 1-2-3 RELEASE 2 FILES WITH 1A

I'm presently using two versions of *1-2-3*; at home, I have *1-2-3* Release 2 on an IBM PC, and at work I use *1-2-3* Release 1A on a Wang PC. While I can use Release 2 on the IBM to retrieve files created on the Wang, *1-2-3* on the Wang won't accept files created using *1-2-3* Release 2 on the IBM. Is there any way I can overcome this problem?

Thomas C. Allsbury
Alexandria, Va.

You will get the error message Not a valid worksheet file *if you try to retrieve a Release 2 file with a WKS file name extension directly into* 1-2-3 *Release 1A.* 1-2-3 *Release 2 has a Translate program to translate Release 2 files into 1A files. But one version of this utility file, called WR1WKS.XLT, has a bug in it. If you get the error message* Formula translation error *or* Worksheet full, *the translation won't work until you delete all of the range names in the* 1-2-3 *Release 2 file. Select /Range Name Table to create a list of your range names, then select /Range Name Reset to cancel all of the range names. Resave the file before you translate it to* 1-2-3 *Release 1A. Once you retrieve the file on the Wang, use the range name table to help re-create your range names. This bug has been fixed in Release 2.01.*

UPGRADING YOUR FILE EXTENSIONS

I noticed that when I retrieve a *1-2-3* Release 1A worksheet file with Release 2 or 2.01 and subsequently save the file, the program beeps and displays the message *File will be saved as .WK1.* If I proceed to save the file, I then have two versions of the file: the original with the WKS extension and the new one with the WK1 extension. To avoid having to erase the old Release 1A files, use the DOS RENAME command to change the file extension of your old WKS files to WK1: Enter at the DOS prompt *rename *.wks *.wk1.*

The RENAME command does not change Release 1A worksheets into Release 2 or 2.01 format — that only occurs when you retrieve and resave them with Release 2 or

2.01. However, when you do retrieve and resave the worksheets thus renamed, you will no longer be left with two versions of each.

Eddie Lee
Soltex Corp.
Houston, Tex.

You can use the same command to change the file extension of Symphony *Release 1 and 1.01 files after upgrading to Release 1.1 or 1.2. Enter at the DOS prompt* rename *.wrk *.wr1 *to change the file extensions from WRK to WR1. Refer to your DOS manual for more information on the RENAME command.*

INCOMPATIBLE FILE COMBINATION

I discovered a compatibility problem between *1-2-3* Release 1A and Release 2 while I was combining some old Release 1A files into a single Release 2 worksheet. To reproduce the problem, enter the formula +A2 in cell A1 of a Release 1A worksheet and save the file under the name TEST. Now go to cell A2048 in Release 2. Select /File Combine and specify the file named TEST. The formula reads +A1 instead of the expected and proper +A2049.

You need to retrieve TEST and save it as a Release 2 file to solve this problem. Combining the new TEST file with the Release 2 worksheet will then work as it should.

Richard G. Andreasen
Baylor Health Care System
Dallas, Tex.

This problem is not a direct result of the formula-wrap feature. The Release 1A file that you combine into the Release 2 worksheet does not realize that its new environment has expanded to 8192 rows. The formula therefore wraps around the new worksheet in the old way, referring to row 1. This reaction is an adjustment of the formula to its relative position in the new worksheet.

Try this to better understand what is happening: Place the formula +A2 in cell A1 of a Release 1A worksheet. Now copy this formula to cell A2048. Note that the formula in cell A2048 is +A1 — the same formula you find when you combine your original Release 1A worksheet into a Release 2 environment.

You will also have to save the Release 1A version of TEST as a 1-2-3 Release 2.01 file if you want to combine TEST with a Release 2.01 worksheet.

FILE EXTENSIONS

Please provide a list of possible file-name extensions associated with *1-2-3*, *Symphony*, PrintGraph, and DOS files.

Margaret Griffin-Sarmento
Texet
Arlington, Mass.

Here's the list:

FILE-NAME EXTENSIONS	FILE TYPE
.APP	*Symphony* add-in application file
.BAS	BASIC file
.BAT	DOS batch file
.CCF	*Symphony* Communications Configuration file
.CMP	*1-2-3* Release 2/2.01 and *Symphony* program file
.CNF	*1-2-3* or *Symphony* configuration file
.COM	Command or compiled program file
.CTF	Character Translation file
.DLB	*1-2-3* and *Symphony* driver library
.DRV	Device driver file
.DYN	*1-2-3* and *Symphony* file for add-in applications
.EXE	Executable program file
.FON	*1-2-3* Release 1A PrintGraph font file
.FNT	*1-2-3* Release 2/2.01 and *Symphony* PrintGraph font file
.HLP	*1-2-3* and *Symphony* Help file
.LBR	Library file
.PIC	Picture file (PrintGraph)
.PRN	ASCII print file
.SET	Driver set file
.SYS	DOS System file
.TUT	*1-2-3* Release 1/1A and *Symphony* tutorial file
.WK1	*1-2-3* Release 2/2.01 worksheet file
.WKS	*1-2-3* Release 1/1A worksheet file
.WRK	*Symphony* Release 1/1.01 worksheet file
.WR1	*Symphony* Release 1.1/1.2 worksheet file
.XLT	*1-2-3* Release 2/2.01 and *Symphony* Translate file

INDICATING INPUT AREA WITH LABELS

Release 2 of *1-2-3* generally runs worksheets developed with Release 1A. You will run into problems, however, when you use labels to indicate where data is to be entered.

One of our cash-flow worksheets uses a string of dots to indicate input areas. The dots disappear when a number is entered: the number is then used in the calculations elsewhere on the sheet. If an input area doesn't apply, Release 1A treats the dots as zeros and completes the calculations. Release 2, however, returns ERR for any formula that involves numbers and individually specified labels, such as +A1+A2, if A1 contains a number and A2 a label.

The solution is to erase all labels from the input area and add the labels to the cells immediately to the left of the input area, adding spaces to the beginning of the labels so that the contents overlap the input cells. The labels seem to be in the input cell but are actually in the cells to the left. Since the input area remains blank, there is no problem with mixing labels and numbers in calculations.

G.K. Tribes
Chilliwack, British Columbia

Another solution is to leave the input areas as they are and adjust the formulas that refer to them by using Release 2's @N function. @N(range) returns the numeric value of the top-left cell in range. *The numeric value of a label is 0; the numeric value of a number or numeric formula is the number or value itself. For example, if one of your formulas referring to cells in the input area is + A1 + A2, change the formula to @N(A1) + @N(A2). After you enter the formula, 1-2-3 converts it to refer to ranges: @N(A1..A1) + @N(A2..A2). Symphony doesn't — you must enter @N(!A1) + @N(!A2) or @N(A1..A1) + @N(A2..A2).*

When cells A1 and A2 contain the string of dots, the new formula returns 0 instead of ERR. When you enter values in cells A1 and A2, the formula evaluates the same as + A1 + A2.

The advantage of this solution is that it makes it easier to indicate the input areas; you don't need to append dots to labels and adjust spacing. The advantage of your solution is that the resulting worksheet is compatible with both Release 1A and Release 2 of 1-2-3.

ASCII GRAPHICS CHARACTERS

An undocumented and unsupported capability of *1-2-3* Release 1A allows you to display ASCII characters corresponding to the codes 1 through 31 and 128 through 255. Some people use these characters to make boxes and borders in their worksheets. However, in *1-2-3* Release 2/2.01, as in *Symphony*, these codes display characters from the Lotus International Character Set (LICS). This allows you to display and print characters such as the British pound (£) and Japanese yen ( ).

Worksheet files using the unsupported characters still function after being read into Release 2/2.01 or *Symphony*, but they look quite different from the way they were designed. Codes 1 through 31 are invisible, except through a *Symphony* DOC window, and codes 128 through 255 are represented by international characters.

Another undocumented and unsupported use for ASCII codes 1 through 31 in Release 1A was to represent each macro keyword: {UP}, {DOWN}, and so on. However, the macro processor in Release 2/2.01 and in *Symphony* doesn't interpret these characters as macro commands.

1-2-3/SYMPHONY MIGRATION

I often have to exchange data files created in *1-2-3* or *Symphony*. With all the different versions available, how do I know which files can be retrieved in which releases and how to accomplish these file transfers?

Natraj Singh
New York, N.Y.

The compatibility chart below shows, for example, that to use Symphony *Release 1 to retrieve data files created in* 1-2-3 *Release 2.01, the files must first be translated to* Symphony *Release 1 using the* 1-2-3 *Release 2.01 Translate utility.*

```
                    123/SYMPHONY FILE COMPATIBILITY

                      File Created Under:

                    1-2-3      1-2-3      SYMPHONY   SYMPHONY
                    REL        REL        REL        REL
                    1/1A       2/2.01     1/1.01     1.1/1.2
Program       -------------------  ----------  ----------  ----------  ----------
Currently     -------------------  ----------  ----------  ----------  ----------
Being         1-2-3 REL 1/1A       A           B           C           D
Used:         -------------------  ----------  ----------  ----------  ----------
              1-2-3 REL 2/2.01     A           A           A*          A*
              -------------------  ----------  ----------  ----------  ----------
              SYMPHONY 1/1.01      A*          E           A           F
              -------------------  ----------  ----------  ----------  ----------
              SYMPHONY 1.1/1.2     A*          A*          A           A
              -------------------  ----------  ----------  ----------  ----------

A   Directly retrievable, no need to translate

A*  When using 1-2-3 to retrieve a file created in Symphony,
    or vice versa, you must specify the file name with extension.  For
    example, in 1-2-3 select /File Retrieve and enter TEST.WRK,
    or in Symphony select SERVICES File Retrieve TEST.WKS. Or,
    to choose from a list of all 1-2-3/Symphony worksheet files,
    press Escape to clear the present filename and extension and type *.w??

    Program file extensions include:

    .WKS 1-2-3 Release 1/1A
    .WK1 1-2-3 Release 2/2.01
    .WRK Symphony Release 1/1.01
    .WR1 Symphony Release 1.1/1.2

B   Translate 1-2-3 Release 2 to 1A

C   Create print (ASCII) file in Symphony Release 1/1.01
    and import into 1-2-3 Release 1/1A

D   Translate Symphony Release 1.1/1.2 to 1-2-3 Release 1A

E   Translate 1-2-3 Release 2/2.01 to Symphony Release 1/1.01

F   Translate Symphony Release 1.1/1.2 to Release 1/1.01
```

RETRIEVING NON-ENGLISH LANGUAGE FILES

Are there any problems retrieving *Symphony* files saved in one language into a *Symphony* version for another language?

Linda Keady
Bryn Mawr, Pa.

You can retrieve worksheet files created with Spanish, French, Italian, Swedish, Dutch, and German versions of Symphony *with no problems. The program translates @functions within the worksheet into the proper format for the language into which the file is being retrieved. It also translates currency formats appropriately. It cannot translate macros, because they are saved as labels. Also, driver sets aren't transferable between languages, even if they are the same version number, but this shouldn't affect worksheet retrieval.*

THE TUTORIAL LESSONS

The files on the Tutorial Lessons disk used to reside on our hard disk in the same directory as all of our worksheet files, and the processes of retrieving, listing, and saving were very slow. To speed things up, I erased the lesson files from the hard disk. But we still need to use the tutorial occasionally. How can we use the tutorial without replacing the lesson files on the hard disk?

Harry R. Borgman
First National Bank
Oelwein, Iowa

You didn't specify whether you are using 1-2-3 *or* Symphony, *so here are both ways.*

You cannot use the Symphony *TUTORIAL.APP file from the hard disk and, at the same time, access the Tutorial Lessons Disk from the A drive. If you want to get around this, try the following:*

Place the Symphony *Program Disk in drive A, enter* A:, *then type* access *or* symphony *at the A> prompt to load* Symphony. *Once in the program, replace the* Symphony *Program Disk with the Help and Tutorial Disk. Select SERVICES Application Attach and choose TUTORIAL.APP from the menu. Select Invoke and press Return.* Symphony *will prompt you to replace that disk with the Tutorial Lessons Disk. You now have the Tutorial menu on the screen.*

For 1-2-3 Releases 1 and 1A, place the Tutorial disk in drive A, type tutor *at an A> prompt, and press Return. This loads the tutorial program named TUTOR.EXE into memory. Make sure that you've installed drivers onto the Tutorial disk. If you haven't, copy the driver files onto your Tutorial disk in drive A:. With the DOS prompt visible, and the 1-2-3 subdirectory current, use the DOS command copy ??.drv a:.*

2

Using Different Machines

USING LOTUS PROGRAMS ON MORE THAN ONE COMPUTER
Can I install my Lotus disks for use on a Compaq and also use them on my IBM PC?

Steve Ameida
Brookline, Massachusetts.

You can use both 1-2-3 *and* Symphony *on multiple computers. To change computers with* 1-2-3 *Release 1A, you must rerun the Install program and make the appropriate selections. You can do this as often as needed.*

1-2-3 Release 2/2.01 and Symphony's *Install programs allow you to create multiple driver sets, each of which you may use with a different computer (or printer). Give the default name of 123.SET (LOTUS.SET in* Symphony*) to the driver set you will use most often. Give the other sets appropriate names. For example, if you use an IBM PC at work and a Compaq at home, 123.SET would contain drivers for the IBM and COMPAQ.SET would contain drivers for the Compaq.*

To use 123.SET, enter lotus *or* 123 *(in* Symphony*, access or symphony) at the DOS A> prompt. To use COMPAQ.SET, enter* lotus compaq *or* 123 compaq *at the DOS A> prompt.*

MAKING MULTIPLE CONFIGURATION FILES
Microcomputer labs at schools and corporations that purchase multiple packages of a software program are faced with the task of configuring each package to work with the computers at the lab. The easiest solution is to configure one package of the software, then copy the resulting configuration files to the remaining packages. At our lab, we ran the Install program on one of our 16 packages of *1-2-3* Release 2, then used /Worksheet Global Default to save the desired defaults for the data directory and printer setup string. Returning to DOS, we then formatted a blank disk and copied to it the files COMMAND.COM (from the DOS disk), 123.SET and 123.CNF (from the newly installed and configured *1-2-3* disk). With this disk in drive A, it is simply a matter of copying these three files to each of the remaining 15 packages.

Bob Dougherty
Fort Collins, Colo.

This technique applies to Symphony *as well. Copy LOTUS.SET, SYMPHONY.CNF, and any CCF files from your program disk to a blank disk. If different computers have different configurations (color versus monochrome monitor, for example), you can save different driver sets in one Install session by assigning a unique name to each set. Then copy the appropriate one to the other packages of* 1-2-3 *or* Symphony. *While being copied, the driver sets can be renamed to 123.SET (for* 1-2-3) *or LOTUS.SET (for* Symphony) *to serve as the default driver set for that package.*

MULTIPLE CONFIGURATION FILES

When several people, each needing a different configuration, use the same copy of *1-2-3* or *Symphony*, changing the settings for each person can take time. Our alternative is to make one version of the configuration file for each person and then use a DOS autoexecuting batch file to control which version people use each time they start the program.

The first step is to set up subdirectories for each person. Next, switch to the directory that contains the *1-2-3* or *Symphony* program files, and make a second copy of the existing configuration file. With the DOS prompt on the screen, enter:

    copy 123.cnf standard.cnf
    or
    copy symphony.cnf standard.cnf

Then load *1-2-3* or *Symphony* and enter the desired configuration settings for the first person. In *1-2-3* select /Worksheet Global Default Directory; in *Symphony* select SERVICES Configuration File. Make sure to designate the appropriate subdirectory name for that person as the default directory name, such as \123\BRUCE. Select Update to save the revised configuration in the file. Exit from the program and make a renamed copy of the new configuration file with the following DOS command:

    copy 123.cnf xxx.cnf
    or
    copy symphony.cnf xxx.cnf

Replace the *xxx* with the last part of the newly configured default subdirectory name, for example, BRUCE.CNF. Repeat this process for each person.

Change to your root directory or to the directory you use for batch files. If you use the PATH command, you must list this directory before the directory that contains the Lotus program files. In this directory, create a file named LOTUS.BAT by entering:

    copy con:lotus.bat
    cls
    cd\lotus

```
pause insert lotus disk in drive a:
if exist 123.cnf erase 123.cnf
if exist %1.cnf copy %1.cnf 123.cnf
if not exist 123.cnf copy standard.cnf 123.cnf
lotus
erase 123.cnf
^z
```

In the line that reads *CD\lotus,* you should substitute the full path and name of the directory that contains your program files. *Symphony* users should replace all occurrences of *1-2-3* with *SYMPHONY* and replace the last *LOTUS* with *ACCESS.* On an IBM PC, press the F6 function key followed by the Return key to get ^z.

When a person starts the program, he or she enters *lotus xxx,* where *xxx* is replaced by the name of his or her own subdirectory. Merely entering *lotus* starts the program using the standard default configuration. One warning: When several people want to use *1-2-3* one after the other, each person must exit from the program and move to the subdirectory containing the LOTUS.BAT file before entering the appropriate command.

I have also set up GRAPH.CNF for use with PrintGraph in a similar manner.

Bruce Burson
Hoover, Alabama

If the only configuration difference for each user is the name of his or her default directory, it is easier for the user to load the program and then select his or her own directory from a menu. In 1-2-3 *you can enable the file containing the menu to load automatically when the program is started by naming it* AUTO123. *In* Symphony *select SERVICES Configuration Auto, enter the file's name, and then select Update to include this information in the Configuration file. You can also set up the macro that creates the menu to execute automatically when the file is loaded by naming it \0. In* Symphony *select SERVICES Settings Auto-Execute Set and then point to the first cell of the macro. One more note:* 1-2-3 *Release 2/2.01 can be loaded directly from the hard disk without placing the Program disk in drive A, so users of these later releases could leave out the PAUSE command in the batch file.*

IBM PC AT

Can I use *1-2-3* and *Symphony* on my IBM PC AT? Do I need to make any special adjustments to do this?

Alma Carter
Mobile, Alabama

Both products run on the IBM PC AT. Symphony users, however, must first reset the high-density disk drive in the AT to low-density mode. To do this, enter a DOS command, such as dir a:, *at the DOS prompt. This lets the machine discover that you are using low-density mode. A second option is to reselect* Symphony *after you receive the error message following your initial attempt to load your software.*

If you are switching between an AT and a PC or XT, remember to save your data in the low-density mode. The PC and XT cannot read high-density files.

The AT also contains a nonstandard nine-pin serial port. You must purchase a cable converter to connect a standard serial printer to the AT. Even with this adjustment, hardware differences between the AT and the rest of the IBM family of computers cause certain peripheral configurations to malfunction.

AT&T AND ZENITH

When I used the *1-2-3* Release 2.01 Install program to copy the protection scheme to the hard disk of my AT&T PC, the transfer terminated prematurely, and I got the error message *Hard disk incompatible.* What next?

Sarah Oakland
Arlington, Va.

If you're using MS DOS 2.11, you can't use the Install program to copy the protection scheme to the hard disk. Instead, use the COPYHARD command that is outlined in the pamphlet "A Note to Hard Disk Users."

If you are using a Zenith ZW 150 series computer, you cannot copy the protection scheme to the hard disk unless your PC has a ROM revision 2.2 or higher. To obtain the current ROM revision, contact Zenith Parts Replacement at 616-982-3571 and ask for ROM sets 444-229 and 444-260. You can run 1-2-3 from the hard disk using your key disk until you receive the updated ROM revision.

MORE MEMORY FOR HP-150

The Hewlett-Packard Touchscreen (HP-150) includes *Personal Applications Manager (PAM)* software, which greatly simplifies system operation. However, this is achieved at the price of additional memory use, so the largest *1-2-3* spreadsheet you can ordinarily store in the base system memory (256K) is 47,948 bytes.

Instead of purchasing extra memory, you can more than double the amount of available memory for the price of a single floppy disk. You disable the loading of the *PAM* file during a "soft boot" of the system (Control-Shift-Reset), thereby making an additional 55,248 bytes of memory available for spreadsheet use. The technique is to make an additional copy of the MS-DOS COMMANDS directory on a blank, formatted disk and change the name of the CONFIG.SYS file so that *PAM* will not be loaded upon a soft boot of the system.

When formatting the blank disk, be sure to select the COPYSYSTEM option. After installing the MS-DOS COMMANDS directory on the disk, insert it into the default drive (for example, drive A on a HP-9121) and touch REREAD DISCS, or select

Softkey f1. Then touch FILE MANAGER (f5), RENAME FILE (f7), and select the block titled CONFIG.SYS. Type in a new file name such as CONFIG.SAV, then press Return. Press START RENAME (f1), EXIT RENAME (f8), then EXIT FILE MANAGER (f8). The disk is now ready to use.

To use *1-2-3* with this version of the Command disk, insert the disk into the default drive and execute a soft boot by pressing Control-Shift-Reset. Respond to the date and time prompts, then insert the *1-2-3* disk in the default drive. Enter *1-2-3* and proceed as usual. When you exit from *1-2-3* by selecting /Quit Yes, the DOS A> prompt appears. You then load PrintGraph by inserting the PrintGraph disk into the default drive and entering *Graph*.

To get back into *PAM*, save whatever you're working on, insert the original and unmodified MS-DOS COMMANDS disk into the default drive, and execute another soft boot.

Stephen C. Schiff
Planning Systems Inc.
McLean, Va.

3

Translate

ERASING UNNEEDED TRANSLATE FILES

The Translate utility that comes with *1-2-3* Release 2/2.01 and *Symphony* translates data between *1-2-3* and *Symphony* and other PC software. It consists of the translation "engine," called TRANS.COM, and a series of modules (XLT files) that take data from a particular program and convert it into Lotus format, and vice versa. You can save disk space by copying only the XLT files that you need to your hard disk. The list below is of the XLT files that come with *1-2-3* Release 2/2.01 and *Symphony*.

XLT FILES

DBF2.XLT	*dBase II* to and from *1-2-3* or *Symphony*
DBF3.XLT	*dBase III* to and from *1-2-3* or *Symphony*
DIF.XLT	DIF files to and from *1-2-3* or *Symphony*
JZZLOTUS.XLT	*Jazz* to all releases of *1-2-3* or *Symphony*
VCWRK.XLT	*VisiCalc* to *1-2-3* or *Symphony*
WR1WKS.XLT	*1-2-3* Release 2/2.01 and *Symphony* 1.1/1.2 to *1-2-3* Release 1A
WR1WRK.XLT	*1-2-3* Release 2/2.01 and *Symphony* 1.1/1.2 to *Symphony* Releases 1 and 1.01

One other file, WRKWR1.XLT, doesn't actually do any translating. It contains messages that tell you that you don't need to use Translate to do the conversion you just requested. For example, you don't need to translate *1-2-3* Release 1A files to *1-2-3* Release 2/2.01 — Release 2/2.01 can read 1A files directly.

The Translate utility senses which XLT files are available and adjusts its menus accordingly.

Don Domzalski
Buffalo Grove, Ill.

The names of these files vary from release to release, but the principle is the same: You can keep just the ones you use on your hard disk. However, don't erase the XLT files on the original disk — there's no telling when you might need them.

DBASE II TRANSLATE PROBLEMS

I have had some problems doing *Symphony* Release 1 to *dBase II* translations. No matter what *Symphony* default column width I specify, my *dBase II* column widths are nine characters wide. Also, the translate process loses all the numbers to the right of the decimal place of certain values but not of others.

Reggie Knight
Chicago, Illinois

There are solutions to both problems. The Symphony *Release 1 Translate utility doesn't read the default column-width setting properly. To control the width of columns, individually assign a width to each column by placing the pointer in the desired column, selecting MENU Width Set, then entering the width number. Once you have set all the individual column widths, use the MENU Settings Width command to set the default column width at a number that is different from the individually set widths. If the default and individually set widths are identical, the Translate program assumes the default setting is the controlling factor but then ignores the default setting and creates a* dBase II *column width of nine. For example, to translate a column width of 15, set the individual column width to 15, then make sure that the default is not 15.*

The Translate program also loses numbers to the right of the decimal point when the cell to be translated has the default format, General. General format does not display a fixed number of decimal characters. However, dBase II *must know exactly how many decimal places to use for particular numbers. Since General format mentions no definite number,* dBase II *assumes that there are no decimal figures and overlooks any that may actually exist. The short-term solution is to change the cell format to one that indicates a specific number of decimal places. Possible formats include Fixed, Currency, %, and Punctuated. To adjust the format, use the MENU Format command. Selecting MENU Settings Format will not work in this case.*

The long-term solution is to upgrade to Symphony *Release 1.2, in which the Translate program assumes two decimal places for General format cells.*

WRK TO DBASE

The *Symphony* Release 1 Translate utility is supposed to allow you to convert either an entire worksheet or a range within a worksheet into a DBF file for use with *dBase*. Unfortunately, the range convert option doesn't work properly if your database is part of a larger spreadsheet. The solution is to select SERVICES File Xtract to separate the database into its own file, retrieve the extracted file, then save it once again.

You must go through this last Retrieve/Save process because *Symphony* Release 1 can't translate extracted files. [Subsequent releases of *Symphony* have corrected this problem, so you no longer need to go through the extra Retrieve/Save process before translation.]

In addition, prior to translating a *Symphony* database into DBF, you must format all numeric fields in the first record by selecting MENU Format and setting the Fixed, Scientific, Currency, or Percent options to the number of decimal places desired in the *dBase* file. Merely selecting the Global Format option is not sufficient since the *Symphony* Release 1 Translate utility treats all globally formatted values as whole numbers. [Subsequent releases treat Global format as Fixed, 2 decimal places.] You must specifically format the first record since *Symphony* determines the field type, field width, and number of decimal places to be used in the translated file based on the database's first record — the second row of the database range.

Don Domzalski
Buffalo Grove, Ill.

DBASE III TO 1-2-3/SYMPHONY

Is there any way to transfer a *dBase III* file into a *1-2-3* worksheet? I know *1-2-3* Release 1A has a Translate utility for *dBase II*, but what about *dBase III?*

Bob Zurek
Houston, Tex.

1-2-3 Release 2/2.01 and Symphony *Release 1.2 have a Translate utility that works to and from* dBase III. *Although neither* 1-2-3 *Release 1A nor* Symphony *1/1.1 has a Translate utility for use with* dBase III*, you can still do the translation. The* dBase *COPY TO command combined with the DELIMITED and WITH modifiers will produce a file you can import into* 1-2-3 *and* Symphony. *Each record in the database will occupy one line of text in the file. Fields will be separated by commas, and labels will be delimited with quotation marks.*

Suppose that the dBase *file you want to transfer is called TEST and consists of four fields, defined as follows:*

Field	Name	Type	Width	Decimal Places
001	NAME	C	20	
002	COMPANY	C	20	
003	RATING	N	3	1
004	TIME	N	3	1

The records in the file might look like this:

Wu	ABC Co.	2.0	1.0
Jones	Toys Inc.	2.0	1.0
Thomas	XYZ Co.	1.0	2.5
Lee	Sea Inc.	3.0	1.5

Issuing the dBase *command:*

COPY TO test.prn DELIMITED WITH''

will create a print file, TEST.PRN, that will look like this:

"Wu","ABC Co.",2.0,1.0
"Jones","Toys Inc.",2.0,1.0
"Thomas","XYZ Co.",1.0,2.5
"Lee","Sea Inc.",3.0,1.5

You can now read the file into 1-2-3 *or* Symphony *using the File Import Numbers (Structured in* Symphony*) command, producing a worksheet four columns wide.*

TRANSLATING FROM DBASE III TO 1-2-3/SYMPHONY

I have *1-2-3* Release 2.01, *Symphony* Release 1.2, and *dBase III*. Occasionally I translate *dBase III* files into *1-2-3* or *Symphony*, which works fine. I have problems when I make changes to a file and try to translate the file back to *dBase III*. The *1-2-3* Translate utility gives me the error message *There is data missing from one or more fields in the database*, and when I try to use *Symphony*'s Translate utility, my computer locks up. What's happening? Can I fix it?

Lauren Plukas
Newton, Mass.

In 1-2-3 Release 2/2.01 and Symphony *Release 1.2, the Translate utility places unnecessary label prefixes in the first row of the file. For example, if your database contains field names in range A1..D1, the Translate utility may include unnecessary label prefixes in range E1..J1. When you translate this file back to* dBase III, dBase *interprets the label prefixes as field headings. Because range E1..J1 contains label prefixes without data records, and since* dBase *needs an entry in each field of a database, you get an error message.*

To work around this problem, use the File Xtract command to extract the portion of the file that contains your data. Retrieve the file, resave it, and then translate the file.

4

Back Up and Restore

BACKING UP AND RESTORING FILES TO A HARD DISK

If you have a hard disk, you can use the COPYON or COPYHARD procedure to run *1-2-3* Release 2 without a key disk in drive A. This procedure is described in *How to Start 1-2-3 Directly from a Hard Disk*, the brochure that comes with your documentation. These procedures copy *1-2-3*'s protected information to the hard disk. However, if you plan to back up and then restore *1-2-3* files to your hard disk, you should use COPYOFF or COPYHARD/U to remove the protected information from your hard disk before doing so. Then run COPYON or COPYHARD again. *1-2-3*'s protected files cannot be backed up and restored properly to the root directory of the hard disk. If you must restore files to your hard disk without removing *1-2-3* Release 2's protected information, do not restore the read-only files.

Jerry Rivers
Olympia, Wash.

UNAUTHORIZED DUPLICATE ERROR MESSAGE

I had to restore my hard disk with the DOS RESTORE command. Now when I attempt to load *1-2-3* Release 2, I get the error message *Unauthorized duplicate.* What's wrong?

John Neenan
Lowell, Mass.

If you have run the COPYON or COPYHARD installation procedure and find it necessary to restore your hard disk, you must use the DOS RESTORE/P command. (Release 2.01 users need to use only RESTORE without the /P parameter.) When the command asks if you want to restore read-only files, answer No; otherwise, the protected files will be damaged and you won't be able to load 1-2-3 without a key disk in drive A.

Because you didn't use the RESTORE/P command, you have two alternatives. You can use the COPYON or COPYHARD procedure from the Backup System Disk to copy the protected files onto the hard disk, or you can use the key disk (either the

System or Backup System Disk) in Drive A. Before you can use the key disk, you must clear the copy-protection files from the hard disk. If you don't, the program will continue to look for the copy protection on the hard disk. In 1-2-3 Release 2, exit to DOS and with the PrintGraph disk in drive A enter COPYHARD/P *at the A> prompt. In 1-2-3 Release 2.01, exit to DOS and with the Utility disk in drive A enter* zap *at the A> prompt. You will get the message* Product protection system damaged possibly caused by root directory restore. Do you want to continue (Yes/No)? *Answering Yes means that you will purge the copy protection from the hard disk.*

SECTION
4

SAVING AND
RETRIEVING FILES

A computer's memory is a volatile place. Anything in RAM (Random Access Memory) will be lost the moment the computer is turned off. That's why it is so important to regularly save your work to disk, as frequently as every couple of minutes or before you make major changes. The disk version of a file is relatively permanent, staying exactly as you left it until you overwrite the old version with a newer one or until your disk is eaten by the family dog.

But the more files you have, the harder it becomes to keep track of where those files are located. Using directories helps, but what happens if you use floppies to back up your important data? It's pretty easy to forget which floppy contains the most recent version of which file. The eight-character limitation on file names imposed by DOS is another problem — Macintosh users have a big advantage with the 40-plus characters allowed by their machine.

Speed is also an issue. A big file seems to take forever to load into memory or be saved on disk. The fact that *1-2-3 Release 2* originally had a bug that lengthened the process didn't help. In addition, File Save places an exact copy of the worksheet currently in memory without disturbing the monitor display. Once the save operation is complete, there is no way to know (without first exiting to DOS) when you last saved the file. So if you walk away from your computer for a while, then return, it's hard to tell if you remembered to save before you left or if your disk version needs updating.

Finally, windows are a special capability of *1-2-3* that allow you to see two parts of your worksheet at once, or the same part using two different formats. The ability to keep your windows synchronized as they scroll is a very useful tool that was lost in the transition to *Symphony*.

This section covers it all: saving, retrieving, getting around bugs, knowing when you've already saved, and using windows.

1

Using Hard and Floppy Disks

SAVING FILES ON A HARD DISK

We recently purchased an IBM AT with a hard disk. Using DOS, we issued the MD (make directory) command to make subdirectories for Lotus programs and worksheets. We copied all the Lotus programs and worksheet files into their own subdirectories named \LOTUS and \FILES, respectively. But now our files are saving to the root directory and we can't retrieve the worksheets we copied into the \FILES subdirectory. What are we doing wrong?

Pal V. Rao
Eastern Illinois University
Charleston, Ill.

For 1-2-3 and Symphony *to retrieve and save files in a particular subdirectory, the program must be set up to look in that subdirectory.*

Because hard disks can store so many files, you should divide them into sections to better organize both the software and the files you use with each program. Otherwise, the program must scan the entire hard disk to access any file you try to retrieve. There are limits to the number of files in a root directory anyway. The DOS command MD\NAME or MKDIR\NAME creates a subdirectory named NAME. You can create a subdirectory for each software product and its accompanying files, as illustrated on the next page. The highest level, the root directory, is indicated with the backslash (\ ). This is the first directory you see when you turn on your computer.

All directories below the root directory, subdirectories, are indicated by the path \NAME. Each subdirectory can contain as many files and additional subdirectories as disk space allows. You can create as many subdirectory levels as you need. However, no path specification can consist of more than 63 characters, including backslashes. (This number may vary with different versions of DOS.)

To retrieve and save data files in subdirectories, first select /File Directory (1-2-3) or SERVICES File Directory (Symphony), to indicate the desired subdirectory for the current session. In Symphony *and 1-2-3 Release 2/2.01, you can also supply* *a path while retrieving or saving files by pressing the Escape key when prompted for a file name and entering the path. If you want to change the default subdirectory, select /Worksheet Global Default Directory (1-2-3) or SERVICES Configuration File (Symphony), specify the drive letter (C:\) and directory name, press Return, and select Update. The Update command saves the specified subdirectory name in the configuration file, which is stored on the System or Program disk.*

In your case, use /Worksheet Global Default Directory, specify c:\files, press Return, then select Update. To move the previously created but misplaced files, exit from 1-2-3 to a DOS C> prompt and copy the files saved in the root directory (C:\) to the subdirectory C:\FILES with the command:

copy c:\ *.w?? c:\files

Before you erase files from the root directory, verify that the files reside in the C:\FILES subdirectory by entering DIR *at the DOS prompt. If you're not in C:\FILES, enter* DIR C:\FILES *at the DOS prompt. Then enter the command:*

erase c:\ *.w??

The asterisks and question marks are wild cards. An asterisk stands for any number or combination of characters, while each question mark stands for any single character. That is, W?? *stands for any three-character file-name extension that begins with a* W *(for example, WRK, WR1, WKS, and WK1).*

READING SUBDIRECTORIES

If you use *1-2-3* Release 2/2.01 or *Symphony* with a hard disk and have a variety of subdirectories, you can navigate among them while using the File Retrieve command. When you select /File Retrieve (in *Symphony*, SERVICES File Retrieve), you will see a menu of *1-2-3* or *Symphony* worksheet files in the current directory and any subdirectories directly subordinate to the current directory. To see a menu of the worksheet files contained in the directory above the current directory, called the

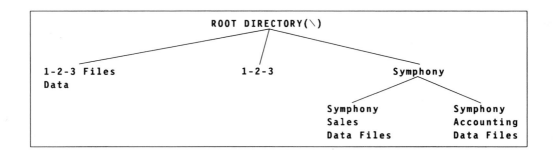

parent directory, press the Backspace key. To see the files in any subordinate directory, highlight that directory's name and press Return.

Stephen Nebel
Fairbanks, Alaska

You can also edit the directory specification in the control panel to change from one directory to any other unrelated directory or disk. After entering the File Retrieve command, press the Escape key and the cursor will appear in the control panel beside the current file specification. Press Home to move the cursor to the beginning of that specification, edit the disk-drive specifier, and enter the directory name you desire (make sure that the specification ends with a backslash — for example, C:\ACCOUNT*.W??). Press Return and you will see a list of worksheet files in the directory you specified.

CANNOT CREATE FILE

I recently encountered the error message *Cannot create file* when I attempted to save the 112th worksheet file on a disk, even though more than 60,000 bytes of disk space remained. The *1-2-3* manual states that I am trying to store too many files on the disk. Is there a limit of 111 files, or does it depend on the size of each file?

Norm Rostocki
Helena, Mont.

There is a limit on the number of files that can be stored in the root directory of a floppy disk. Single-sided disks can store 64 files; double-sided disks can store 112 files. There is a way around this. Subdirectories aren't limited in the number of files they can contain, just in the amount of space. If you create a subdirectory on the disk using the DOS MD (Make Directory) command, the subdirectory counts as one file. Depending on the size of the files, this might allow you to save more files on a double-sided disk. The maximum number of files that can be stored on a hard-disk root directory depends on the size of the partition (if there is a partition).

FROM HARD DISK TO FLOPPY

Here's a technique that enables you to save a file on your hard disk or on a floppy disk. This technique is helpful if, as a safety measure, you often copy a file onto a floppy disk.

First make sure that the hard disk is the default drive: Select /Worksheet Global Default Directory (in *Symphony*, SERVICES Configuration File) and enter *c:* or *c:\subdir*, where *subdir* is the name of the default directory on drive C. Then select Update Quit. If your hard disk is designated as drive D or some other letter, substitute that letter for the letter C when you set the default directory in the preceding instructions.

Press slash (in *Symphony*, MENU), select File Save, and enter the name of the file (you must save the file once manually before these macros will work properly). From the macros shown below, select the two that correspond to the program you use, and enter them on your worksheet. Where you see the word *filename* in each macro, substitute the name you used when you saved the file.

	A	B
1	\c	/WGDD{ESC}c:\123~Q
2		/FS{ESC}
3		filename
4		~R{ESC}
5		
6	\a	/WGDD{ESC}a:\~Q
7		/FS{ESC}
8		filename
9		~R{ESC}
10		

1-2-3 Release 1A

	A	B
1	\c	/FS{ESC 2}
2		filename
3		~R{esc}
4		
5	\a	/FS{ESC 3}a:\
6		filename
7		~R{esc}
8		

1-2-3 Release 2/2.01

	A	B
1	\c	{SERVICES}FS{ESC}
2		filename
3		~Y{ESC}
4		
5	\a	{SERVICES}FS{ESC}a:\
6		filename
7		~Y{ESC}
8		

Symphony

Assign the labels in column A as range names for the adjacent cells in column B: Place your cell pointer on cell A1 and press slash (in *Symphony*, MENU), select Range Name Labels Right, and indicate range A1..A5 (in *1-2-3* Release 1A, indicate range A1..A6). Now hold down the MACRO key (Alt on most computers) and press C to save your file on the hard disk or press MACRO-A to save your file on the floppy disk in drive A. If you wish to save the file on a floppy disk in a different drive, change the letter A in the first line of the macro named \a to the letter indicating that drive.

R. B. Harper
Newington, Conn.

As long as you remember to save your file once manually before using it, this technique appears to work under all circumstances.

VARIABLE DEFAULT DIRECTORY

For my data files, I have several subdirectories, broken down by category. As a result, I found myself changing my working directory (using the File Directory command) as soon as I entered *1-2-3*. I've discovered an easier way to do that from DOS.

I place a line in my AUTOEXEC.BAT file to set the path to the subdirectory containing my *1-2-3* program files, allowing me to load the program from any subdirectory. Since my program files are stored in the subdirectory LOTUS, the new line in my AUTOEXEC.BAT file is *path = c:\lotus*. (Instead of using a batch file, you can enter that command from the keyboard.) I also reset *1-2-3*'s default directory so that it automatically sets itself to the current subdirectory (select /Worksheet Global Default Directory, press the Escape key, press Return, and select Update Quit; in *Symphony* select SERVICES Configuration File, press Escape, press Return, then select Update Quit).

Before I load *1-2-3* I change to the subdirectory containing the worksheet files I want to use. When I load *1-2-3*, the default directory is automatically set to the current directory.

Jerome Kiel
Bloomfield, Conn.

FILE LIST

Whenever I try to execute the File List command in *1-2-3* , my computer locks up and will not accept any further commands. My LOTUS subdirectory contains approximately 200 worksheet files. Is this too many?

Michael R. Quinn
TXO Production Corp.
Shreveport, La.

When you're using 1-2-3 Release 1A and select /File List, your current directory can hold no more than 151 worksheet files. If you have more than 151 files in one subdirectory, the system will lock up in Wait mode, and you'll have to start over by turning the computer off and back on. Even pressing Control-Alt-Delete won't break you out of the lockup. The solution is to separate your large subdirectories into multiple subdirectories. The problem does not exist in Symphony or 1-2-3 Release 2/2.01.

2

File Names and Safety

EDITING DEFAULT FILE NAMES

The *1-2-3* Release 2 *Tutorial* book tells me that I can edit the default file name when I am resaving a file. I am unable to do this — the Backspace key beeps, the Escape key backs up to the previous menu, and any alphanumeric key starts a new file name. Only the Spacebar can be pressed to avoid losing the default file name. By entering a space and then pressing the Backspace key, you can move the cursor to edit the file name. If you press the Spacebar, but then fail to delete the space character by pressing the Backspace key, *1-2-3* tells you that you have entered an illegal character and requires you to press Escape and start over. Am I missing something in the documentation?

Chase Davis
Olympia, Wash.

The Tutorial *book for* 1-2-3 *Releases 2 and 2.01 is incorrect. Pressing any Arrow key or the Backspace key causes* 1-2-3 *to beep at you and prevents you from changing the file name. To edit file names, press the Spacebar, press Backspace to delete the space you just added, then use the Arrow keys or the Backspace key to modify the file name.*

FILE-NAME EXTENSIONS

I used *1-2-3* Release 1A for quite some time but have recently switched to *Symphony*. When I retrieve a file, the file-name extensions are WRK for both worksheet and document files. For example, my files are named BUDGET.WRK and MEMO.WRK. What happened to the WKS extension that appeared after *1-2-3* file names? Why is WRK the extension for both worksheet and document *Symphony* files? Am I saving my files correctly?

Seth Avakian
Concord, Massachusetts

You are saving correctly. Symphony *worksheet files are slightly different from* 1-2-3 *worksheet files, so they have a different file-name extension. Also,* Symphony *spreadsheets and documents may look different on your screen, but because* Symphony *is an integrated product, the information in both is stored in the same kind of worksheet file. This explains the common file-name extension. Both* Symphony *and* 1-2-3 *use PIC and PRN file-name extensions to indicate graph-image and print files respectively.*

DON'T OVERWRITE FILES

When starting a brand new disk, I first save a blank file named AA. I began doing this after losing some files. The problem was that I learned to automatically run through the /File Save Return Replace keystrokes needed to save a file. This works fine unless you are working with a disk that already contains a file. If you are working on a new, unsaved file and you type this sequence, you quickly overwrite the first file in your File Save menu. This is because *1-2-3* Release 1A displays file names in the order in which you originally created them. By making sure that the first file saved on each disk is the dummy AA file, I protected myself against the agony of data loss.

Bruce Weiler
National Lime and Stone
Findlay, Ohio

Because Symphony *and* 1-2-3 *Release 2/2.01 arrange files in ASCII order rather than date-of-creation order, users of these programs should name their dummy file* !! *to make sure that it is always the first one listed.*

PROTECTING FILES FROM BEING OVERWRITTEN

Many of my files serve as templates for my work. For example, I have a LETTER file that contains preset margins, my address and closing, and so on. When I want to create a letter, I retrieve the LETTER file, write the letter, then save the file under a new name. This way I don't need to create a letter from scratch each time. The only problem is that I sometimes forget to change the name before saving the finished letter and I overwrite the template file. But I found a solution. By using the ATTRIB command that comes with DOS 3.0 and later versions, I make the template file a read-only file, which means that I can retrieve the file but cannot change it or delete it. The technique works for all DOS files. I'll use a *Symphony* file as an example.

To make LETTER.WRK a read-only file, at the DOS prompt I type

```
attrib +r letter.wrk
```

When I try to overwrite or erase the file, I am denied access. When I need to change the template, I convert it back to a read-write file by typing

```
attrib -r letter.wrk
```

William Douglas
Houston, Tex.

ATTRIB (which stands for attribute) is an external DOS command, so you must have the DOS disk in a drive when you execute the command (or have the program on DOS's search path if you use a hard disk). If you use DOS 2.0 or 2.1, which lacks ATTRIB, you can use one of the various DOS utility packages. For example, The Norton Utilities, *version 3.1, has a File Attribute command that can make files read-only, as well as hidden.*

FILE-NAME TABLE IN 1-2-3

After seeing *Symphony*'s ability to create a table of file names on the worksheet, I developed a way to achieve the same result in *1-2-3 Release 1A*. I create a PRN file containing my directory information. At the DOS prompt, I type *dir>filename.prn*. The greater-than sign tells DOS to redirect the output of the DIR command to the file named FILENAME.PRN. I can import this file into my *1-2-3* worksheet using the File Import Text command. I then use the Data Parse command to divide the name, extension, date, and size information into separate columns.

Josselyn Roush
New Orleans, La.

3

Retrieving Files

SLOW RETRIEVAL IN RELEASE 2

I have encountered a problem with *1-2-3* Release 2. A file that takes 85 seconds to load in Release 1A takes more than five minutes to load in Release 2. It doesn't seem to matter what Release 2 file I retrieve, they all load slower. Is there a way to correct this problem?

Daniel R. Berger
Shaumberg, Ill.

The problem you describe results from a bug in 1-2-3 Release 2 that has been corrected in 1-2-3 Release 2.01. To get around this during the current work session, save a blank worksheet, then select /File Combine Copy Entire-File to combine this blank worksheet into the current worksheet. From here forward, 1-2-3 will retrieve files more quickly.

QUICKER ACCESS TO EXTRACTED DATA

A file you save using /File Xtract (in *Symphony*, SERVICES File Xtract) takes longer to retrieve than a file saved with /File Save (in *Symphony*, SERVICES File Save). If you extract data that you will be using a lot, retrieve the extracted file and save it with /File Save. Subsequent retrievals will be much faster.

Rebecca Gutin
New Haven, Conn.

KEEPING TRACK OF FILES

Because I have trouble keeping track of which files are on each disk, I created a *1-2-3* Release 1A macro that automatically gives me a full-screen menu of file names, followed by the regular file-name menu, from which I can then make a selection. The macro has two lines:

```
'/FLW
'/FR{?} ~
```

The first line selects the /File List Worksheet command. When I'm done looking, I have to press a key to move to the second line of the macro. This line selects the /File Retrieve command and then pauses while I point to the desired file. Because I named the macro \Ø, it automatically executes whenever I retrieve the worksheet. I named the worksheet LIBRARY and put a copy of it on each of my floppy disks.

John DiStanfano
Brookline, Massachusetts

INDEX FILE

With the eight-character limitation for naming files, you may have difficulty remembering a file name or contents, even when using subdirectories. Create a worksheet file called INDEX on each floppy disk or in each subdirectory of your hard disk. The first column of the worksheet should list all the file names on this disk or subdirectory. The second column should contain a full description. Creating an index like this is particularly helpful when several people use the same disks or if someone uses your disks in your absence. It is also a good idea for any disk of archived files.

Jeff Kimball
Bothell, Wash.

Symphony *users can select SERVICES File Table to create a list in the current worksheet of all the files in the current directory or on the current disk.*

SOLVING MULTIUSER FILE CONFUSION

Four people in our accounting department take turns using *1-2-3* on the same IBM XT. Not only do the four fight for time on the machine, but they also tend to give the same name to different files. This causes everyone to endure the agony of searching through seemingly endless lists of unfamiliar file names when saving or retrieving.

To solve these problems, we created separate subdirectories for each person and now use autoexecuting macros to switch each person to the correct subdirectory. Our *1-2-3* program files are in a directory called LOTUS. Using the DOS make-directory command (MKDIR), we created four subdirectories under LOTUS:

```
C > MKDIR\LOTUS\BETH
C > MKDIR\LOTUS\ART
C > MKDIR\LOTUS\SUSAN
C > MKDIR\LOTUS\TOM
```

We copied each person's files to the appropriate subdirectory. Then in a blank worksheet, we entered the following macro:

```
/WGDD{ESC}c:\lotus\tom ~ Q/WEY
```

We named the macro \Ø, which causes it to be invoked automatically when anyone retrieves the file. We then saved the file under the name TOM in the LOTUS directory. We did the same thing for each of the other three people by using the appropriate names, and we made one file called MAIN for the LOTUS directory.

Now when Tom, for example, sits at the computer, he retrieves his namesake file with a couple of keystrokes: /FRtom and Return. The current directory is automatically adjusted, and he proceeds with no further problem.

John B. Ford
Glen Allen, Virginia

The Symphony *macro version is:*

   {SERVICES}CF{ESC}c:\lotus\tom ~ Q{SERVICES}NY

To make it autoexecuting, select SERVICES Settings Auto-Execute Set, and point to the first cell of the macro.

PART OF FILE MISSING

While retrieving a worksheet file recently, I received a *Part of file is missing* error message and could not retrieve that particular file. The rest of the files on the disk were fine. What would have caused this error, and what could I have done to retrieve my file?

Lisa Palumbo
Harris Teeter Supermarkets
Charlotte, N.C.

The Part of file is missing *message is displayed for any of the following reasons: The data disk has been damaged; the file did not close properly due to a power surge or some kind of interference while you were saving it; or you tried to create a print file (PRN) and neglected to close the file properly (by selecting Quit from the main Print menu). Try the following ideas to salvage your file:*

1. *If it's a print file (ASCII text file), use a text editor to add Control-Z (^Z) at the end of the file. However, worksheet files are not in ASCII format.*

2. *If you have a backup copy of the data disk, use that copy as your starting point and update it. This is often easier than recovering a lost file.*

3. *If you don't have a backup copy, try retrieving the file, then pressing the Escape key. Some of your file may be successfully loaded into RAM. Save this data with a new file name on another disk. Use this as a starting point to rebuild your file.*

4. *If every data file you attempt to retrieve from that disk displays this error message, then the disk's File Allocation Table, which keeps track of the location of each file, could be damaged. Use steps 2 and 3 on each file, or try one of the file-recovery products such as* The Norton Utilities.

5. *If you can retrieve all other data files without getting an error message, you should copy them onto another disk and check each file for accuracy. Part of the damaged file may have accidentally become attached to another file.*

6. *If all files retrieved from all disks display this message, it could be a problem with your System Disk* (1-2-3), *Program Disk* (Symphony), *or your machine. Try your System Backup disk to see if the program is damaged. To see if your computer is causing the problem, try saving files on another machine using the same copy of* 1-2-3 *or* Symphony.

RELEASE 2 PRINT FILES

I created a print file in *1-2-3* Release 2 by selecting /Print File, entering the file name, specifying the range, and selecting Align Go Quit. Whenever I select /File Import Text (or Numbers) in *1-2-3* Release 1A and attempt to import the file, I get the error message *Part of file is missing*. What am I doing wrong?

Tuti Efron
Reshon, LeZion, Israel

1-2-3 Release 2/2.01 print files do not have the ^z (Control Z) end-of-file marker that 1-2-3 Release 1A places at the end of print files. Just press the Escape key at the message — the file will come without problems.

4

Saving Files

SAVING LARGE WORKSHEETS

My floppy disks can hold up to 360K. However, I often create spreadsheets that are larger than 360K. How can I split up and save my worksheet?

Dan Bills
Granite Financial Corporation
Sacramento, California

Use the File Xtract command to save separate sections of your worksheet in separate files, one per disk. Then use the File Combine command to paste the files back together in your computer's memory. Make sure to place each segment in exactly the same position that it originally occupied. One problem with this method is that the Combine command does not retain range names found in the incoming worksheet. You may need to write a macro that renames relevant cells.

To avoid this problem, you might also explore breaking your big spreadsheet into smaller worksheets, placing the key data from each worksheet in a special range, and then combining that range into a central worksheet.

ALREADY SAVED INDICATOR

My bigger worksheets used to take me a long time to save, so I'd start the process, then work on something else until the process was completed. When I returned to the computer, I would often have forgotten if I'd actually saved the file, so I'd save it again just to be sure.

To avoid this confusion and waste of time, I now use a macro that enables protection, recalculates the whole worksheet, saves the file, then erases the screen. When I return, the screen is clear and I know it's safe to go on.

/WGPE{CALC}/FS~R/WEY

David N. Lindbergh
Temcor
Torrance, Calif.

Make sure you've already saved the worksheet under its current name at least once before you invoke this macro. Otherwise, you will overwrite the first worksheet on your file-name menu.

The Symphony *version is:*

$$\{SERVICES\}SGYQ\{CALC\}\{SERVICES\}FS \sim Y\{SERVICES\}NY$$

If you want to save the worksheet but intend to continue working on the file, you should keep it in memory. However, you may want a signal to let you know that the file has just been saved. Instead of erasing the worksheet from memory, change the last part of the macro to send the pointer to the bottom-right corner of the sheet, cell IV2048 or IV8192, depending upon which Lotus worksheet product you use.

CAN'T ESCAPE DRIVE A

As instructed, I use drive A for my program disk. I place my data disk in drive B. Why does *Symphony* go to drive A when I select File Retrieve or File Save?

Fred Jones
Fort Worth, Tex.

Symphony *and 1-2-3 contain several built-in assumptions, called defaults, which you can change.* Symphony *uses drive A as the initial default for saving and retrieving files. To change this for the current session only, select SERVICES File Directory, press the Escape key to clear the default setting, and enter the desired drive, for example,* B:\.

To change the default so that the program automatically uses another drive in future sessions, select SERVICES Configuration File, press Escape to clear the default setting, and enter B:\ *or whatever drive you have chosen for your default. To save your new settings in* Symphony's *configuration file (SYMPHONY.CNF), select Update from the SERVICES Configuration menu.*

The initial default drive is drive B for 1-2-3 Release 1A and drive A for 1-2-3 Release 2/2.01. To change it for the current session only, press slash and select File Directory. To change it for future sessions, press /Worksheet Global Default Directory, enter the new drive specification, then select Update.

5

Windows

WINDOW INDEPENDENCE

Why is it that when I change the width of a column in one window, it doesn't affect the same column as displayed in other windows?

Linda M. Graham
Pontiac, Michigan

Each window is an independently controlled display area. The underlying contents of the cells are the same no matter which window you are in. In other words, if you enter a value into a cell through one window, all other windows will reflect the effect of the new value. However, if you change the Global format of one window, it will not affect the displayed format in other windows. This was done to provide maximum display flexibility — for example, it allows you to see the same data in different ways simultaneously.

UNDOING SPLIT WINDOWS

In *Symphony* is there any way to undo the effects of selecting SERVICES Window Pane other than selecting Layout and expanding the window back to full size? The problem with this solution is that all the previously created windows still exist, take up memory, and clutter my worksheet.

Robert B. Searl
Rich's
Atlanta, Ga.

The Window Delete command eliminates unwanted windows. If you've created a window you don't need now but you may need later, you can select SERVICES Window Hide. To reveal a hidden window, you must select SERVICES Window Use and point to the name of the window. The SERVICES Window Isolate command hides all but the current window in a worksheet. The SERVICES Window Expose command reveals all the windows you've hidden.

56

CREATING WINDOW RESTRICT RANGES

After you create a new window and select Restrict Range, *Symphony* has the annoying habit of ignoring the window's location and offering the "parent" window's Restrict range as the new restricted area. To stay connected to the window location when indicating a Restrict range for a newly created window, first place the pointer in the upper-left cell of the new window area with that cell in the top-left corner of your screen. Follow the usual procedures for creating a new window.

After you have highlighted the window area and the Window settings sheet becomes visible, select Restrict Screen then Restrict Range. The entire area of the window is highlighted as the current Restrict range, and you can expand or contract the Restrict range as you desire, with the advantage of having started from the current window area.

George Fitzgerald
Medford, Massachusetts

You can also start with the cell pointer in the cell that will become the top-left corner of the new Restrict range. Position the cell pointer and create the window. When the Window settings sheet becomes visible, select Restrict Range, then press Backspace to cancel the default range and press Tab to anchor the cell pointer. Now you can highlight the Restrict range for the new window.

SECTION
5

FORMULAS AND CALCULATIONS

It's not surprising that this is the longest section of this book. Entering, rearranging, and analyzing data are the core of what we do with worksheets. These tasks also involve some of the most difficult conceptual aspects of spreadsheet use, in particular the meaning of absolute, relative, and mixed cell references — a topic made even more complicated since the File Combine commands adjust all incoming formulas as if they were relative.

The good ideas in this section run the gamut from editing cell entries to calculating year-to-date totals, from speeding recalculations to copying relative cell references, from using @functions to moving the pointer, from naming ranges to laying out a worksheet.

For most of us, this is the section we'll come back to most often, each time finding a new trick that speeds up some repetitive task. Don't wait until you have a problem needing an instant solution. Prepare yourself by leafing through these tips and tricks before disaster strikes.

There are some items in this section that show users of *1-2-3* Release 1A how to get around limitations in that product that were eliminated in later releases. For example, transposing a range was a technical trick in the original versions of *1-2-3* but a simple matter of selecting the Range Transpose command in later releases. On the other hand, simplifying the process of calculating running totals or year-to-date consolidations is of interest to all spreadsheet users. Forecasters and anyone creating budget projections will find valuable ideas listed under "Statistics and Random Numbers," while the tips on creating a clearly defined input area will benefit people who create worksheets for themselves as well as people who prepare models for others. We have tried to avoid duplication. Often, however, our readers will provide us with several different solutions to the same problem or alternative methods of speeding up a particular technique.

1

Moving, Editing, and Keeping Track of Data

TRANSPOSING ROWS AND COLUMNS

In *1-2-3* Release 1A when I want to transpose a table of numbers laid out rowwise into a columnwise layout, I extract the range into a separate file, translate the file into data interchange format (DIF) with the Translate utility, then translate it back to WKS format using the columnwise option. When I combine the file into its original location, I have what I want.

Harriet C. Barry
Wayne, Pennsylvania

In 1-2-3 Release 2/2.01 you can select /Range Transpose (MENU Range Transpose in Symphony*) to accomplish the same thing.*

TRANSPOSING RANGES

In a previous Good Idea a reader explained how to use DIF files to transpose a table of numbers. You can also accomplish this using the @LOOKUP function, a much simpler method that is also dynamic as changes in the original table are carried into the transposed range when the worksheet is recalculated. The example uses @VLOOKUP, but @HLOOKUP would work as well. The range name *table* refers to cells A2..D4.

	A	B	C	D	E
1	YEAR	X	Y	Z	
2	84	15	17	21	
3	85	18	24	26	
4	86	19	27	30	
5					
6		YEAR	84	85	86
7	1	X	15	18	19
8	2	Y	17	24	27
9	3	Z	21	26	30

You have to enter the labels and the year numbers manually. You must also enter an index column (A7..A9) that contains the offsets for the original table. The formula entered in cell C7 is:

@VLOOKUP(C$6,$table,$A7)

Note the use of mixed references, which makes the copying work, and the dollar sign in front of the range name, which makes it absolute.

Mark D. Pankin
Arlington, Va.

COPYING TO EVERY OTHER CELL
Suppose cell A1 contains a formula that you want to copy to cells A3, A5, A7, and so on down to cell A23. Copy using a FROM range of A1..A22, and a TO range of A3. If you need to copy to every third cell, use the same FROM range but change the TO range to A4. I don't know why it works, but it does!

Patrick MaGee
Bellevue, Washington

Nice trick! Here's why it works. When copying a range to a single target cell, both 1-2-3 and Symphony copy the entire FROM range to the TO cell. The copy is placed so that the top-left corner of the range is located at the TO cell. The program places the contents of the first cell of the FROM range (A1) in the first cell of the TO range (A3). Then it copies the contents of the second cell of the FROM range (A2) to the next cell after the initial TO cell (A4). No surprises so far. But when the program goes to copy the contents of the third cell in the FROM range (A3), it discovers the formula that has just been entered into A3 and copies the formula into cell A5. The process continues for the number of cells contained in the original FROM range.

USING THE ABSOLUTE KEY IN EDIT MODE
Is it possible to make the ABS key operable in Edit mode in *1-2-3*?

W.A. Seedorff Jr.
Mas Minerals Associates
Sunnyvale, Calif.

You cannot do this if you are using 1-2-3 Release 1A. However, in 1-2-3 Release 2/2.01 you can edit a cell that contains an absolute cell reference by pressing the EDIT key and then pressing the ABS key repeatedly until you get the proper combination of absolute and relative references. For example, suppose you type A5 + N8 in cell A1 and you really want A5 + $N8. Place the cursor on cell A1, press the EDIT function key, and then press the ABS function key twice. The last cell address changes. If you want to change A5, you must place the cursor on or near A5 and then press the ABS key. In the case of a function such as @SUM(A5..A10), when you use the ABS key, both addresses change simultaneously.

POINTING IN EDIT MODE

When editing formulas in Edit mode, it's often easier to reenter ranges by pointing to the cell addresses.

First press the EDIT key, then press the Backspace key to erase the cell address you wish to reenter. The line should now end with either a comma, an arithmetic operator (such as + or *), or an open parenthesis. Move the cell pointer up or down with the Arrow keys to switch from Edit mode to Point mode. Now you can move anywhere in the worksheet in Point mode. Press Return to return to Edit mode and to insert the new cell address in the formula you are editing.

John Predmore
Fairport, N.Y.

This method works only when you are removing the rightmost argument from a formula. Arguments contained within the formula are unavailable for Point mode editing.

USING THE NUMERIC KEYPAD

You can use the numeric keypad to enter numbers and still have access to the Arrow keys. When you want to use the keypad, just press Shift and a keypad number. Release the Shift key to enable the cursor-movement Arrow keys. You can also press Num Lock to enable the keypad and press the Shift key when you want to enable the cursor-movement Arrow keys.

Joan Ferrara
Syracuse, New York

SYMPHONY SHEET TIPS

1. Occasionally, you may wish to place notes to yourself in a spreadsheet; however, you may not want to print out these notes with your sheet. To create nonprinting lines, go to column A and enter the vertical bar label prefix (¦) followed by your text. Even though you may include your note in the print range, the note will not appear on your printout.

2. Many of *Symphony*'s @functions, such as @S, @N, and @CELL, require a range as an argument although only a single cell is involved. For example, @S(G1) won't work; you must indicate starting and ending cell locations, even though they are both the same — for example, @S(G1..G1). To simplify the entry, enter an exclamation mark (!) as the first coordinate — for example, @S(!G1). The program interprets and subsequently displays this as the single cell range G1..G1. This works very nicely within macros and is also useful when you reference a range name that begins with a number — for example, @SUM(!1040).

3. The entry form visible in a FORM window can also be used to enter data into a spreadsheet. You can display prompts and instructions, pass the input through

validity checks, transform incoming values with a formula, compute additional items based on other data, and include default entries. After you've generated the form, issue the FORM window MENU Settings One-Record command (or the SHEET window MENU Query Settings One-Record command). The database accepts only one record, which can be used as the input for a spreadsheet because each field name is also a range name that can be referenced in formulas. You can see spreadsheet computations in a SHEET window while you are using the entry form in a FORM window.

To erase an old record prior to entering new data into your spreadsheet, the FORM window must be current. Select MENU Initialize to return all fields to their default values, then enter new data for another spreadsheet session.

If you have more than 32 input items, just create a second form in another FORM window.

Anne Gaston
New York, New York

INTERNAL TABLE OF CONTENTS

In my worksheets, I include a number of associated but separate computations. First I assign a range name to each worksheet work area. Then, starting in cell A1, I place a list of the range names and the cell addresses of the upper-left and lower-right corners of the ranges. I always press Home before saving the worksheet to insure that my internal table of contents is the first thing visible when the file is retrieved. This practice not only provides a quick reminder of the worksheet's contents but also allows me to use the GOTO key and avoid the annoyance of having to tab or use PageDown to find desired work areas.

Brian Brenegan
Milwaukee, Wisconsin

In 1-2-3 Release 2/2.01 you can select /Range Name Table to give you a list of range names and their cell coordinates (MENU Range Name Table in Symphony).

CHANGING CONTENTS OF TITLES CELLS

You don't have to clear your Titles settings in order to edit the titles. Press GOTO, Home, then Return. Two copies of the titles area appear on your screen with the pointer inside one of them. Make your changes, then press PageDown (with horizontal titles) or Control and RightArrow key (with vertical titles) to get back into the spreadsheet. You can also use the Copy and Move commands to transfer cell contents into the title area. Once you are in Point mode, you can move into the title area to indicate the destination for moving or copying titles.

John E. Predmore
Fairport, N.Y.

SPACE IN VALUE CELLS

I need to create a *1-2-3* worksheet that adds columns of values, but I want these values to appear right-aligned without the space at the end of each cell. Entering values with quotation marks places them right-aligned, but then these values can't be used in any calculations. Why is the space there, and is there any way to get rid of it?

Don Nummi Jr.
Superior, Wis.

In 1-2-3 *Release 1A you can't get rid of the space at the end of each value cell. The space is there to separate columns of numbers visually and also for closing parentheses around negative numbers in currency format.*

In 1-2-3 *Release 2/2.01 and* Symphony, *you can enter values as labels and still manipulate them with formulas. To do so, use the @VALUE function. The @VALUE function returns the numeric value of a label and allows labels, regardless of their alignment, to be used in calculations. For example, if cell A1 contains the label ''2 and cell B1 contains the label ''3, then @VALUE(A1) + @VALUE(B1) evaluates to 5.*

FLAGGING VARIABLES

To indicate that the numbers in one range of my worksheet are variable, I enclose them in parentheses by preceding the numbers with a minus sign and selecting /Range Format , (Punctuated in *Symphony*). The problem is that formulas read these numbers as negative and calculate accordingly. What I want is a formula that evaluates these numbers as positive. Can you help?

Benita Gaines
Atlanta, Ga

As you've discovered, numbers enclosed in parentheses are evaluated as negative numbers. You might want to modify the way you flag variables. For example, you could insert a one-character column in which you enter an asterisk next to variables, or you could separate the variables from the constants and label them accordingly.

If you still want to use your method of flagging variables, use the @ABS function, which takes the absolute value of a value or cell address. For example, @ABS(B1) evaluates to 500 even when cell B1 contains (500).

2

Cumulative, Running, and Year-to-Date Totals

YEAR-TO-DATE — I

I created a short macro to accumulate year-to-date totals in a two-column worksheet area. I enter the current figures in column A under the heading *current*, then the macro calculates and enters the running totals in column B under the heading *YTD*, which is also the range name of the first data cell below the heading. The macro is named \t:

```
{GOTO}ytd~
{EDIT}+{EDIT}{LEFT}~
{EDIT}{CALC}{DOWN}
/RNDytd~
/RNCytd~ ~
/XIytd<>0~/XG\t~
{UP}{END}{UP}{DOWN}
/RNDytd~
/RNCytd~ ~
```

This avoids the whole process of combining files.

Martin E. Pirrman Jr.
Sure Foundation Fellowship
Buffalo, Okla.

This macro works by switching back and forth between EDIT and VALUE modes — a process you start by repeatedly pressing the EDIT key. You must, however, have empty cells above the YTD label. With 1-2-3 Release 1A you need an empty cell or label below the last item in the column. Symphony and 1-2-3 Release 2/2.01 have a Range Values command that negates the need for a macro. However, the macro listed above will work in 1-2-3 Release 2/2.01 just as well as in Release 1A.

YEAR-TO-DATE — II

You've previously described various ways of creating and updating a running year-to-date total. Here's another:

When you set up your spreadsheet, put each time period's entry section in a distinct column, then insert a new column each time you wish to enter new data. The YTD formula in cell D2 reads @SUM (B2..C2). In this example, I would insert a new column between FEB and YTD when it was time to enter March data.

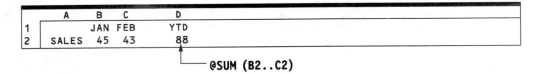

Don Schlosser
King Videocable Co.
Seattle, Wash.

This approach assumes that you don't need to see an entire year's worth of data and that you've constructed your worksheet so that you can insert columns. Even so, as set up, your model requires you to adjust the @SUM range each time you insert a new column. To avoid that, leave a one-character-wide blank column just to the left of the YTD column and include that column in the @SUM range.

If you place the pointer on the blank column when you select Insert, the new column is placed to the left of the blank column, and the @SUM range automatically expands to include the new data. In the example shown here, YTD would move to column E, and column D would be blank.

YEAR-TO-DATE TOTALS

As part of my job, I am responsible for determining the year-to-date total for a set of numbers. Typically, I have 12 months' worth of data, some actual history, and some estimated future figures. At the end of each month, I'd like to include one more month in the sum headed *YTD Actual*. I have tried massive @IF statements, logic calculation formulas, and macros that reset and recopy the formula. Is there some easy way to accomplish this task?

Bill Leetham
Candle
Los Angeles, California

	A	B	C	D	E	F	G	H	I	J	K	L	M	N	O
1								selector		number >>				9	
2															
3		Actual									¦ Outlook			YTD	
4		Jan	Feb	Mar	Apr	May	Jun	Jul	Aug	Sep	Oct	Nov	Dec	Actual	Projected
5	***														
6	widgets	1	2	3	4	5	6	7	8	9	8	7	6	45	66
7	...	3	4	5	6	7	8	6	54	3	45	6	5	96	152

FIGURE 1. The formula in cell N6 is: @CHOOSE(N1,Ø,B6,B6+C6), @SUM(B6..D6), @SUM(B6..E6), @SUM(B6..F6), @SUM(B6..G6), @SUM(B6..H6), @SUM(B6..I6), @SUM(B6..J6), @SUM(B6..K6), @SUM(B6..L6), @SUM(B6..M6)). The formula in cell O6 is @SUM(B6..M6). Cell N1 contains the selector number: the month that *YTD Actual* should accumulate up through should be entered here. In this example, *YTD Actual* is up through September (month 9), therefore the *YTD Actual* accumulates up through month 9.

Try @CHOOSE(selector-number, argØ,arg1,arg2, …). If the selector-number is Ø, the function returns argØ; if it is 1, the function returns arg1, and so on. In Figure 1, the different arguments are @SUM functions that total different ranges. The larger the month number you place in cell N1, which is referred to as the selector-number value, the more cells are included in the range.

SEPARATING OUT PARTS OF A WHOLE

I need to keep a running total by dozens. The cumulative columns must be in whole numbers; that is, 2.5 dozens must be changed so that the 2 is in one cell and the .5 is translated into 6 units and placed in a different cell. Part of my problem is that fractional numbers are rounded up when I format the cells with Fixed Ø. In the example below, what formula should I enter into cell C4? How do I avoid rounding up display errors? And how do I get the partial dozens cumulatively added, divided into dozens and units, then entered into cell D4?

George Ebbinghousen
Polo Ralph Lauren
Carlstadt, New Jersey

	A	B	C	D
1	Overage		Cumulative	
2	DOZ	UNITS	DOZ	UNITS
3	1	6	1	6
4	1	7	?	?

Assume you manually enter each day or week's average in columns A and B. In cell C3 enter the following formula:

 @SUM(A3..A3) + @INT(@SUM(B3..B3)/12)

And in cell D3 enter:

 @MOD(@SUM(B3..B3),12)

 Now copy these formulas down next to the entries in columns A and B.

 The absolute reference used as the first part of the @SUM ranges anchors the range at the top of each column of data. If you leave the second reference relative, it can adjust as you copy the formula to lower rows. The result is that the SUM range stretches to cover all entries in each column.

 The first formula adds the total number of dozens to the integer remaining after the total number of units is divided by 12.

 The second formula returns the remainder, as a whole number, after dividing the total number of overage units by 12.

CUMULATIVE SUM FORMULA REVISITED

In a past tip you suggested using the hybrid reference @SUM(B2..$B3), then copying the formula down a column of data for a running cumulative sum. I found an alternative way to accomplish the same thing. Enter +B2 in cell C2 and +B3+C2 in cell C3, then simply copy C3 down the column.

Robert C. Davey
Electrical Engineering
Honolulu, Hawaii

EASY SUMMING OF RANGES CONTAINING SUBTOTALS

Here's a way to total a column that already contains subtotals. As long as each entry is contained in a subtotal within the column, all entries are essentially in the column twice. Simply total the column using the @SUM function, and divide the result by 2.

Cell	Entry
A1:	1
A2:	2
A3:	3
A4:	@SUM(A1..A3)
A6:	6
A7:	7
A8:	8
A9:	@SUM(A6..A8)
A10:	\-
A11:	@SUM(A1..A9)/2

A slight modification of this technique will work for lower levels of detail (sub-subtotals). Just divide the sum of the column by the number of times each value has been included.

Jim Puiia
Massachusetts General Hospital
Boston, Mass

QUICK ACCUMULATOR

We need to keep running totals in the column to the right of the column containing monthly sales or expenses. Here's the simplest route we've found to do it. Position the pointer in the cell directly to the right of the first cell in which you wish to keep a total, and enter a special @SUM formula referencing the cell in the column to the left. For example, to keep a running total of data that begins in cell B2, enter the formula @SUM(B$2..B2) in cell C2.

	A	B	C
1	Month	Sales	YTD
2	Jan	123	123
3	Feb	134	
4	Mar	232	

When you copy the formula down column B, *B$2* locks the first part of the range specification at the top of the column, while *B2* will change to reference the cell currently to the left of the formula. For example, if you copy the original formula down the column to cell C4, the entry in cell C4 would read @SUM(B$2..B4).

	A	B	C
1	Month	Sales	YTD
2	Jan	123	123
3	Feb	134	257
4	Mar	232	489

The concept works both columnwise and rowwise. You can also embed the formula in an @IF function to display the year-to-date total only if the cell next to it has a total:

@IF(B5,@SUM(B$2..B5),0)

1-2-3 and *Symphony* evaluate the first argument of the @IF function (B5) as "true" if the argument returns a nonzero value. If the first argument is true, the function returns the value of the second argument, @SUM(B$2..B5). If the first argument is false, the function returns the value of the third argument (0). Since blank cells return the value 0, if cell B5 is blank, the first argument will be "false," and the function will return the third argument, 0.

As written, the @SUM range will always begin in row 2. However, when copied to another column, the formula will adjust to reference the new column to its left.

Steve Cox
Parkersburg, W.Va.

CUMULATIVE TOTALS

In one of our worksheets, we need to enter numbers repeatedly into column A and have column B display the cumulative total. If in column B we place a formula that adds column A to column B and then recalculates the worksheet, column B adds all of the numbers in column A a second time. How can we set up our spreadsheets so that previous entries in column A are not erroneously re-added?

Joe Castellana
Carol McCarthy
HCHP Hospital
Boston, Mass

To accumulate in column B entries made in column A, try the following technique. First, enter the current values into the input area, which in this case is A2..A5.

	A	B
1	Current	Cumulative
2	126	6000
3	560	7000
4	600	5000
5	790	4000

Select /File Xtract Values (1-2-3) or SERVICES File Xtract Values (Symphony), enter a file name, and specify the range A2..A5. Move the cell pointer to cell B2 and select /File Combine Add Entire-File (1-2-3) or SERVICES File Combine Add Entire-File Ignore Values (Symphony). Then specify the file name that contains the extracted values from column A. After this procedure, your file will look like this:

	A	B
1	Current	Cumulative
2	126	6126
3	560	7560
4	600	5600
5	790	4790

Because column B cells don't contain formulas referencing column A, changing the numbers in column A will not affect column B. You can automate this process with a macro.

3

Summary Worksheet:
File Combine

COPY, ADD, OR SUBTRACT?

When using the File Combine command, when is it appropriate to use Copy, Add, or Subtract?

Kevin L. Holleran
Buffalo, N.Y.

The File Combine command is useful in combining data or entire worksheets from several different sources or in accumulating similar sets of data.

Use the Copy option when you want to replace a range that you have in your current worksheet with a range from another worksheet, or when you want to append a range or worksheet to the current worksheet. The Copy option will begin placing incoming values, labels, and formulas wherever your cell pointer is positioned at the time of combining and will overwrite cell contents on the current worksheet. If incoming cells are blank, the current values remain intact. Position the cell pointer in the upper-left corner of the range where you want the incoming file to be placed. Make sure to save the current file before you combine another file into it. This will reduce the consequences of a mistake such as overwriting needed cells from the current file.

Use the Add or Subtract options when you want to consolidate numbers — adding or subtracting a group of values in one file to or from a group of values in another file.

The Add option adds incoming values to the numeric values in the current worksheet. If an incoming value overlays a cell containing a numeric value, 1-2-3 and Symphony *add the two values. If the incoming value overlays a label or a formula, 1-2-3 and* Symphony *ignore the incoming value and leave the label or formula undisturbed.*

The Subtract option subtracts incoming values from the numeric values in the current worksheet. 1-2-3 and Symphony *consider blank cells to have a value of zero, so positive values subtracted from a blank cell produce negative values (for example, 0–240 = –240).*

FILE COMBINE

I just bought an IBM PC XT, with one floppy-disk drive. When I was using an IBM PC (dual drive), the worksheet I created was too large to fit on a single disk, so I split it into six worksheets and saved them on six separate disks under different file names. Each worksheet uses columns A through AQ and has identical labels and formulas in the respective columns. The rows vary from 40 to 60.

Now that I have an XT, how can I combine all six worksheets into one and save it on the hard disk? I don't want to overlay the data, I just want to attach each file of information to the next.

Richard C. Dehmel
Short Hills, N.J.

Let's assume that the files you want to combine are named FILE1, FILE2, *and so on. You can use the following procedure to combine your worksheets:*

1. *Starting with a blank worksheet, place the cell pointer in the cell where you want the file to begin. Save this blank worksheet onto your hard disk in the directory in which you want it to reside and call it MASTER. Place the disk containing* FILE1 *in drive A. If you have the default directory set to a drive other than A, select /File Directory (in* Symphony, *SERVICES File Directory) and type A:\ to specify A as the current directory. This will allow you to combine worksheets that reside in the A drive.*

2. *Select /File Combine Copy Entire-File (in* Symphony, *SERVICES File Combine Copy Entire-File Ignore Formulas). A menu of file names will appear. Select* FILE1 *and press Return. The file is combined into the blank worksheet.*

3. *Replace the disk in drive A with the disk containing* FILE2. *Move the cell pointer down column A to the top-left cell in which you want* FILE2 *to begin. Repeat step 2, but this time select* FILE2 *as the file to combine.*

4. *Repeat steps 2 and 3 until you've combined the data from all six files into this worksheet.*

5. *Select /File Save (in* Symphony, *SERVICES File Save) to save your worksheet with its file name MASTER.*

If you run into the Memory full *error message, the combined file you are attempting to create is too large to fit in your computer's RAM. You will have to keep at least two files.*

SUMMARY WORKSHEET

We have 11 branch offices. I want to construct a summary worksheet that adds together the information we receive each month from each office. All the offices have *1-2-3* and can create files for my use.

Laura A. Lasky
NRS Magazine
North Olmsted, Ohio

Create a master worksheet model that you distribute to all branches. By using a common model, you ensure that the summary data of each office's report are in the same range. For example, the total monthly telephone bill is always placed in cell C4, the total utility bill is in C5, and so on. Give the summary area a range name, such as summary. *You then add all these subtotals together by retrieving your own consolidation file, which has a similarly structured summary area, placing the cell pointer in the top-left corner of the summary area, selecting /File Combine Add Named-Range (SERVICES File Combine Add Named-Area in* Symphony*), then entering* summary *and the file name. Do this for each of the files sent to you by the branch offices. The File Combine Add command is applicable to many file consolidation tasks.*

COMBINING FORMULAS INTO OTHER FILES

I have built a check register using *1-2-3*. I use macros to enter the amount of disbursement in the appropriate column headings. After finally removing all the problems, I tried to combine the column totals into another worksheet file using the File Combine Copy command. For some reason all the combined cells contain 0.00. The range that I attempted to combine contains @SUM formulas. Help!

Paul Amicucci
Juneau, Alaska

The File Combine Copy command copies entries from a worksheet stored on disk into the current worksheet. The incoming formulas replace existing formulas, and the cell references in those newly arrived formulas now refer to cell addresses in the current worksheet. For example, if the incoming formula that gets placed in cell A452 is @SUM(A400..A450) and if range A400..A450 in the current worksheet doesn't contain any values, the formula will evaluate to 0.

4

Recalculations

BEEP TO SIGNAL END OF RECALCULATION

You've previously published a macro used to trigger a beep at the end of a long recalculation to let you know the computer is ready for further use. For those people who shy away from macros, and for those who write them and then forget to use them (such as myself), there is an alternative.

After pressing the CALC key to start the recalculation process, press a string of nonsense command letters, for example, /bbb Esc. The keyboard buffer stores these keystrokes until the computer finishes the recalculation and is ready to accept additional input. At that point, since no command begins with the letter B, the program beeps three times, which signals the end of the recalculation. The final press of the Escape key eliminates the menu from your screen.

Mary A. Conti
Brookline, Massachusetts

This technique also works in a Symphony *SHEET window.*

SPEEDIER RECALCULATION METHODS

In the old days, spreadsheets recalculated row by row or column by column. Unfortunately, if a formula in cell A1 was dependent upon another formula in B2, the first formula would be calculated before the second. Consequently, you had to calculate the spreadsheet two or more times to get an accurate result.

Both *1-2-3* and *Symphony* ordinarily use natural order of recalculation. This means that cells containing information needed in a formula are calculated before the formula cell. For example, if cell A1 contains a formula that references cell B2, cell B2 is calculated before cell A1. Natural order of recalculation lets you place data and formulas anywhere in a spreadsheet. Lotus programs also default to automatic recalculation, which means that the entire worksheet is recalculated every time new information is entered. This ensures that all formulas display up-to-date results.

However, as your spreadsheet gets larger, the recalculation time increases. To avoid recalculation delays, change your recalculation method to manual. In *Sym-*

phony select MENU Settings Recalculation Manual; in *1-2-3* select /Worksheet Global Recalculation Manual. Now the worksheet will not recalculate until you press the CALC function key. To remind you, the *Calc* indicator appears on the bottom of your screen whenever you enter information and remains visible until you press CALC.

The natural order of recalculation is slower than row or column recalculation methods. If you have a very large worksheet and if your model contains no forward references, you might save some time by switching to one of these alternatives. For access to these options, in *Symphony* select MENU Settings Recalculation Order, and in *1-2-3* select /Worksheet Global Recalculation.

RECALCULATING ONE CELL

You've previously shown how users can recalculate one cell in a worksheet set to Manual Recalculation by placing the pointer on the cell, pressing the EDIT key, then the CALC key. One problem with this is that if you then press Return, the original formula is lost and only the current value is entered into the cell. To avoid this problem, you must press Escape after EDIT and CALC. Another method is to copy the cell to itself. This also works for updating values in a range. When you use this technique, remember that all other cells remain unchanged, even if they reference the recalculated cells. In addition, you must follow certain guidelines to make sure that a single copy-to-itself command properly updates all cell values in a range. First, any formulas in the range that reference other cells in the same range can only reference cells that are to the left and above. Second, be sure to use the default Natural recalculation order.

Ronald L. Seaman
Decatur, Georgia

SPEEDING UP CALCULATION OF DATA TABLES

One of the most time-consuming operations in *1-2-3* is the calculation of complex data tables (what-if tables in *Symphony*). I have found a way to reduce this calculation time drastically by using one-way instead of two-way data tables.

For instance, I have a table that is 100 clients deep and eight employees across. If I use a two-way data table, placing an @DSUM formula in the upper-left corner, *1-2-3* has to calculate the spreadsheet 800 times, once for each client/employee combination. However, if I set up eight @DSUM formulas across the top of the table, *1-2-3* has to recalculate the spreadsheet only 100 times, once for each client. It takes longer for each recalculation, due to the seven additional formulas, but this is more than made up for by the 700 fewer recalculations. In this particular example, the table takes 15 minutes instead of 45.

To use this technique, you have to set up multiple Criterion ranges, one for each @DSUM formula. Each Criterion range would consist of two fields: *Client* and *Employee Number*. The employee number would vary from 1 to 8, and the client entry in the first Criterion range would be the input cell for the one-way data table. The *Client* fields in all subsequent Criterion ranges could then reference this cell for their input.

Jack Griffith
Fort Worth, Tex.

SPEEDING TABLE RECALC

I have a huge worksheet that contains a large database and several two-way data tables (called what-if tables in *Symphony*). To calculate the tables, the program had to recalculate the entire worksheet for each pair of input cells in each table. Because of all the formulas involved, this recalculation took about eight hours for the whole macro-driven process.

I finally discovered a way to expedite the process. Now I move the formulas needed for the table to a spot close to the table area. I then issue the /File Xtract Values command to extract the rest of the worksheet, including the database, into a separate file. Next I issue the /File Combine Copy command to combine the extracted material back into the worksheet in the same position that it originally occupied. Finally, I issue the /Data Table command. This cut the run time down to 40 minutes!

Michael J. Benson
George A. Hormel and Company
Austin, Minnesota

MULTIPLE RECALC NEEDED

Our large worksheet is set to Manual recalculation, but we have to press the CALC function key three or more times to make the calculations carry through to the bottom row. Why should this be?

Karen Scholtes
Christian Science Monitor
Boston, Massachusetts

You may have one or more circular references that require multiple recalculations before reaching a final figure. In addition, check if you have accidentally changed the Natural calculation settings to Rowwise or Columnwise, either of which could cause the problem you describe. To correct it, in 1-2-3, select /Worksheet Global Recalculation Natural; in Symphony, select MENU Settings Recalculation Order Natural.

There are times when you need multiple calculations of a spreadsheet. For those occasions, use the Recalculation Iteration command to control the number of recalculation repetitions.

5

Rounding

ROUNDING UP

You previously supplied one way to round numbers up to the next-highest integer. Here's a way that works on negative as well as positive numbers, calculates more quickly, and requires fewer characters than your approach. In addition, you can use this method to round to any number of decimal places as well as to integers:

@ROUND(*cell* + 0.499999,0)

To round to different decimal places, simply move the decimal point in 0.499999 to the left. For example, to round up to one decimal place, use 0.0499999.

Michael Gallagher
Concord, Mass

You can also control the sensitivity of the rounding-up process by varying the number of nines. The fewer nines you use, the less sensitive the process is to minute fractions. If the number of staff positions to be rounded is 3.00000001, do you still want to hire four people? When it comes to negative numbers, remember that rounding up *means reducing the absolute value. For example, rounding –1.2 up returns –1, not –2.*

ROUNDING UP TO NEAREST MULTIPLE

One of your good ideas presented a formula that rounds up to the nearest multiple, solving such problems as: If I need 980 bricks, and bricks come in bundles of 76, how many bundles do I need? You suggested the following formula to round the value in *cell* up to the nearest multiple of 76:

@INT(cell/76) + (@MOD(cell,76) > 0)

A much more compact formula is:

@INT((cell + 75)/76)

If *round* is a cell containing the rounding factor, such as 76, the formula becomes:

@INT((cell + round–1)/round)

The @MOD statement is unnecessary.

Richard E. Ozaroff
New York, N.Y.

If you use only whole numbers, your technique works fine. However, if you are using decimal numbers, you can get erroneous results. The formula as written will mis-round values that are less than one unit above a particular multiple of the rounding interval. For example, assume the correct rounding interval is 76: @INT((152.5 + 76–1)/76) returns 2, though the correct result is 3. To make the formula more reliable, change the factor you add to cell *to reflect decimals; for example, @INT((cell + round–.001)/round) will mis-round only numbers that are less than .001 greater than a multiple. Or use the @MOD formula, which has no problems with decimal numbers.*

ROUNDING TO THE NEAREST NICKEL

I need a formula to round a dollar amount to the nearest nickel. Can you help?

S. Manning
Seattle, Wash.

Here's a way to round a dollar amount to the nearest nickel using string functions. Enter a dollar amount in cell A1 and the following formula in cell A5:

> *@IF(@RIGHT(@STRING(A1,2),1)< = ''2'',@INT(A1*10)/10,@IF (@RIGHT(@STRING(A1,2),1)< = ''6'',@INT(A1*10)/10 + 0.05,@INT(A1*10)/10 + 0.1))*

   If the last digit of the dollar amount is less than or equal to 2, the number is rounded down; for example, 10.22 would be rounded to 10.20. If the last digit is greater than 2 and less than or equal to 6, the number is rounded to 5; for example, both 10.23 and 10.26 would be rounded to 10.25. Finally, all numbers ending with a digit greater than 6 are rounded up; for example, 10.27 would be rounded to 10.30.

ROUNDING-ERROR MACRO

After building a large spreadsheet, I usually find some rounding errors. I have created a macro to take care of this problem without the keystrokes that are normally necessary. I place the pointer on the cell that caused the rounding error and invoke the macro. This version rounds the cell's contents to two decimal places. You can adjust the number of decimal places by changing the number at the end of the macro.

{EDIT}{HOME}@ROUND({END},2)~

R. I. Levine
Washington, D.C.

If memory space is a problem and you don't mind freezing the cell at its current value, you can add {CALC} just before the tilde to change the formula into a hard number.

TRUNCATING DECIMALS

I recently needed to truncate a decimal answer to nine decimal places but did not want to round off the value.

1-2-3 and *Symphony* do not have a truncate function for decimals, but the @INT function will truncate a mixed number. I used the following formula to truncate the decimal to nine places:

@INT((*cell*)*1000000000)/1000000000

The formula multiplies the results of the *cell* calculation by 1,000,000,000 (one billion), thereby moving the decimal point nine places to the right. The @INT function then returns only the integer portion of the number. Dividing the integer portion of the number by 1,000,000,000 moves the decimal point nine places to the left, resulting in a decimal truncated to nine places. The formula replaces the decimal places 10 through 15 with zeros.

You can use this formula to truncate a decimal value to any number of decimal places simply by changing the multiplication/division factor (one billion, in this example).

Douglas Linton
Long Beach, Calif.

6

@Lookup

LOOKUP TABLE CONFUSION

The numerical values in an @VLOOKUP table's lookup column, the first column in the table, must be in ascending order. If the lookup column doesn't contain an exact match for the *testvalue*, the first argument in the @function, the function uses the largest value that doesn't exceed the *testvalue*. For example, assume that your table, named *lookup*, is located in B1..C3 and contains the following:

	B	C
1	CODE	PRICE
2	1003	$4.35
3	1021	$0.89

Also assume that cell A1 contains code number 1018, which represents a new product you haven't yet had time to insert in the table. If you enter @VLOOKUP(A1,$LOOKUP,1) into an empty cell, the @function returns $4.35. This probably isn't the correct answer, but it could take you a while to find the error.

I protect myself by filling gaps in the lookup column with values that are slightly above the previous value, then making that new value return ERR. My revised table looks like this:

Code	Price
1003	$4.35
1004	ERR
1021	$0.89

If I accidentally use an illegitimate code number, the function returns ERR, which lets me catch the error.

John E. Predmore
Fairport, N.Y.

You can also use this system to protect yourself against data-entry mistakes and typographical errors. Another approach is to use a logical formula such as:

@VLOOKUP(A1,$LOOKUP,1)/(@VLOOKUP(A1,$LOOKUP,0)=A1)

LINEAR INTERPOLATION

The @VLOOKUP function looks up a given value in a list and returns a result related to that value. If the value is not in the list, @VLOOKUP returns a result related to the largest number in the list less than the specified number. But I often want the function to interpolate for me — if the given value is not in the list, return a value based on it anyway, not on another value in the list.

For example, range A1..A5 in the following model contains the list of values being looked up, and range B1..B5 contains the values returned by the @VLOOKUP function. The formula @VLOOKUP(14,A1..B5,1) tells *1-2-3* to look down the leftmost column of the lookup range (A1..B5) until it finds the value 14. Since 14 is not in the list, *1-2-3* moves to the cell one row above the first value greater than 14. The next highest value is 16, and the cell above that contains 12. Since the third argument in the lookup function (the offset number) is 1, *1-2-3* moves one column to the right of the 12 and returns the contents of that cell, which is 0.3. However, I would rather have *1-2-3* figure out that 14 is halfway between 12 and 16, which are in the list, and return the value halfway between the values corresponding to 12 and 16, or 0.31. This process is called linear interpolation. Here's how to do it:

	A	B	C
1	4	0.17	0.023333
2	7	0.24	0.012
3	12	0.30	0.005
4	16	0.32	0.016666
5	19	0.37	
6			
7	14	0.31	

In column C enter formulas that calculate the slope of the linear relationship between the two lists of values in columns A and B. In cell C1 enter the formula (B2-B1)/(A2-A1).

Copy the formula to C2..C4. Leave blank cell C5, which corresponds to the last pair of values. Assign the name *table* to range A1..C5. Enter the value 14 in cell A7. Now enter the following lookup formula in cell B7, which returns a result based on a value given in A7:

@VLOOKUP(A7,table,1)+(A7−@VLOOKUP(A7,table,0))
    *@VLOOKUP(A7,table,2)

B7 returns 0.31, the interpolated value corresponding to 14.

With this formula, *1-2-3* determines exactly where the lookup value lies between two entries in the column A list and returns the value that is the same distance between values in column B. If the value being looked up is less than the first value in the list, the above formula returns ERR. If the value being looked up is greater than the last value in the list, the formula returns the last value in column B. You can insert an @IF function into the formula to test whether the value being looked up is within the bounds of the list.

Cheng-yi Lu
NASA Lewis Research Center
Cleveland, Ohio

MORE EXACT LOOKUP TABLES

I prepare price quotations by pulling information from a database, which I use as a lookup table. The vertical lookup uses the following syntax:

@VLOOKUP(*selectorvalue, searchrange, offset*)

When this function is calculated, *1-2-3* looks down the leftmost column in the search range for the selector value. The values in this column must be in ascending numeric order. When *1-2-3* finds the selector value, it returns the contents of the cell the *offset* number of columns to the right, with the search column having an offset number of zero.

If it doesn't find the selector value, however, the program moves down to the largest value that doesn't exceed the *selectorvalue* and returns the value found *offset* columns to the right in that row. This may work for some applications, but I ended up with inaccurate results. I need a way to know instantly if the desired selector value is absent from the database/table range.

In my worksheet I enter the selector value in one cell and put the @function in an adjacent cell. The values I want the @VLOOKUP to return from the table are located one column to the right of the search column, so I need an offset value of 1.

To test if the search column has the contents of my selector value cell — in this case B2 — I nest two @VLOOKUPs within an @IF. The first argument of the @IF, the test, is a logical equation that checks if the @VLOOKUP, when used with an offset of zero, finds the selector value in the search range. If the selector value is returned as the value of the @function, the logical equation is true and evaluates to a value of 1.

In this case the @IF function returns the result of the second argument, the true value, which is the @VLOOKUP formula with an offset of 1. If the selector value is in the search column, the first @VLOOKUP returns the next higher value, the test equation is false and evaluates to zero. This makes the @IF function return the third argument, the false value, which is a long line of nines. Since this number is too long to fit into the cell's width, it is displayed as a series of asterisks. This lets me know that I need either to enter the needed prices manually or to revise my database.

For example, here is one of my formulas, where *select* is the range name of the cell containing the selector value, and *table* is the range name of the lookup table:

@IF(*select* = @VLOOKUP(*select,table,*0),
  @VLOOKUP(select,table,1),99999999)

Robert H. Scheibe
AAA Trucking Corporation
Trenton, New Jersey

Users of Symphony *and* 1-2-3, *Release 2/2.01, can use either label or numeric selector values in the horizontal and vertical lookup functions, and the function will return labels as well as numbers. When you use a label as the selector value, however, the function returns* ERR *if no exactly matching label is found in the table.*

@HLOOKUP WITHIN @VLOOKUP

I often use an @HLOOKUP function within an @VLOOKUP function to perform a double lookup.

In the following example, when you enter a salesperson's name in cell B10 (such as Pradeep) and a month for which sales data is desired in cell B11 (such as Jan), the formula @VLOOKUP(salesperson,A1..C7,@HLOOKUP(month,A1..C7,0)) in cell B14 returns the value at the intersection of the *Pradeep* row and the *Jan* column (30.6).

	A	B	C
1	Salesperson	Jan	Feb
2	Alhad	10.6	23
3	Dhanu	11.4	25
4	Girish	29.8	12.8
5	Pradeep	30.6	20.1
6	Sudhir	1.1	15
7	Upendra	12.9	12.6
8			
9			
10	Salesperson	Pradeep	
11	Month	Jan	
12			
13	Sales	30.6	

The @HLOOKUP first returns the column offset for month, and then the @VLOOKUP returns sales data for salesperson.

Girish S. Thakar
University of Oklahoma
Norman, Okla.

This is one of the few cases where it doesn't matter if the @HLOOKUP or the @VLOOKUP goes first. Therefore, an equivalent alternative, in this case, would be @HLOOKUP (month, A1..C7,@VLOOKUP(salesperson,A1..C7,0)).

USING @HLOOKUP WITH @DSUM

@DSUM and similar database functions require that the offset column number indicate the field to be used for the computation. However, if you add or delete fields in the database, the @D function will refer to the wrong column. Using @HLOOKUP in place of the offset solves this problem by anchoring the offset to the desired field name in the first row of the database.

Suppose you have three fields: *Name, Address,* and *Balance.* The result of @HLOOKUP("Balance",database__db,∅) is 2, meaning it is two columns to the right of the first field in the database. This is exactly the number needed for the offset value. Incorporating this into the @DSUM formula yields:

@DSUM(database__db,@HLOOKUP ("Balance",database__db,∅), database__cr)

This will remain accurate no matter how many fields you insert or delete in the database.

David C. Schlosser
Gresham, Oreg.

This technique doesn't work in 1-2-3 *Release 1A.*

CROSS-REFERENCED LOOKUPS

Recently I was asked to come up with a way to extract a value from a table based on both a horizontal and a vertical lookup value. I had often used the lookup functions but had never tried to combine the two in one operation. After a few tries, I settled on the following solution. First, add a column to the far right of the table. In this new column, select /Data Fill (MENU Range Fill in *Symphony*) and indicate a range from the second row to the bottom row of the table. Enter a Start value of 1 and a Step value of 1, then press Return to accept the default Stop value. The @VLOOKUP function uses this column to return an offset number for the @HLOOKUP function. In the example below, the table consists of mileages between the cities listed. I have given the range name *input* to the entire table, including the added column.

	A	B	C	D	E	F
1		Concord	Dover	Keene	Laconia	
2	Concord	0	39	52	24	1
3	Dover	39	0	93	45	2
4	Keene	52	93	0	76	3
5	Laconia	24	45	76	0	4
6						

Input

For example, to find the distance between Laconia and Keene, create the table shown above, define the Input range, and enter the following formula into any cell:

@HLOOKUP(''Keene'',input,@VLOOKUP(''Laconia'',input,5))

Donald Hubbard
Somersworth, N.H.

When using lookup tables, remember that when offset number equals Ø in @HLOOKUP, the value returned is the column number; when offset number equals Ø in @VLOOKUP, the value returned is the row number.

7

Formulas to Values

TURNING FORMULAS INTO VALUES QUICKLY

There are two common methods of converting formulas into values in *1-2-3* Release 1A. The first is to point to a cell containing a formula, press the EDIT and CALC keys, and press Return to save the value. This procedure is slow and laborious if you have many formulas to convert. The second technique is to select /File Xtract Values and specify the range of formula cells. This extracts the values into a separate file, which you can then combine into the current worksheet by selecting /File Combine. This is also slow, and can fail altogether if the disk is almost full.

A much faster method is to treat the formulas as if they are in a database and use the /Data Query Extract command to copy the values to another location in the worksheet. Although you must set up the database ranges, the actual conversion of formulas to values is very fast, making it worth the setup time if you have a lot of data to handle. The only restriction is that the formulas you're converting must be in a continuous column with a blank cell at the top.

In the following simple example, cells B2 through B9 contain the formulas to be converted into values. Treat these entries as a column in a database. First, enter a "field name" in cell B1; I have used *name*. Next set up Criterion and Output ranges for your "database." The Criterion range is C1..C2 (C2 is blank), and the Output range is D1..D9. (Although *1-2-3* allows you to specify a single cell as an Output range, don't do that here, since that would cause all of column D to be erased when you extract the data.)

	A	B	C	D
1		name	name	name
2	20	+A2*20		400
3	30	+A3*20		600
4	40	+A4*20		800
5	50	+A5*20		1000
6	60	+A6*20		1200
7	70	+A7*20		1400
8	80	+A8*20		1600
9	90	+A9*20		1800

Now select /Data Query Extract. This command copies data meeting the specified criteria into the Output range as values, even if the database contains formulas. Since cell C2 is blank, all "records" in your database are selected, meaning that all the formulas in column B are converted into values in column D.

You can easily automate this technique with a macro.

Rosalind B. Marimont
Silver Spring, Md.

In 1-2-3 Release 2/2.01 select /Range Value to convert formulas to values (MENU Range Values in Symphony).

FREEZING FORMULA VALUES WITH PRINT FILE

You have previously pointed out that formulas can be turned into hard numbers at their current value by moving the pointer to the formula cell and pressing EDIT, then CALC. The process could be automated for a column of formulas with a macro.

```
'{EDIT}{CALC}{DOWN}
```

This turned out to be too slow for our column of 450 formulas, so we've come up with an alternative method.

We make a print file of the column, making sure to select /Print File Clear All and then Options Other Unformatted before selecting Go and Quit. With the pointer at the top of the column, we then select /File Import Numbers to pull the file containing the column, which has been converted to current value hard numbers, back into the worksheet. We think this is even quicker and easier than the /File Xtract Values approach you mentioned. One word of caution, however: The formulas containing @ROUND will return the rounded value rather than the full value with its 15 decimal-point precision.

This technique has other benefits. Values take up less memory than formulas. So, where particular sets of no longer changing but originally calculated values — such as the results of previous runs of a financial model — are to be kept in a worksheet, it makes sense to save them in separate print files for recall as needed.

Peter Williams
Association of County Councils
London, England

1-2-3, Release 2/2.01, and Symphony let you turn formulas into their current values with the Range Value command.

With 1-2-3 the only problem with saving data in a print file instead of a worksheet file is that you can't leave any blank or label cells between data cells in the same row. This is because the process of making a print file turns each row of cell entries into a single line, ignoring blank and label cells as it does so.

8

Labels and Numbers

CONVERTING LABELS TO NUMBERS AND VICE VERSA

I have a very large worksheet full of numbers that I've centered. When I created this worksheet, I didn't realize that I couldn't use centered numbers in formulas. Is there an easy way to change these labeled numbers into formula numbers?

Herbert Shah
GTE Sylvania
Needham, Mass.

If the columns are adjacent, specify the range of labeled numbers as the print range in a print file. Select /Print File (in Symphony, *SERVICES Print Settings Destination File) and specify the print range as the entire block of cells. Set the left and top margins to zero, and choose Print File Options Other Unformatted (in* Symphony, *SERVICES Print Settings Page Breaks No) to suppress header, footer, and page-break spaces before selecting Go and Quit. Then position the pointer in the upper-left corner of the range of labeled numbers and select File Import Numbers (1-2-3) or SERVICES File Import Structured (Symphony). The data will be imported as numbers without the label prefix.*

If your columns are spread out on the worksheet, create a separate print file for each column and import one file at a time, making sure that the cell pointer is in the correct column before each import. Incoming values will replace the old label contents of each cell in the range.

If you wish to go the other way, print each separate column of numbers into a print file, then select File Import Text. You must convert each column separately. Each column of numbers will now be labels. They will appear right-justified, but they will actually be preceded by spaces.

1-2-3 Release 2/2.01 and Symphony *users have another option: the @VALUE and @STRING functions. To convert labels to numbers, enter the @VALUE(cell) formula in a separate cell on the worksheet. To convert numbers to labels, enter @STRING(cell,decimal places) in a separate cell on the worksheet. In either case, use the Copy command to copy the formula for as many cells as you want converted to values or labels. Select MENU Range Values (Symphony) or /Range Value (1-2-3 Release 2/2.01) to copy the new cell contents back into the original cells. You can then erase the range containing the @VALUE and @STRING formulas. For example, @VALUE (B3) where B3 contains the characters '300 would equal 300. @STRING(C4,2) where C4 equals 1234 would equal '1234.00.*

USING @VALUE WITH CALCULATIONS

I am having a problem using the @VALUE function with some strings. It's supposed to turn strings that look like values into the corresponding value, but if I try to reference a cell that contains '4000*2 with the @VALUE function, I get ERR in the cell containing the @VALUE function. This is puzzling, since if I try to reference a cell that contains '4000/2 with the @VALUE function, I get the correct answer, 2000. Why does the @VALUE function do division but not multiplication?

Randy Reed
South Hampton, N.Y.

The @VALUE function will not perform mathematical calculations. However, it will convert a fraction to its decimal equivalent. So when you enter @VALUE ('4000/2), it isn't performing division, it's converting a fraction to a decimal. To solve your problem, you could enter '4000/(1/2), which turns the multiplication into a fraction. Even this trick has its limits however: @VALUE(4000/(1/2)) works but @VALUE(A1) returns ERR if A1 contains '4000/(1/2).

USING NUMBERS AS LABELS

When we entered dates or Social Security numbers that began with a zero into our worksheet, the initial digit would not appear. Also, unless we formatted the cell for Text, a date entered as 12-2-84 or 12/2/84 would appear as the solution to a subtraction or division problem, respectively.

The following macros alleviate both these problems and also automatically move the pointer down one row. Remember to enter each line of the macro as a label.

For dates:

	A	B	C
1	\d	/XLEnter Date: ~~	
2		{DOWN}	
3		/XG\d~	

For Social Security numbers:

	A	B	C
1	\s	/XLEnter SSN: ~~	
2		{DOWN}	
3		/XG\s~	

Vicki Owens
Baltimore, Maryland

Your macros work because they enter the numbers as labels by preceding each number with a label prefix, such as an apostrophe. If you're willing to sacrifice the Enter Date *and* Enter SSN *prompts, you could use an even simpler macro:*

	A	B	C
1	\m	'{?}{DOWN}	
2		/XG\m~	

All of these macros are "infinite loops." You stop them by holding the Control key and pressing Break.

Symphony *users should substitute the following second line:* {BRANCH \m}.

To retain the prompts, the Symphony *versions of your macros would be slightly more complicated because the* {GETLABEL} *statement requires a specific cell address as an argument. You can write the macro as a string formula and use the* @CELLPOINTER *function to return the current cell address. You must also precede the statement with* {CALC} *to update the* @CELLPOINTER *formula (located in a cell named* next *in the following example). This example will also work in 1-2-3 Release 2/2.01.*

For dates, use the following:

	A	B	C	D	E	F	G	H
1	/d	{RECALC next}						
2	next	+"{GETLABEL Enter Date ,"&@CELLPOINTER("ADDRESS")&"}"						
3		{DOWN}						
4		{BRANCH \d}						

9

Copying Relative
Formulas Absolutely

COPYING RELATIVES ABSOLUTELY

If you need to copy an existing formula but want to preserve all its cell references as absolute (meaning the copied formulas will still refer to the originally referenced cells), you can avoid changing every relative reference to an absolute reference. With the pointer on the formula, press EDIT Home, type a label prefix (such as an apostrophe), and press Return. Now copy the formula as a label as many times as you need to. When you are finished, remove the label prefix from each label to turn them into formulas again.

If, after entering a long, complex formula, you find that *1-2-3* or *Symphony* won't accept it, and you cannot correct the problem immediately, enter a label prefix to its left and press Return. You can then print it out or study it on the worksheet to determine the problem without losing all the time you spent entering it. When you locate the problem, remove the label prefix and finish the formula.

Ginger Scalet
Brookings, S. Dak.

Your choice of methods — making each cell reference absolute or copying the formula as a label — depends on two factors. The more cell references you need to make absolute, the more likely the method described will save you time. On the other hand, the more copies of the formula you need to make, the more likely that changing the cell references is more efficient.

RELATIVELY ABSOLUTE REFERENCES

If you have a formula that contains absolute references — for example, @SUM(B5..B17) — you can copy it to a new location in the worksheet and have the addresses adjust as if they were relative while retaining their absolute reference in the new location. Instead of using the Copy command, select /File Xtract Formulas and point to the range of formulas you wish to move. You can call the new file containing the extracted formulas TEMP. Then place the cell pointer on the top-left corner of the new location and select File Combine Copy, using TEMP as the file to be drawn into the current worksheet. The formulas reappear in the desired new locations with their cell references relatively adjusted even though they retain their absolute character. For example, if you extracted @SUM(B5..B17) and combined it one column to the right, it would read @SUM(C5..C17).

Michael S. Alexander
Northern Trust Company
Chicago, Illinois

MOVING FORMULAS BETWEEN WORKSHEETS

I started with two large worksheets that contained identical formulas and structures but that I used for two separate tasks. Over time the sheets evolved and diverged. On one of the worksheets I developed a particularly useful but complex task, located in cells S34..W54. But when I tried to transfer these source cells to the other worksheet, I discovered that these cell addresses were already occupied by another complex series of formulas that I could not move. Consequently, I needed to bring the source cells into the target worksheet into a location different from the one they had occupied in the original worksheet. But relocating them by selecting /File Xtract Formulas, then /File Combine Copy Entire-File would not work because the Xtract/Combine process treats cell references as if they were relative, even if they are actually absolute. This would make the formula references of the source cells end up pointing to the wrong data.

I could retype everything, but then I discovered that I could use a "dummy" worksheet as an intermediate aid. First, in the target worksheet, I note the top-left cell of the area into which I wish to move the source range. Next I retrieve the source worksheet, select /File Xtract Formulas (SERVICES File Xtract Formulas in *Symphony*), enter the file name DUMFILE1, and point to the source range. In a new worksheet, I place the pointer in the same top-left cell as the range's original location, and select /File Combine Copy Entire-File DUMFILE1 (SERVICES File Combine Copy Entire-File Ignore Formulas DUMFILE1 in *Symphony*). In this file, I use the Move command to relocate the code to the desired target cell. The Move command preserves the original cell references of the formulas. The formulas are now in the desired location, referring to the proper cells. Some of the formulas will display ERR. I give the source cells a range name, such as *temp*, then save the worksheet. Finally, I retrieve the target worksheet, place the pointer in the top-left cell of the target area, select /File Combine Copy Named-Range (Named Specified-Range in *1-2-3* Release 2/2.01 and Named-Area in *Symphony*), and enter *temp*.

Ed Fine
Stoughton, Massachusetts

Another method is to point to the source formula cells, press EDIT, then Home, type a label prefix and enter the label into the source cell. Give the cell a range name and save the file. Retrieve the second worksheet and use the File Combine Copy command to bring the source range into the desired new location. Edit out the label prefix to return it to a formula that still refers to the desired cells.

10

Reusing Worksheets

ERASE DATA, SAVE FORMULAS

Is it possible to erase data on a spreadsheet without losing the formulas? I have a fiscal-year report I would like to reuse next year with the formulas in place but without the old data.

Richard D. Horning
University of Michigan
Flint, Michigan

When you enter new data, the new numbers will replace the existing cell contents. However, a more elegant approach is to create and name specific input and assumption areas you can easily erase. For example, you put explanatory labels in column A, then place your entries and assumptions in column B. All your formulas are located in other parts of the worksheet, and they all refer back to the appropriate cells in column B. It is then a simple matter to erase column B whenever you wish to start again.

REUSING SPREADSHEET TEMPLATES

As state auditors, we audit the same agencies every two years. We often need to reuse the same spreadsheets; however, the input data changes from year to year. The layout of the worksheet makes it difficult to use the Range Erase command; we would risk losing formulas inadvertently. Here's the solution we developed.

Retrieve the file you wish to reuse. Position the pointer on cell A1 and select /File Combine Subtract Entire-File (in *Symphony*, SERVICES File Combine Subtract Ignore Formulas) and choose the file you just retrieved. That operation subtracts the file from itself, leaving all values and formulas set to zero.

Edison Vizuete and Leroy Chomley
Bismarck, N.Dak.

Users of 1-2-3 Release 2 should avoid this technique due to a bug that was corrected in Release 2.01. If you use the File Combine Add or File Combine Subtract commands to combine formulas that reference strings, 1-2-3 Release 2 will occa-

sionally handle the operation improperly. A variety of unusual results have been reported, including LICS characters appearing in the cell in question or the keyboard locking up. Since the problem doesn't occur consistently, don't assume you can use the technique if you try it once successfully.

11

@Functions and Miscellaneous Tips

@FUNCTION FLEXIBILITY

Several @functions are more flexible than most people realize. For example, you probably know that certain @functions take range arguments, such as @SUM(A1..B5), which sums a group of contiguous cells. But @SUM can also find the total of noncontiguous cells. All you have to do is separate each group of contiguous cells with commas. Range names are acceptable, for example:

@SUM(A1..B5,D3,C1..C45,subtotal)

Dave Streifford
St. Louis, Missouri

This technique works with most @functions that the 1-2-3 *and* Symphony Reference Manuals *describe as accepting a* list *as an argument.*

USING NESTED @IF STATEMENTS

I am a teacher and I've been averaging my students' scores using the @AVG function. I recently found a way to use nested @IF functions to assign each average score the proper letter grade, making it a cinch to complete report cards.

Enter a student's grade-point average in cell F3 and this formula in cell G3:

@IF(F3<60,"F",@IF(F3<70,"D",@IF(F3<80,"C",@IF(F3<90,"B","A"))))

If cell F3 contained an 89, the formula in cell G3 would return a B.

Karol McClosky
St. James, N.Y.

This is just one application using nested @IF functions and the ability of 1-2-3 *Release 2/2.01 and* Symphony *to manipulate strings. The concept behind this formula can easily be applied to many applications. Investigate the @VLOOKUP and @HLOOKUP functions if you need to look up data in more complex tables.*

RELIABLE ONE-CELL @COUNT RANGE

Normally the @COUNT function returns 1 when its argument is one cell, even when that cell is empty. For example, @COUNT(A1) returns 1 whether or not cell A1 contains an entry. I have found a way to use @COUNT with a one-cell range and get 0 if the cell is empty. I'll assume you want to test A1, which is currently empty.

Move to the cell where you want the formula to appear. Enter @COUNT(A1). The numeral 1 appears. Now press EDIT and change the formula to read @COUNT(A1..$A1). The formula now returns 0. Enter something in cell A1; the formula now returns 1. @COUNT returns the desired result for a one-cell range when you repeat the cell reference but use a different address type (mixed or absolute).

This technique works in both Release 1A and Release 2/2.01 of *1-2-3*. The technique's only disadvantage is that you can't copy the formula — since one of the cell references is mixed or absolute, the copy maintains at least part of the original cell address.

John R. Mertz
Endicott, N.Y.

In Symphony, *@COUNT(A1) also returns 1 when A1 is empty, but you can work around the problem more easily in* Symphony. *Enter the formula as @COUNT(!A1), which* Symphony *converts to @COUNT(A1..A1). This formula has a value of 0 when A1 is empty, otherwise it is 1. You can also copy the formula wherever you want. (Both releases of* 1-2-3 *automatically convert @COUNT(A1..A1) into @COUNT(A1), so you need the $ to force the range specification.)*

GRABBING DECIMALS

I needed a formula to return the value of the first decimal position (tenths) from another value. The obvious solution was this formula:

@INT(10*(A1–@INT(A1)))

Unfortunately, the formula works for some values but not for others due to the way it rounds off the result. I developed this formula instead:

@VALUE(@MID(@STRING(A1,5),@FIND(".",@STRING(A1,5),1) + 1,1))

In this case, cell A1 contains the value, and the 5 in the @STRING portions of the formula is the maximum number of decimal places that could be in the value. This number can be increased to test values with a greater number of decimal places. If you change the last 1 in the formula to 2, the formula will return the first and second decimal places: change it to 3 to add the third decimal place, and so forth.

Ed English
Boulder, Colo.

This formula will work in 1-2-3 *Release 2/2.01 and* Symphony.

CHANGE VALUES USING MATRIX MULTIPLICATION

I use *1-2-3* Release 2.01. I would like to divide each of 200 numbers in a column by two. Is there an easy way to do this without creating a macro or using another column to hold formulas?

Janis Fantasia
Boston, Mass.

There is a rather simple way to do this using the 1-2-3 Release 2/2.01 Data Matrix Multiply command. Any column of numbers can be thought of as a matrix: A column of 200 numbers is a 200-by-1 matrix, and a single cell can be thought of as a 1-by-1 matrix. If the center dimensional terms of these matrices are equal, the matrices can be multiplied; for example, (200x1)*(1x1) = (200x1) in which the center terms are the 1's that face each other next to the multiplication sign (*).

Enter the multiplication factor, in this case .5, in an empty cell. Select /Data Matrix Multiply and enter the column of numbers as the first matrix, the single cell containing the multiplication factor as the second matrix, and the top of the column of numbers as the Output range. The new values will then overwrite the old ones in the original column.

The Matrix Multiplication capability is also available in Symphony *Release 1.2. First you must attach the STAT.APP add-in by selecting SERVICES Application Attach and selecting STAT.APP. You can then select MENU Range Matrix Multiply to perform the matrix multiplication.*

MATRIX MULTIPLY

My spreadsheets consist of wholesale and retail parts prices. Often, I have to increase or decrease all of the prices by a certain percentage. I used to enter formulas that multiply the prices by a percentage and then use the Range Values command to copy the values returned by the formulas back into the original database. However, because of the two additional columns used for the formulas, I would often run very low on memory. Also, copying and recalculating the formulas would take quite a long time. Using /Data Matrix Multiply is a memory-efficient and much faster solution.

	A	B	C	D
1	Wholesale	Retail	0.9	0
2	$125.00	$250.00	0	0.9
3	$70.00	$140.00		
4	$200.00	$400.00		
5	$225.00	$450.00		
6	$150.00	$300.00		

In my example, I want to decrease all of the prices by 10%. First create the table above, then set up a 2-by-2 matrix by entering .9 in cell C1 and cell D2. Zeros are entered in cells C2 and D1. Next, select /Data Matrix Multiply and specify range A2..B6 as the second matrix, and A2..B6 as the Output range. The results are put right back into the database.

Byron Lee
Andover, Mass.

DIVIDING BY ZERO PROBLEM

One of our worksheets records how many of each item we sell and then performs various calculations. However, if an item had zero sales, the result of a calculation involving division would be ERR. Assuming the sales figure is in cell B1 and D3/B1 represents our calculation, we avoid this problem by placing the following formula in our report area: @IF(B1 = 0,0,D3/B1). Now, if sales are zero, the calculation returns a zero.

Sharleen M. Thiel
Alma Products Company
Alma, Michigan

PRESERVING REFERENCE NUMBERS

Every time I enter a new number into an @SUM range, I change the value returned. How can I get an adjacent cell to show the current @SUM total but not change until I want it to, no matter how many changes I make to the values in the summed range?

Herb Berks
PAFB, Florida

You need a quick macro that enters a formula to reference the current @SUM value, then turns the formula into a hard number. The number will remain constant until the next time you invoke the macro. Assuming that the @SUM cell has the address E34 and the adjacent cell has the range name here, *the macro would read:*

    {GOTO}here ~
    + E34{CALC} ~

Symphony *and 1-2-3 Release 2/2.01 users can build their macros around the Range Value command. The* Symphony *version is:*

    {GOTO}E34 ~
    {MENU}RV ~ {RIGHT} ~

The 1-2-3 Release 2/2.01 version of the macro would be:

    {GOTO}E34 ~
    /RV ~ {RIGHT} ~

Both of these macros copy the value of the @SUM formula to cell F34.

ADDING ONLY POSITIVE NUMBERS

How can I add only positive values in a column that contains both positive and negative values?

Vicki L. Sena
The Kingsford Co.
Louisville, Ky.

The simplest way to add positive values in a column that contains both positive and negative values uses the @DSUM function with a database Criterion range. The @DSUM function uses the criteria to decide which values in a specified range to include in a sum. Consider the following example:

	A	B
1	Sales	Sales
2	$1,000.00	1
3	($240.00)	
4	$3,670.00	
5	($1,452.00)	
6	$2,000.00	
7	$1,300.00	
8	=========	
9	$7,970.00	

The positive values to be added reside in range A2..A7. That range also includes two negative values, in cells A3 and A5, which will be excluded from the sum. If your column of values doesn't have a field name like the one in cell A1, enter one and copy the field name into an empty cell, cell B1 in this example, making sure there is an additional blank cell beneath. Range B1..B2 is the Criterion range. Cell B2 contains the formula +A2>0. The formula in cell B2 tests against the first record (cell A2) of the database (A1..A7) to see if the value it contains is greater than 0; it returns 1 because the value in cell A2 is greater than 0 (1 indicates true, 0 indicates false). The formula @DSUM(A1..A7,0,B1..B2) entered in cell A9 follows the form @DSUM(input range, offset, criterion). Range A1..A7, including the field name at the top, is the Input range, the range to be tested. You count (starting from zero) from the leftmost column of the Input range to the column being tested to determine the offset value. Since you wish to sum values from only the first column, the offset value is 0.

MAXIMUM NUMBER OF CHARACTERS IN A CELL

I have a problem concerning a lengthy formula in *1-2-3*. The formula is 243 characters long, but *1-2-3* only allows me to enter 240 characters. It beeps when I try to enter another character and doesn't display an error message. What can I do?

Kevin R. Hamm
American National Bank
Abilene, Texas

You must split up the formula. Take a part of the formula, place it in another cell, and refer to it in the original formula. For example, @IF(@SUM(range),0,@IF(... can be divided so that the @SUM is in one cell and the @IF is in another. You could also replace all range coordinates (B5..C6) and multicharacter range names (total) with single-letter range names (A).

FACTORIALS

Is there an easy way in *1-2-3* or *Symphony* to calculate *n* factorial, the product of all integers between 1 and *n*?

Robert Wass
Manchester, N.H.

Since 1-2-3 and Symphony do not have a factorial function, here are Symphony and 1-2-3 macros that will do the job for you.

For 1-2-3 Release 1A:

	A	B	C	D
1	number	6		
2	count	1		
3	factor	720		
4				
5				
6	\a	/XNEnter number: ~number~		
7		/Cnumber~block~		
8	Loop	/DFcount~count-1~~~		
9		/DFfactor~factor*count~~~		
10		/XIcount=1~/XQ		
11		/XGloop~		

For Symphony and 1-2-3 Release 2/2.01:

	A	B	C	D
1	number	6		
2	count	0		
3	factor	720		
4				
5	\f	{GETNUMBER "Number ? ",number}		
6		{LET factor,1}		
7		{FOR count,number,1,-1,fact}		
8		{CALC}		
9				
10	fact	{LET factor,factor*count}		

Select /Range Name Labels Right (1-2-3) *or MENU Range Name Labels Right* (Symphony) *to assign the labels in column A as names for the adjacent cells in column B for the range A1..A10. For the 1-2-3 Release 1A macro, you also must assign the range name* block *to cells B1..B3. To invoke the macro, press Alt-A for the 1-2-3 Release 1A macro and Alt-F for the* Symphony/1-2-3 *Release 2/2.01 macro. If you use the second macro in* Symphony, *change the command in cell B8 to* {DRAW}. *This command updates the screen more quickly than does the* {CALC} *command.*

NONMACRO FACTORIALS

A previous reader asked for an easy way to calculate *n* factorial (the product of all integers from 1 to *n*) and was advised to use a macro because *1-2-3* and *Symphony* do not have a factorial function. However, you can use the following formula to calculate *n* factorial to an accuracy within .001 percent of the exact value:

@ROUND(((1 + 0.08367334/n)*n^n*@EXP(-n)*(2*@PI*n)^(1/2)),∅)

So if you aren't bothered by a slight inaccuracy, you don't need to resort to a macro to calculate factorials.

Sam Reyburn
Bronx, N.Y.

A MATTER OF MATHEMATICS

In working with *1-2-3* and *Symphony*, I've found some discrepancies with scientific notation and exponentiation. For instance, why isn't 6*(10E −6) equal to 6*(10^−6)?

Joseph A. Menard
Bellevue, Wash.

The following table shows the mathematical order of operations in solving these equations:

Scientific Notation	Exponentiation
6*(10E − 6)	6*(10^ − 6)
6*(1E − 5)	6*(1/10^6)
6*(0.00001)	6*(1/1,000,000)
0.00006	6*(0.000001)
	0.000006

In scientific notation, the value to the right of the E moves the decimal place that number of spaces to the right for a positive value or to the left for a negative value. In this example, 10E − 6 equals 1E − 5, which is 0.00001. With exponentiation, the value preceding the caret is multiplied by itself the number of times specified by the value following the caret — in this example, 10^{-6} (or $1/10^6$). Hence, these numbers are not equivalent.

ADDING MIXED RANGES

When I use an @IF function such as @IF(A1 = B1,A1,''''), where the false condition is an empty string, *Symphony* and *1-2-3* Release 2 read that empty string as a label. If I later try to add the cells in a range containing both values and empty strings, the formula evaluates to ERR. How can I create numeric empty space so that I can add a range of @IF statements?

Peter R. Wunsch
Facts On File Publications
New York, N.Y.

To avoid ERRs, use @ISNUMBER with the @DSUM function. This method tests to see whether cell entries are numbers. If they are numbers, they are used in the @DSUM calculation. Use the following example to help you with your problem:

	A	B	C
1	First	Last	Total
2	0	10	
3	1	1	1
4	2	12	
5	3	3	3
6	4	14	
7	5	5	5
8	6	16	
9	7	17	
10	8	8	8
11	9	19	
12	Grand	Total	17
13			
14		Total	
15		0	

Columns A and B contain the numbers that are compared in column C. Cell C2, named total, *contains the formula @IF(A2 = B2,A2, ''''). The formula in cell C2 is copied to the range C3..C11. Cell B15 contains the formula @ISNUMBER (*total*). Cell C12 contains the formula @DSUM(C1..C11,Ø,B14..B15), where C1..C11 is the range to be totaled, Ø is the offset, and B14..B15 is the Criterion range that specifies only numbers to be added.*

1-2-3 Release 2.01 solves this problem for you by treating labels as having a value of zero.

AREA OF IRREGULAR POLYGONS

We recently had to calculate the areas of many irregular polygons. Rather than tediously adding and subtracting partial areas, we developed the following system.

We began with the following formula, which relates the XY coordinates of vertices to the area of any polygon:

$$\text{Area} = \tfrac{1}{2}((x_1 y_2 + x_2 y_3 + \ldots + x_n y_{n-1} + x_n y_1) - (x_2 y_1 + x_3 y_2 + \ldots + x_n y_{n-1} + x_1 y_n))$$

Listing may start at any vertex but must proceed around the polygon in a counterclockwise direction. Using a transparent overlay, we selected a coordinate system such that $(x_1, y_1) = (0, 0)$. The area formula then became:

$$\text{Area} = \tfrac{1}{2}((x_2 y_3 + \ldots x_{n-1} y_n) - (x_3 y_2 + \ldots + x_n y_{n-1}))$$

We constructed the following spreadsheet and entered the data in counterclockwise order. In this example, the area equals 4.8 square inches, which appears in cell E14.

	A	B	C	D	E
1	Area calculation				
2		X	Y		
3	----------------------------------				
4	1	0	0		
5	2	1	1		0.5
6	3	0.5	2	2	3.4
7	4	1.7	1.7	0.85	4.25
8	5	2.5	2.5	4.25	1.25
9	6	0.5	2	5	-2
10	7	-1	3	1.5	-3
11	8	-1	-0.4	0.4	
12					
13				14	4.4
14	Area in square inches				4.8

Columns B and C contain the coordinates of the eight points of the polygon whose area you want to measure. Calculations are done in columns D and E. Cell D6 contains the formula +B5*C6, which is copied to cells D7..D11. Cell E5 contains the formula +B6*C5, which is copied to cells E6..E10. D13 and E13 sum the values in columns D and E, respectively. The area is calculated in E14 as 0.5*(D13−E13), or 4.8.

The example given is for an eight-sided polygon, as shown on the next page, but the system can be easily expanded or reduced. The permissible polygon is limited only by the size of the spreadsheet, and the accuracy of the result is limited only by the accuracy of the vertex designations.

L. Clark Arnold and Steven D. Van Nort
Lowell Mineral Explorations
Tucson, Ariz.

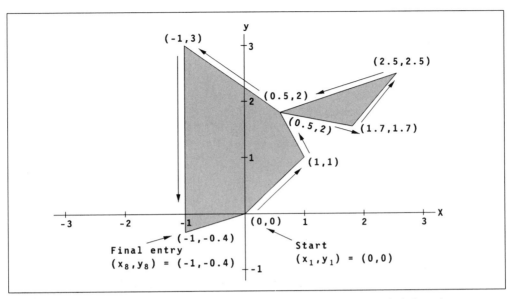

To measure the area of this irregular polygon, you must list the coordinates in counterclockwise order, as indicated by the arrows.

HISTOGRAMS

I have found the + / − cell format (Bargraph in *Symphony*) to be a quick and easy way to set up a histogram of my data. Using the + / − cell format, I am able to include a rough but highly effective graphic representation of my data right in my printed reports.

For example, suppose you have the following entries in cells A1..A5: 25, 40, −15, 0, 55. Set the width of column A to 72 by selecting /Worksheet Column Set-Width (in *Symphony*, MENU Width Set) and entering 72. To format the entries as a bar graph, select /Range Format + /− (in *Symphony*, MENU Format Other Bar-Graph) and indicate range A1..A5.

The program represents positive numbers with a quantity of plus signs equal to the integer portion of the underlying value, negative numbers with a quantity of minus signs equal to the integer portion of the underlying value, and zeros with a single period. If the underlying value is greater than the number of spaces in the width of the column in which it resides, the program will display asterisks across the cell (reduce the column width to 54 and observe the change in cell A5).

Randy L. Smith
Honeywell Inc., Sperry Aerospace Division
Albuquerque, N.M.

12

Named Ranges

RANGE NAME TABLE

To keep track of my range name locations, I create a table in the upper-left corner of every spreadsheet. However, instead of entering the upper-left cell of each range location as a label, I enter it as a formula (for example, +B7) and then format the cell for Text (*1-2-3*) or Literal (*Symphony*). In this way I create a table of contents that adjusts itself whenever I rearrange the worksheet. If I want to show both upper-left and lower-right corners, I use either two cells or a single formula such as +B7+R4.

David B. Herst
New York, N.Y.

You can use the Range Name Table command in 1-2-3 *Release 2/2.01 and* Symphony *to create a range name table in the worksheet that alphabetically lists all range names and their corresponding addresses.*

RESTORING DELETED RANGE NAMES

While naming a range with the Range Name command, I have several times mistakenly selected the Reset command, thereby eliminating all of my named ranges. I now keep a table of range specifications and their associated names (created with the Range Name Table command) in a blank area of my spreadsheet. In the event that I repeat my error, I can use the table as a guide to reconstruct my range names. However, in the case of worksheets containing large numbers of named ranges, it's time-consuming to reenter all the range names. To remedy that, I developed a way to convert the table into a macro that will rename all the ranges for me.

	A	B	C
1	/RNCMAIN~Z4~	MAIN	Z4
2	/RNCMENU_1~AA5~	MENU_1	AA5
3	/RNCBALANCE~P1..S40~	BALANCE	P1..S40
4	/RNCTOTAL~A45..R45~	TOTAL	A45..R45
5	/RNCSUB_1~AA10~	SUB_1	AA10

The following formula resides in cell A1 of the illustration on the preceding page:

+ ''/RNC''&B1&''~''&C1''~''

I copy the formula in cell A1 as far down the column as there are entries in column B. As you can see from the example, the result of the formula is a macro. To run it, name the first cell \a: Select /Range Name Create (MENU Range Name Create in *Symphony*), enter \a, indicate cell A1, and press Return. Run the macro by holding down the MACRO key (Alt on most computers) and pressing A. The macro will stop when it reads the first blank cell (in this case, cell A6). Be sure to update the table if you add more range names to your worksheet.

Dan Ehrmann
Chicago, Ill.

In Symphony *use the following formula in cell A1:*

+ ''{MENU}RNC''&B1&''~''&C1&''~''

INSERTING AND DELETING ROWS IN NAMED RANGES

I use a database in which I delete and add rows on a weekly basis. I use the Data Query commands to sort and extract records, but then the named range for the database readjusts. This causes problems since we rely on that count to be accurate.

Merril Robinson
Hughes Aircraft Co.
Goleta, Calif.

Named ranges do adjust, depending on where you insert and delete rows by selecting /Worksheet Insert or Delete Row (in Symphony, *MENU Insert or Delete Rows). The following illustrates various effects of adding and deleting rows:*

	A	B	C
1	Name	State	Code
2	Jones	MA	C
3	Adams	RI	D
4	Locke	FL	A
5	Deane	RI	B

Range A1..C5 is the database named dbase. *Range names are defined in* 1-2-3 *and* Symphony *by the upper-left and the lower-right corners of the range. In the example, cells A1 and C5 identify the range named* dbase. *If the Delete command is used on either cell, the range name becomes invalid. Therefore, if you delete the first or last row of a named range, the range name's references are lost.*

However, if you delete one row in the middle of this range — row 2, 3, or 4 — dbase *is adjusted to range A1..C4. Similarly, if you add a row in the middle of this range — by placing the cell pointer on row 2, 3, 4, or 5 and selecting /Worksheet*

Insert Row (MENU Insert Rows in Symphony*) —* dbase *adjusts to refer to A1..C6.*

There is one tricky aspect to inserting rows. If you add a row by placing the cell pointer on the first row of the database (row 1), the inserted row pushes the entire range down so that dbase *refers to the same cell contents as before but down one row (range A2..C6). If you add a row when the cell pointer is in the last row of the database (row 5), the inserted row pushes the lower-right corner cell down and expands the range-name definition to cover the database plus the new row you added (range A1..C6).*

To avoid making mistakes in calculations, remember not to delete the first or last row of a named range. Instead, use the Range Erase command (MENU Erase in Symphony*) to get rid of the contents of these range-name identifiers. Erasing a cell's contents does not affect its status as an identifier. If you want the range to include more records, insert a row below the top row of the named range.*

13

Worksheet Layout
and Display

HIGHLIGHTING INPUT CELLS

Suppose you want to distinguish between input cells and formula cells, or you have modified particular cells and need a quick way to identify them visually. You can select /Range Unprotect (MENU Range Protect Allow-Changes in *Symphony*) and indicate the cells you want highlighted.

Todd C. Minor
Southmark Funding
Dallas, Tex.

ADJUSTABLE DASHED LINES

You can use the backslash (\) label prefix to repeat any combination of characters across a cell. To display a continuous line across your worksheet, enter a backslash followed by a hyphen into a cell, and copy that label to adjacent columns. While such lines help set off titles and subtotals, I think they are more effective if they are separated by a blank space. To accomplish that, I make them one character less than the width of the cell they occupy (see figure).

	A	B	C	D
1		Jan	Feb	Mar
2		-------	-------	-------
3	Sales	9253	9471	9855
4	Cogs	7894	8011	8123
5		-------	-------	-------
6	G.P.	1359	1460	1732

1-2-3 Release 1A gives you just one way to generate the lines illustrated: You must enter a label prefix followed by a specific number of hyphens, then manually add or subtract hyphens from the line whenever you change column width. *1-2-3* Release 2/2.01 and *Symphony* contain @functions to simplify the job.

These functions allow you to generate a line that adjusts its length to whatever column you place it in. It will also adjust to changes made with the Column-Width Set command. Since the formula uses @functions, it has to be recalculated to change the line length, and, unfortunately, it will not do that automatically. The formula that creates the subtotal line in cell B2 is:

@REPEAT("–",@CELL("WIDTH",!B1)–1)

The formula works by repeating the hyphen (which must be in quotations to be recognized as a string) as many times as the cell is wide, minus one. The @CELL function calculates the width of the cell specified in the formula. Since I want the subtotal line to be one character less than the column width, I also subtract one more.

It's a simple formula; nonetheless, it makes printouts easier to read and saves lots of time over the method required in Release 1A.

John Campbell
Claremont, Calif.

When you change the column width, all cells in the column change, but the length of the dashed line remains unchanged. Press the CALC key and the dashed lines will assume their proper length. The cell reference in the formula (B1 in the above example) should not be the same cell that the formula resides in, or a circular reference results. Choose another cell in the same column.

There are a few drawbacks to keep in mind. First, the convenience offered by the formula comes at some cost in memory: 80 bytes per entry versus 22 for the simpler method described earlier (\–). The difference could be pivotal in larger applications. Second, be sure to exclude such a formula from a range referenced by an @SUM function in 1-2-3 Release 2 and any version of Symphony, as including it will produce an error. You can, however, include this cell within an @SUM range in 1-2-3 Release 2.01.

QUICKER UNDERLINING

When setting up my worksheet, I use rows of underlines or equal signs to separate the various segments of the report. However, even if I use the repeating label prefix, it can be time-consuming to enter the label (__), copy it across the row, then copy the row each time I want to insert a dividing line. Instead, I give the entire row of underlines a range name such as *L* for the underline and *LL* for the equal sign. Whenever I want to insert a divider line, I enter /Copy L Return Return (MENU Copy in *Symphony*).

Jay Farr
Overland Park, Kansas

ZERO SUPPRESSION — I

I use *1-2-3* Release 2, and I'm having trouble with zero suppression. I don't understand how the command Worksheet Global Zero Yes can affect less than the entire worksheet, but it seems to affect some cells and not others. Please explain.

Harry A. Darius
Electric Power Research Institute
Palo Alto, Calif.

If you widen the cells containing 0 that appear to be unaffected and format them for 15 decimal places, you'll see previously undisplayed numbers to the right of the decimal place. 1-2-3 stores the binary equivalent of a number, which is not always the same as the number itself.

Use the @ROUND function to round the results of your formulas to two decimal places. For example, the following formula rounds the result of the @SUM formula to two decimal places:

@ROUND(@SUM(A1..A10),2)

ZERO SUPPRESSION — II

I had a problem suppressing zeros after selecting /Worksheet Global Zero Yes, saving the file, and then retrieving it. Although Lotus Development Corporation designed *1-2-3* Release 2/2.01 not to save suppression, many of the worksheets I create and use need it.

My solution is simple. I create an auto-executing macro (naming the macro \0 tells *1-2-3* to run the macro immediately after the file is retrieved). The macro contains the instructions /WGZY (the keystrokes for the command sequence /Worksheet Global Zero Yes). When I retrieve the worksheet, the zeros are automatically suppressed.

Larry Heyman
Pomona, N.Y.

Thanks for the addition.

NEW CELL-FORMATTING OPTIONS

I frequently want to designate values as measurements in inches by appending a quotation mark to them. However, since I use these values in calculations, I do not want to enter them as labels followed by a quotation mark. I found that in *1-2-3* Release 2/2.01 I can select /Worksheet Global Default Other International Currency (in *Symphony*, SERVICES Configuration Other International Currency), change the dollar sign to a quotation mark, and select the Suffix option. I can then format values as inches by selecting the Currency format.

George B. Wilhelm
Albany Medical Center Hospital
Albany, N.Y.

This technique can be adapted to use any character — including special LICS characters — as suffixes or prefixes to values. A significant limitation of this technique is that it makes the original Currency format unavailable in the same worksheet (you can't apply different symbols to different ranges). You should also be aware that this technique resets the Currency format for any worksheet you use during this session. If you retrieve another worksheet previously created using the original Currency format, that worksheet will show the new inches format instead. To reverse that effect, you'll need to repeat the procedure described above and change the quotation mark character back to a prefix dollar sign. To make the setting the default for future sessions, when you select the new format, also select Update before returning to Ready mode.

FORMAT COMMANDS

I cannot format specific columns in my worksheet. As an example, look at the following:

	A	B	C
1	$1,234.00	$1.00	$23.54

I wanted column C to be in the Fixed format with no decimal places, so I selected /Worksheet Global Format Fixed 0. Yet all three entries in row 1 continued to display a currency format with two decimal places.

I then went back to column A and reformatted it by selecting /Worksheet Global Format Fixed 0.

	A	B	C
1	1234	1	24

What's going on?

Craig F. Knowlton
Puyallup, Wash.

By selecting /Worksheet Global Format Fixed 0, you change all cells in the entire worksheet that haven't already been formatted with the Range Format command. The Worksheet Global commands (MENU Settings Format in Symphony*) establish overall standards that can be overridden for particular cells with the Range Format commands (MENU Format in* Symphony*). To specify a format for a particular range, select /Range Format (MENU Format in* Symphony*).*

ASCII GRAPHICS CHARACTERS IN A WORKSHEET

A previous item mentions that an undocumented capability of Release 1A of *1-2-3* allows you to use ASCII characters corresponding to codes 1 through 31 and 128 through 255. These characters include single and double rules, which some people use to draw boxes and borders in their worksheet. Several readers wanted to know the technique. Please keep in mind, however, that this capability is not supported by

Lotus Development Corp. It works reliably for us here at *LOTUS* magazine, but if you want to try it, you are on your own.

The June 1984 issue of *Absolute Reference* offered the following technique. It has been modified slightly here and is reprinted with permission from Que Publishing. The technique works only for *1-2-3* Release 1A. Release 2/2.01 and *Symphony* use the Lotus International Character Set for codes 128 through 255. A technique that works with *Symphony* is presented on the next page.

1. Load *1-2-3*. If necessary, clear the worksheet (/Worksheet Erase Yes).
2. Enter the one-character label *e* in cells A1 through A256.
3. Save the worksheet file with the name ASCII.
4. Exit to DOS and then load BASIC. If you have a floppy-disk system, copy ASCII.WKS to the disk containing BASIC, insert your BASIC disk and type *Basica*. If you have a hard-disk system, copy ASCII.WKS to the directory containing BASIC, change the current directory to the BASIC directory, and type *Basica*.
5. Create this BASIC program:

```
10 OPEN "R",1,"ASCII.WKS",12
20 I = −1
30 FIELD 1,6 AS A$,1 AS B$,5 AS C$
40 I = I + 1
50 IF I > 255 THEN 150
60 GET 1,105 + I
70 LSET B$ = CHR$(I)
80 PUT 1,105 + I
90 GOTO 40
150 CLOSE 1
160 SYSTEM
```

6. Run this program by typing *Run* and pressing Return. If an error results, check your program for typographical errors. If you still have problems, your version of BASIC might be different from IBM's BASIC and your program may need to be modified. See your BASIC manual for help.

This program opens ASCII.WKS and replaces each *e* label with the character corresponding to the row of the worksheet (cell A1 contains the character for the ASCII code 0, the null string; A2 contains a happy face, ASCII 1; A68 contains a *C*, ASCII 67; A197 contains a horizontal rule, which is code 196 in IBM's extended character set, and so on through A256, ASCII 255). The program ends by returning you to DOS.

You can now retrieve the transformed ASCII.WKS in *1-2-3* and use any of the graphics characters in your worksheets. You can create boxes, for example, by copying and moving the appropriate characters and using the repeating-label prefix

(\) to fill a cell with a rule. Give a range name to the box and when working in another worksheet, use /File Combine Named Range to pull in the box. If you retrieve into *1-2-3* Release 2/2.01 a Release 1A worksheet containing ASCII values greater than 127, the characters are converted to the corresponding LICS characters. For example, ASCII 196, a horizontal rule, will be converted to LICS 196, the letter *A* with an umlaut.

Note, however, that you cannot print these box-drawing graphics characters unless your printer has the same extended character set (only a few do, such as IBM's Quietwriter, the Diablo 630 IBM ECS, and the Star Micronics SB and SR printers). Most printers use different characters for ASCII 128 through 255. The Epson FX 80, for example, prints these characters mostly in italic letters, not graphics characters. Also, don't try to print characters corresponding to codes 1 through 31; they are control codes that specify such functions as line-feeds, form-feeds, and carriage returns.

In *Symphony* you can use the following technique to display box-drawing characters in a DOC window.

1. In a new worksheet, select MENU Range Fill to enter the numbers 1 through 32 in cells A1 through A32.
2. In cell B1, enter the formula @CHAR(A1).
3. Copy B1 to the range B2..B32.
4. Select MENU Range Values to copy the formulas in column B to column A, overwriting the numbers. The formulas in column B should now read ERR.
5. Delete column B.
6. Switch to a DOC window. The graphics characters now appear. They can be copied and moved but can only be displayed in a DOC window. These characters cannot be printed.

14

Moving the Pointer

KEEPING TRACK OF CELL-POINTER POSITION

When I want to look for some data and then return to the current cell, I need to keep track of the location of my cell pointer prior to doing so. I found a trick that does just that. I press the plus key before I start moving around the worksheet. Then once I have found what I am looking for, I can press the Escape key once to return to the cell that I started from, and then press it again to return to Ready mode.

Wendy Schuman
Woodbridge, Va.

CHECKING DISTANT VALUES

I have a very large worksheet and often want to see the current value of a cell that is far removed from where I am working. Instead of going to the cell in question, and perhaps losing my place on the worksheet, I use *1-2-3* as a calculator. Assuming the cell whose value I want to check is named *far*, at Ready mode I type *+far* and press Calc. The current value of *far* is now displayed on the control panel. I can then press Return to store that value in the current cell, or press Escape to clear the control panel and return to Ready mode.

Dwayne Rutland
Percy, Ind.

QUICK-REFERENCING RANGE NAMES

To move the cell pointer directly to a named range, press the GOTO key, immediately followed by the NAME key. This will display a list of the range names (five at a time on the third line of the control panel) for selection.

You can also press the NAME key when *1-2-3* requests a range and you want to specify a previously created name. A list of range names for selection will appear.

Both of these methods are generally faster than typing in the range name, and they provide a list of assigned names, avoiding the problem of forgetting or misspelling names.

Leslie Williams
Peacock, N.H.

In Symphony *press the MENU key to select a range name when prompted for a range.*

FINDING TOP OF COLUMN, BEGINNING OF ROW

I recently had to figure out how to jump quickly to the leftmost cell in any row or the topmost cell in any column without knowing which row or column the pointer would be in and without repeatedly pressing LeftArrow or UpArrow. The solution is simple: use the Titles command. The macro code /WTH{HOME}/WTC moves the pointer to the first cell of the row. To move to the top of a column, just substitute a V for the H.

N. J. Williams
Data Logic Ltd.
London, England

If you regularly use titles, you must start by clearing the old titles and end by restoring them. An easier method would be to press End and UpArrow to move to the top of a column. Press End and DownArrow to move to the bottom of a column.

MOVING TO THE END OF A LIST

In *Symphony*, when working with long columns of numbers, I often need to get to the last occupied cell in a column. If all cells in the column contain entries, I can simply press End DownArrow. If there are empty cells in my list, I can press PageDown, but if the list is long, I may have to do so many times. I discovered that I can press End PageDown to move to the bottom row of the worksheet. Once there, I press End UpArrow to travel to the last row in my list.

Dan R. Ellis Jr.
Monroe, N.C.

USING WINDOW FOR EXPLORATION

In my *Symphony* models, I use many windows restricted to specific areas of the worksheet. While this makes for an efficient and secure application, it also makes it hard to move around the worksheet when I want to do some debugging or modifying. So I name one window EXPLORE and define its Restrict range as A1..IV8192; that is, the entire worksheet. Using this window I can easily move about in the model and change and verify data without revising individual window settings (and having to change the settings back later).

J. Richard Belville
Stratford, Conn.

15

Statistics and
Random Numbers

USING A WEIGHTED AVERAGE

Some advice for summarizing a table of data: It is often misleading to calculate an average percentage by averaging a column of percentages. A better, more meaningful figure is a weighted average, in which you sum the two columns of numbers used to generate the individual percentages and then calculate the ratio of the sums. In the example below, the 48 percent weighted average for margin, calculated in cell C8 as + A6/B6, indicates the overall performance more accurately than the simple average, calculated in cell C7 as @AVG(C2..C4). Cell A6 contains the formula @SUM(A2..A4), which is copied to cell B6.

	A	B	C
1	Profit	Sales	Margin
2	$10	$50	20%
3	$2	$10	20%
4	$500	$1,000	50%
5	----------------------		
6	$512	$1,060	
7	simple average:		30%
8	weighted average:		48%

*John Predmore
Fairport, N.Y.*

THE @RAND FUNCTION

Random numbers are an important part of many business simulation models (and games). For example, they are used to calculate the number of salespeople needed when the number of customers randomly varies between 50 and 150 per hour. The @RAND function provides random numbers between zero and one. By multiplying, adding, and rounding off, you can shift the number into any range you desire. @ROUND (@RAND*100 + 50,0) produces values between 50 and 150.

How does @RAND work? There is very little about a computer program that is truly random. Randomness can be approximated, however. For example, *1-2-3* and *Symphony* contain an internal program that takes any number given to it, and produces a number that seems to have no visible connection to the original number. If you feed the new number back into the program, another pseudorandom number is generated. In this way the program produces an endless list of seemingly random numbers. Because of the randomizing effect of the program, it is very unlikely that the same number will appear more than once.

Of course, you need a number to start the process. Both *1-2-3* Release 1A and *Symphony* Release 1 contain the same "seed" number. (Later versions of each product use slightly different pseudorandom number generators.) Feeding the seed number into the code produces the number 0.14175068968. Feeding this first "random" number into the code produces a second "random" number of 0.4141005329, and so on.

Always starting with the same seed means that the same list of numbers is generated every time you turn on *1-2-3* or *Symphony*. How can @RAND serve as a random number generator if the same list of numbers is created each time you turn on the program? It is true that the first time you enter @RAND after starting the program, the same value of 0.1475068968 will always appear. However, each time an @RAND is evaluated, the internal program creates and makes available the next number on the list. If your spreadsheet contains three @RANDs, they are evaluated one at a time. The value of the first @RAND is used as input to create the second, which is then used as input to create the third. As a result, they each display a different value from the random number list. So you can still rely on @RAND to give you random results within each spreadsheet.

RANDOM NUMBER TABLE

I want to generate a table of random numbers between 209 and 3,058. I also want to place the numbers 209 and 3,058 in cells so that I can easily change them. I would like to generate the same table, with identical numbers, anytime I need it. Finally, the table should contain only 25 random numbers between 209 and 3058. Is this possible?

R. David Randall
Framingham, Massachusetts

The @RAND function in all Lotus products returns a number between zero and 1. It returns a different random number every time you recalculate it. To generate a list of random values between and including any two numbers, multiply @RAND by one more than the difference between the two numbers, and then add the lower number. To eliminate the fraction, apply @INT, for example:

@INT(@RAND*(3058–209 + 1) + 209)

To generate a random number between but not including two numbers, multiply @RAND by one less than the difference between the two numbers, and then add one more than the lower number, for example:

@INT(@RAND*(3058–209–1) + 209 + 1)

You can easily substitute cell references for each of the numbers, although you must be careful to use absolute references to the cells containing 209 and 3058. By copying this formula into 25 cells, you can create a table of random numbers that meet your needs. If you are using 1-2-3 Release 1A, you must issue the File Xtract Values command to pull the table out of the worksheet into a separate file. Then when you need the table, select /File Combine Copy to bring it into your current worksheet. With other products, use the Range Values command to turn the formulas into hard numbers.

CALCULATING THE MEDIAN

Is there an @function *1-2-3* or *Symphony* to calculate the median of a range? If not, can you give me a solution?

Jim Caranis
College Park, Md.

No, there isn't a median function, but here are two solutions. Use the @IF and @MOD functions to determine if the range contains an odd or even number of values. Then use the @INDEX function to find the appropriate median value. The following formula calculates the median of a range of contiguous, ordered numbers, where range is the range of numbers:

@IF(@MOD(@COUNT(range),2) = 0,(@INDEX(range,0,@COUNT
(range)/2) + @INDEX(range,0,@COUNT(range)/2–1))/2,@INDEX
(range,0,@INT(@COUNT(range)/2)))

Make sure you sort the data in ascending or descending order before using this formula.

The second formula is slightly shorter and doesn't use @IF:

@INDEX(range,0,@INT(@COUNT(range)/2)) + @INDEX
(range,0,(@INT(@COUNT(range/2)) – (@MOD(@COUNT
(range),2)< > 1)))/2

MORE ON MEDIANS AND MODES

In the past, you published a method for finding the mode and median of a set of data using the Data Sort command and then manually scanning the list to find the required values. If the list contains a lot of data, that would be tedious and prone to error. Why not let *1-2-3* Release 2/2.01 do the work as shown here?

	A	B	C	D	E	F
1	VALUES	OCCURRENCES		\m	{LET critcell,@MAX(occurrences)}~	
2	3	1			/DQIinput~Ccrit~Ooutput~EQ	
3	5	1				
4	5	2				
5	7	1				
6	9	1		COUNT	OCCURRENCES	
7	9	2		15	3	
8	9	3				
9	17	1		MEDIAN:	17	
10	19	1				
11	22	1		MODE:	OCCURRENCES	VALUES
12	27	1			3	9
13	31	1				
14	33	1				
15	34	1				
16	38	1				

First you need to know how many items appear in the list. Assign the range name *values* to the sorted data: Select /Range Name Create, enter *values*, and designate range A2..A16. Determine the number of entries in the list by entering the formula @COUNT(values) in cell D7 and assign that cell the range name *count*. If *count* is odd, the median is the middle value in the list. If *count* is even, the median is the average of the two values that bracket the middle. The formula in cell E9 calculates the median using the @INDEX function:

$$@IF(@MOD(count,2) = 0,(@INDEX(values,0,count/2-1) +$$
$$@INDEX(values,0,count/2))/2,@INDEX(values,0,count/2))$$

To find the mode (the most commonly occurring value), you need a formula to count the number of times each value appears. If *values* begins in cell A2, place a 1 in cell B2 and enter the following formula in cell B3:

$$@IF(A3 = A2,B2 + 1,1)$$

Copy cell B3 down column B parallel to the entries in the *values* column. Assign the name *occurrences* to range B2..B16. Now the entries in *occurrences* can be converted to values and sorted along with *values* to bring the mode(s) to the top. Better yet, use @MAX(occurrences) as a criterion, and use the Data Query Extract command to extract the modes into an Output range. In the example above, a macro beginning in cell D1 performs the latter two operations. Place the pointer on cell C1 and use the Range Name Labels Right command to name the macro. You could also write a macro to perform the entire process rather than just the Data Query operations.

Steven W. Weeks
First National Bank
Cincinnati, Ohio

This is an elegant solution to a common question. Other methods of finding modes often neglect to take into account the fact that there may be more than one mode (for example, bimodal and trimodal distributions). The Data Query operation handles that nicely. The method also works well in Symphony *after substituting the following for line two of the macro:*

$\{MENU\}QSBDinput \sim Ccrit \sim Ooutput \sim QQEQ$

NEGATIVE R SQUARED IN RELEASE 2

When I use the Data Regression command on a set of random numbers, I sometimes get a negative R-squared value, which is theoretically impossible. What's going on?

Jesse White
Swampscott, Mass.

Make sure that you haven't set the intercept to zero (/Data Regression Intercept 0). Forcing the intercept to zero for a set of random numbers will sometimes result in a negative R-squared value.

DATA DISTRIBUTION

How do the Data Distribution *(1-2-3)* and Range Distribution *(Symphony)* commands work?

Gary Duhaine
North Hollywood, Calif.

The Data Distribution (1-2-3) *and Range Distribution* (Symphony) *commands evaluate a list of values to determine how many fall within a series of specified intervals. For example, how many values are greater than 80 and less than or equal to 85? The specified intervals are defined by the values placed in ascending order from top to bottom in a column of cells called the Bin range. The list of values to be distributed is located in the Values range.*

The Values range in the example on the next page is a list of test scores. The Bin range used is in increments of 5 beginning at 50 to represent a grading scale.

	A	B	C	D	E
1	Values	Bin	Results	Description of Results	
2	Range	Range			
3	97	50	0	0 scores <= 50	
4	78	55	1	1 score > 50 and <= 55	
5	55	60	0	0 scores > 55 and <= 60	
6	82	65	1	1 score > 60 and <= 65	
7	88	70	0	0 scores > 65 and <= 70	
8	86	75	1	1 score > 70 and <= 75	
9	85	80	2	2 scores > 75 and <= 80	
10	84	85	7	7 scores > 80 and <= 85	
11	91	90	3	3 scores > 85 and <= 90	
12	93	95	2	2 scores > 90 and <= 95	
13	62	100	1	1 score > 95 and <= 100	
14	75		0	0 scores > 100	
15	85				
16	84				
17	82				
18	77				
19	81				
20	89				

*To find out how many scores fall into each interval, select /Data Distribution (1-2-3) or MENU Range Distribution (*Symphony*) and enter A3..A20 as the* Values *range and B3..B13 as the* Bin *range.* Symphony *and 1-2-3 calculate the number of test scores that fall into each interval and put these in the* Results *column. Note that the* Results *column extends one row below the* Bin *range. This is because 1-2-3 and* Symphony *test to find the number of values greater than the last* Bin *number. Remember that you must leave the column to the right of the* Bin *range blank, as it will display the results.*

PERFORMING A T-TEST

The Data Regression command determines the degree of linear relationship between a dependent variable (Y value) and one or more independent variables (X values). Once the analysis is performed, you usually want to determine the significance of the fit, that is, to test whether the linear relationship is real or due to chance. The most common test uses the correlation coefficient, *r*, which is the square root of the *r*-squared value provided by *1-2-3*. Alternatively, you can perform a t-test by using the following formula to calculate *t*, where *cell1* and *cell2* are the cells where the regression analysis has placed *r* squared and the degrees of freedom, respectively:

@SQRT(*cell1*)*@SQRT(*cell2*)/@SQRT(1−*cell1*)

Given the value of either *r* or *t* and the degrees of freedom, you can use a table of *r* or *t* values in a statistics book to determine the probability that the obtained results were due to chance.

Peter Aitken
Duke University Medical Center
Durham, N.C.

You could also use:

@SQRT((cell1∗cell2)/(1−cell1))

6

CATCHING ERRORS

Who hasn't had this nightmare? You're sitting in a meeting in which the main discussion focuses on figures you've put together and analyzed; everything seems to be going well, and the group is slowly coming around to the position you knew was correct all along; and then someone notices an error. Suddenly the whole analysis is in doubt, as is the trustworthiness of your data!

The good news is that it doesn't take too much extra effort to protect yourself against calculation errors. Aside from the most obvious sources of error, such as the use of inaccurate data and mistakes in data entry, the most common worksheet errors involve formulas. Errors in formulas can be as simple as referencing the wrong range, or as confusing as inadvertently overwriting the formula with "hard" numbers that leave the display on your monitor intact but actually replace the underlying formula with a number. Setting up crossfooting formulas to double-check calculations can help, as can bounds-checking validation tests to make sure your input numbers and final results fall within reasonable limits.

Probably the single most important piece of information this section discusses, however, is that two numbers that appear to be the same aren't always equal, whether because of rounding, display formats, or because of the computer's built-in inaccuracy in the 15th decimal place. A good technique for finding these errors is the use of cross-checking formulas and bounds checking.

It also seems appropriate in a discussion on catching errors to include tips about getting help. Lotus products have always been known for the usefulness of their on-line help systems, but few people use the help system to its maximum potential. And users of *1-2-3* Release 1A need to remember to avoid pressing the HELP key if they've removed the System disk from the computer.

1

Checking Formulas

CROSSFOOTING FORMULAS

I often create tables on my spreadsheet that I total across and down. To make sure those sums agree, I crossfoot them. Because of the way *1-2-3* totals its values, I can't compare them down to 15 decimal places, but for my purposes I need to know only that they are accurate within two decimal places. In the example, cell E6 contains the following formula:

@IF(@ROUND(@SUM(E1..E4),2)–@ROUND(@SUM(A6..D6),2) = 0,
@SUM(E1..E4),@ERR)

	A	B	C	D	E
1	1225	1076	554	1201	4056
2	1687	2231	234	1398	5550
3	1248	2113	764	2462	6587
4	1871	912	449	1377	4609
5	-------	-------	-------	-------	-------
6	6031	6332	2001	6438	20802

This @IF statement checks to make sure that the sum of the totals across equals the sum of the totals down. If they are equal, the formula produces the grand total; otherwise, it produces an ERR to flag that the worksheet does not cross-check. Using this formula is the most efficient method I have found to check my totals because it does not require the use of any extra cells.

Michael Resnick
Bethesda, Md.

A simpler approach is to write a formula that checks to see only if the difference between the two totals is greater than some preset amount, say .0001:

@IF(@SUM(E1..E4)–@SUM(A6..D6)>.0001,@ERR,@SUM (E1..E4))

If the difference is greater than that amount, the formula returns ERR; if not, you get a total. These suggestions work with Symphony *as well.*

"EQUAL" NUMBERS AREN'T THE SAME?

I had set up a logical formula to check my spreadsheet by comparing two numbers. The numbers were the results of two different sets of intermediate calculations, and they appeared to be equal. So my check formula read *cell1 = cell2*. If the result was true, a one (1) would appear, if false, a zero.

Although the numbers seemed to be equal, the check formula kept announcing that the equation was false. Finally, I remembered that the program stores my numbers with 15 decimal points of precision and it normally rounds off only to the number of decimal figures displayed. Therefore, the two seemingly equal dollars-and-cents figures displayed on my monitor could actually be different — for example, $219.69 could actually be 219.6867 or 219.690004. To control the rounding operation, I use the @ROUND function. Now I have a reassuring series of ones running down my check-formula area.

Beth Winston
Vancouver, British Columbia

FORMULA SAFEGUARDS

Incorrectly defined ranges are a common source of worksheet errors. To reduce the frequency of this kind of error, I include extra rows and columns around the outside of the ranges that I use to define @SUM arguments. In the example below, A and D are the extra columns, 1 and 4 are the extra rows. These border cells can be used for labels (column A), underscores (row 4), blanks (column D), or any nonnumeric characters. *1-2-3* and *Symphony* ignore the nonnumeric data. Best of all, any future column or row insertions or deletions will be made inside the range borders.

I even incorporate the larger borders within my double-checking formulas. The formula in E5 checks each of the subtotals against the grand total.

James L. Bailey
The Charter Company
Jacksonville, Florida

	A	B	C	D	E
1		Head1	Head2		Total
2	Item1	1	1		2
3	Item2	1	1		2
4		-----------------------			-----
5		2	2		4

Expanding your rows in this way can cause problems. While @SUM ignores labels, other @functions such as @AVG do not. A safer approach is to include a blank extra row or column as part of your range. You can then add or delete rows or columns between the last row or column of data and the blank cells.

RANGE NAMES CHANGE FORMULAS

When a formula refers to a cell such as B3 by its address and then B3 is given a range name, the formula changes to include that name. The formula will continue to reference the range name rather than the cell address even if the name is subsequently moved to another cell, which changes the whole meaning of the formula. The only way you can prevent this is to delete a range name before using the same name for another cell.

John A. C. Woodley
Georgia Power
Valdosta, Ga.

UNFORMATTED FORMULA VALUES

Occasionally, it is useful to view the unformatted result of a formula or to compare the unformatted results of two or more formulas. It can be tedious to set the number of decimal places, widen the columns sufficiently to display them, and then reverse those settings when done. A quicker way of doing this is to place the cell pointer in the desired cell and press the EDIT key so that the formula displays in the control panel. Now press the CALC key. The control panel now displays the result of the formula with all decimal places visible. Then return to Ready mode by pressing the Escape key twice. If you press Return, *1-2-3* will overwrite the formula on the worksheet with the value in the control panel.

Bruce Balan
Econovest, Inc.
Los Angeles, Calif.

You should be aware of a limitation to this technique. 1-2-3 *and* Symphony *will show only 9 decimal places on the Edit line, as opposed to a maximum of 15 decimal places visible on the worksheet.*

DOCUMENTING FORMULAS

Is it possible to write a macro that will do a PrintScreen? I want to print all the formulas in a column.

Celeste Chernak
Pacific Gas and Electric
San Francisco, California

If your formulas are not longer than 72 characters, you need not write a macro to accomplish this. Format the range of cells containing the formulas to display the actual text of the formula. Select /Range Format Text (1-2-3) or MENU Format Other Literal (Symphony) and then highlight the column of formulas. Select /Worksheet Column-Width (1-2-3) or MENU Width Set (Symphony), then expand the column so that the entire length of the formulas is visible, and print the range.

If you want a printout of the cell-by-cell contents, including formulas, of every cell in your spreadsheet, select /Print Printer Options Other Cell-Formulas (1-2-3) or SERVICES Print Settings Other Format Cell-Formulas (Symphony). In either case, you should also eliminate top and bottom margins and page breaks. This is done in 1-2-3 by selecting /Print Printer Options Other Unformatted, and in Symphony by selecting SERVICES Print Settings Margins No-Margins.

INSERTING AND DELETING ROWS WITH @SUM

When I delete a row from a range covered by an @SUM function, the formula does not readjust but gives me an ERR indication. However, when I insert a row, the formula readjusts properly. What is the cause of this difference?

Tarn Mereness
IBM Corporation
Boulder, Colorado

You can delete any row within the @SUM range except the top or bottom rows. Deleting either of these rows invalidates the range and causes the function to return ERR. When you insert a row, the new row is squeezed into the spreadsheet just above the row containing the cell pointer. If the cell pointer is located in any row of the @SUM range other than the top row, inserting a row expands the range. If you placed the cell pointer in the top row of the range and insert a row, the new row is placed above the @SUM range and is not included in the calculation. If you regularly want to insert rows at the top of the range, you should expand the range to include a blank line above the data lines. When you want to expand, place the cell pointer in the top data line then select the insert command.

FINDING CIRCULAR REFERENCES

On occasion, I inadvertently create a situation where CIRC appears at the bottom of a *1-2-3* worksheet. Because I work with very large worksheets with a number of calculations, it may take an hour or so to discover what is causing the circular reference. Can you suggest an easier way to find the circular reference?

Leslie F. Benmark, Ph.D.
E.I. duPont de Nemours & Co.
Wilmington, Del.

Circular references occur when a cell's value directly or indirectly depends on itself. Whenever 1-2-3 detects a circular reference in a worksheet using the Natural order of recalculation, the CIRC indicator appears at the bottom of the screen. There are three ways to find a circular reference:

1. *You can use 1-2-3 Release 2/2.01 or Symphony to locate circular references in 1-2-3 Release 1A, since these products display the address of a cell that contains a circular reference. /Worksheet Status (in 1-2-3 Release 2/2.01) and MENU Settings (in a Symphony SHEET window) indicate a cell that contains a circular*

reference. If you eliminate the circular reference from one cell, check to see if you have any other problem cells, because the status screen can display only one circular reference at a time.

2. *You can use the 1-2-3 /File Combine Subtract command. Recalculate the worksheet and save the file that contains the circular reference by placing the cursor in cell A1 and saving the file with File Save. Now recalculate the file using the CALC key. Use the /File Combine Subtract Entire-File command, and specify the file you just saved. All cells that involve a value or calculation will evaluate to zero, since subtracting a value from itself will evaluate to zero. Most cells that contain the circular references will not evaluate to zero since 1-2-3 cannot accurately compute these cells. However, if the cells already equal zero, ERR, or NA before the extract, they will still evaluate to zero, ERR, or NA, respectively.*

3. *You can save the file that contains the circular reference, then begin to delete rows from the bottom of the active worksheet. Start by deleting a large chunk of rows. If the CIRC indicator at the bottom of the screen disappears, you will know that the rows deleted contained the circular reference. Retrieve the file that you saved before you deleted the rows, and delete a smaller range of rows to see if it contains the circular reference. If it does, continue retrieving the file, deleting a smaller and smaller number of rows until you find the problematic row.*

2

Checking Data

BOUNDS CHECKING

Suppose you have a column of entries and want to verify that they are all within a given range (say, 100 through 600). I've found that the @IF function handles that nicely. For example, if the first entry you want to check is in cell A1, enter the following formula in cell B1:

> @IF(A1 > = 100#AND#A1 < = 600,"OK","ERROR")

Use the Copy command to copy this formula as far down column B as there are entries you wish to check in column A (there should be one formula in column B beside each entry in column A). If the numeric entries are within the bounds you expect, the formula will return *OK.*

Helena Jones
Tuscaloosa, Ala.

1-2-3 Release 1A can't use strings as arguments in formulas, so if you use Release 1A, you'll need substitutes for the "Error" and "OK" arguments. Rewrite the formula as follows:

> *@IF(A1 > = 100#AND#A1 < = 600,@NA,@ERR)*

The @NA and @ERR arguments are functions, not strings, but they achieve much the same effect as a string when you use them in this way, with NA standing for OK and ERR for ERROR.

@DSUM AIDS ERROR CORRECTION

I had a column that contained 500 entries and an adjacent column that contained a series of @IF formulas. The @IF formulas tested whether or not the entries in the first column met certain conditions. If the @IF formula returned a zero, the entry did not meet the needed criteria. I needed a way to add all the entries that failed to meet my criteria. Therefore, I placed the levels *Data* and *Test* at the top of the entry and test columns, and then designated the columns as a Database (Input) range. I then entered

Test in a nearby cell, placed a zero under it, and designated it as the Criterion range. Finally, I used @DSUM (datacolumn,∅,criteriarange) to produce the needed sum.

M. Constantine
Schnectady, New York

Eliminate the need for the Test *column by putting a formula in the Criterion range.*

+ /– FORMAT

I work at the Kennedy Space Center where we use *1-2-3* to analyze the flow of data. We found that the + /– format (Other Bar-Graph in *Symphony*) solved a problem we had in identifying values in long columns that exceed an important parameter.

The seldom-used + /– format expresses the numerical value of a cell as plus or minus signs. If a cell contains the number 2, it is displayed as two plus signs. If the cell contains –2, it is displayed as two minus signs. The value ∅ is expressed as a period. (In *1-2-3* Release 1A a ∅ is displayed as a blank.)

We used a macro to go down the column and test if each value exceeded, equaled, or was less than the target. If it exceeded that target, 1 was entered in the cell to the right of the tested value. If it equaled the target, ∅ was entered. And if it was less than the target, a –1 was entered. Through the + /– format, these values were displayed as plus or minus signs or as periods and served as quickly visible flags.

Stephen M. Schneider
Lockheed Space Operations Co.
Cape Canaveral, Fla.

Instead of a macro, you could use the @IF function to do the same test. For example, to test entries in Range A1..A100, enter the following formula in cell B1:

@IF(A1 > target,1,@IF(A1 < target,–1,0))

Copy this formula from B1 to B2..B100. Then format range B1..B100 with the + /– (Other Bar-Graph in Symphony*) format.*

CHECKING CRITICAL WORK

I have two people independently post the same data in a large, important application, in order to be sure it is done correctly. Since they both use the same template, each person's worksheet should be identical to the other's. When the two models are finished, I make a copy of each file and retrieve the copy of the first person's worksheet. I move the cell pointer to cell A1, select /File Combine Subtract Entire-File (in *Symphony*, SERVICES File Combine Subtract Entire-File Ignore Formulas), and select the name of the second person's worksheet.

When the operation is complete, all of the identical cells have a value of zero, which I take to mean that the entries are correct. Those that do not evaluate to zero indicate differences between the two worksheets I combined. I then note the location of the discrepancy and retrieve and check each of the original worksheets.

Rob Gallagher
Wheaton, Ill.

LARGEST NUMBER ALLOWED IN CELL

What is the largest number I can place in a cell? How accurately will my Lotus program remember it?

Bonnie Johnston
Concord, New Hampshire

The largest number that you can enter and that a Lotus product will remember is 10 to the 300th power. The largest number that you can see on your screen is 10 to the 99th power. Lotus products store all numbers with up to 15 digits of precision.

CHECKING FOR DECIMAL-PLACE ACCURACY

While posting a worksheet recently, I mistakenly entered 145234.4 instead of 14523.44, which ended up as an error of 130,710.90. This kind of mistake is so easy to make that I decided I needed a method to check for misplaced decimal points. Here's a quick trick I discovered to detect such errors.

If column C contains numbers that range between 100 and 500, insert a column directly to the right of that: Press slash and select Worksheet Insert Column, and press Return to specify the current column. (In *Symphony* press MENU, select Insert Column, and press Return.) The new column should be at least nine characters wide. If yours is set to some other size, select /Worksheet Column Set-Width and enter 9 (in *1-2-3* Release 1A, select /Worksheet Column-Width Set and enter 9; in *Symphony*, select MENU Width Set and enter 9). Enter the formula +C1/100 in cell D1 and copy cell D1 as far down the column as there are entries in the adjacent column. Format cell D1 by selecting /Range Format +/− (in *Symphony*, select MENU Format Other Bar Graph) and then indicate the range containing the new formulas. We'll use the formulas in each cell of column D to error-check the corresponding numbers in column C.

Numbers in column C less than 100 are represented in column D as a single period; numbers greater than 100 appear as a series of plus signs (the number of plus signs equals the number of times the number is divisible by 100). You'll quickly spot numbers that are outside your expected range.

If you see a series of asterisks across a cell, that number is greater than 999. You can use this technique with numbers greater than 999 by changing the divisor of the formula in column D to 1,000 (or any multiple of that).

If you have a problem entry, it's likely to be either the greatest number or the least number in the column, so you might also use another technique to pinpoint problem entries. In blank cells elsewhere on the worksheet, enter the functions @MAX(*cells*) and @MIN(*cells*), where *cells* is the range containing the entries in column C. The results will be the largest and the smallest numbers in the column, respectively. Examine those numbers to determine if they exceed your bounds.

Jack Turner
Chicago, Ill.

DIVIDING BY ZERO

Why do my formulas evaluate to ERR when I try to calculate a percentage dealing with a 0? Am I doing anything wrong? Is there another way to calculate a percentage without getting ERR? In the following figure, cell C1 contains the formula (A1/B1) and cell C2 contains (A2/B2).

	A	B	C
1	1625	0	ERR
2	47	0	ERR

Bonnie L. Breniser
HAPSCO Group
Camp Hill, Pa.

Dividing a number by 0 is undefined in mathematics, and you will get ERR if your formula attempts to do so. To avoid getting ERR and still maintain your calculations where appropriate, enter the following formula in cell C1 of the figure below:

@IF(B1 = 0,0,(A1/B1))

	A	B	C
1	1625	0	0
2	47	0	

Here the @IF function checks whether cell B1 contains 0. If it does, 0 appears instead of ERR. If not, the result of the formula appears. If you have 1-2-3 Release 2/2.01 or Symphony and prefer to see a blank cell instead of 0, enter the following formula in cell C2, where a blank ("") replaces 0 as the first argument in the @IF function:

@IF(B2 = 0,"",A2/B2)

With 1-2-3 Release 1A, as well as all other releases you can use a formula that tests whether the cell evaluates to ERR:

@IF(@ISERR(A1/B1),0,A1/B1)

3

Using Help

BACKING UP IN HELP FACILITY

I just discovered that I can return to previously viewed Help screens by pressing the Backspace key. It's a great way to use one screen as the starting point for a number of screens. I select one topic from the master screen, read the new screen, then simply press Backspace to return.

Jason Smith
Seattle, Wash.

HELP CAN BE DANGEROUS

When you press the Help key, *1-2-3* Release 1A looks for the help file in the drive or directory from which it was originally loaded, regardless of the current settings of the default directory. If you remove the System Disk, then replace it with a data disk and press the HELP key, *1-2-3* loses its pointers. You then must reenter your worksheet data from scratch. So be careful to keep the System Disk in drive A or, if running from a hard disk, a copy of the 123.HLP file in your *1-2-3* directory.

Roger Levinger
Provident Mutual Life
Philadelphia, Pa.

1-2-3 Release 2/2.01 and Symphony *solved this problem by allowing you to designate Help as Instant or as Removable. Selecting Removable lets you take the System Disk out of the original drive from which you loaded* 1-2-3. *In 1-2-3 Release 2/2.01 use the /Worksheet Global Default Other Help Removable command sequence. In* Symphony *use SERVICES Configuration Help Removable.*

HELP FOR HELP

One way to avoid the problems caused by accidentally pressing the HELP key when the *1-2-3* Release 1A System Disk has been removed is to cover the key with a little cardboard box. On an IBM PC the top of the box is ¾ of an inch square, and the sides are ¹³⁄₁₆ of an inch high.

Bill Woodruff
Stone Container Corp.
Chicago, Ill.

SECTION
7

FINANCE

1-2-3 and *Symphony* are used for applications as varied as sailboat navigation and educational games. But the most common application is financial analysis. Creating budgets and projections are the most typical uses, followed closely by the calculation of interest rates and charges, loan balances, mortgage payments, tax levels, discount prices, and rates of return.

Spreadsheets have many advantages for financial analysis. They are extremely flexible, allowing constant updating and revisions. Spreadsheet models are relatively simple to create, easy to use, and quick to recalculate. By entering data and formulas into spreadsheet cells, you are performing a type of programming where the spreadsheet itself is performing a good part of the work. On the other hand, spreadsheets do not contain inherent error-checking facilities, documentation, and auditing functions, or even the ability to do certain types of financial calculations. Nonetheless, the advantages seem to outweigh the disadvantages, and financial analysis is probably the most common application performed on PC spreadsheet software.

This section describes ways to apply *1-2-3* and *Symphony* to many common financial problems such as loan calculations. In addition, it gives tips on overcoming some of the products' limitations. For example, *1-2-3* and *Symphony*'s financial @functions assume end-of-period payments, so there are several tips on dealing with cash flows involving beginning-of-period payments.

You will also find warnings about some quirks and bugs in Lotus spreadsheet functions such as the @IRR (internal rate of return) and the depreciation @functions.

1

Loan Calculations

FINANCIAL FUNCTIONS IN 1-2-3 RELEASES 1A AND 2

There are a couple differences in how the @PMT, @PV, and @FV financial functions work in *1-2-3* Release 2, as opposed to Release 1A. In Release 1A, these functions accept negative numbers, while in Release 2, negative numbers result in ERR. Also, in Release 1A, you can specify a decimal number as the *term* (such as 10.5 for 10½ years). In Release 2, however, decimal numbers are truncated to whole numbers.

If you need to use negative numbers or fractional time periods to calculate periodic payment, present value, or future value with these Release 2 functions, use the formula that underlies the built-in function. The formulas are given in the *1-2-3 Reference Manual* under the appropriate function.

John Miller
St. Louis, Mo.

The bug causing this problem was fixed in Release 2.01.

LOAN AMORTIZATION — I

Is there a formula or function that would allow me to set up an amortization table showing the monthly amount of principal, interest, and remaining balance? The @PMT function only gives me a lump sum.

Judy Thacker
Fresno, Calif.

The example below and on the next page illustrates how you can construct an amortization table. The initial principal is entered into cell A1, the interest rate in A2, and the term in A3. The following formulas reside in the indicated cells:

> *A5: @PMT(A1,A2/12,A3*12)*
> *D2: +A1*A2/12*
> *D3: +F2*A2/12*
> *E2: A5 − D2*
> *F2: +A1 − E2*
> *F3: +F2 − E3*

Cell E2 is copied to cell E3. The contents of cells D3..F3 are then copied down to the range D4..F13. You can expand this model for large loans by changing the principal, interest, and term in cells A1 through A3 and by copying the cells D3..F3 down to the number of payments necessary to calculate zero for the ending balance. The 1-2-3 Release 1A Tutorial Disk provides an amortization schedule called LESND__1.WKS that you can retrieve and use.

	A	B	C	D	E	F
1	$2,000.00	Principal	Term	Int	Princ	End Bal
2	12.00%	Interest	1	$20.00	$157.70	$1,842.30
3	1 Year		2	$18.42	$159.27	$1,683.03
4			3	$16.83	$160.87	$1,522.16
5	$177.70	Monthly	4	$15.22	$162.48	$1,359.68
6		Payment	5	$13.60	$164.10	$1,195.58
7			6	$11.96	$165.74	$1,029.84
8			7	$10.30	$167.40	$862.44
9			8	$8.62	$169.07	$693.37
10			9	$6.93	$170.76	$522.61
11			10	$5.23	$172.47	$350.13
12			11	$3.50	$174.20	$175.94
13			12	$1.76	$175.94	$0.00
14				-------------------		
15				$132.37	$2,000.00	
16				===================		

LOAN AMORTIZATION — II

I used your suggestion to create an amortization table for a 30-year loan. How can I obtain yearly interest totals and still have the formulas continue for next year?

Irene Kassner
Seattle, Wash.

You can use the @SUM formula to determine the annual interest payments.

Using the example amortization table shown above, assign a range name to the rows containing the interest payments. Press slash (in Symphony, MENU) select Range Name Create, enter interest *as the range name, and indicate range D2..D13. Enter the label* Interest Total *in cell A8 and enter the formula @SUM(*interest*) in cell A9 to determine the total interest paid.*

Since your table extends beyond one year, assign a unique range name to each group of monthly interest payments; for example, interest1, interest2, *and so on. Use these range names in your @SUM formulas to obtain the yearly totals.*

CALCULATING REMAINING BALANCE ON A LOAN

I'm an avid *1-2-3* user who used to get frustrated whenever I had to calculate the balance remaining on a loan after some payments had been made. At first the only solution seemed to be creating a large, slow amortization table, but I discovered a formula that can calculate remaining balance directly. If *loan* is the original loan balance, *rate* is the periodic interest rate, *term* is the number of periods in the loan, and *payments* is the number of payments made to date, the remaining balance is as follows:

$$+ \text{loan} - ((1/((1 + \text{rate})\char`\^\text{term})) * @FV(@PMT(\text{loan,rate,term}),\text{rate,payments}))$$

The interest rate must correspond with the payment periods. For example, if the loan requires monthly payments, you must express the interest rate as the monthly rate and the term as the number of months.

Suppose you have a 30-year, 12 percent mortgage for $100,000 and want to know how much you will owe after 10 years. Here, *loan* is 100,000, *rate* is 0.01 (12%/12), *term* is 360 (12*30), and *payments* is 120 (10*12), so the remaining balance is $93,418, or

$$+ 100000 - ((1/((1 + .01)\char`\^360)) * @FV(@PMT(100000,.01,360),.01,120))$$

James Biram
Memphis, Tenn.

Here is an easier way to do it: A loan's remaining balance is the same as the loan's present value at the time in question. You can find the present value with the following formula:

@PV(@PMT(loan,rate,term),rate,term – payments)

In your example, that would be

@PV(@PMT(100000,.01,360),.01,360 – 120)

which also evaluates to $93,418.

REDUCING A LOAN BALANCE

We create many spreadsheets using most of the Lotus financial functions. However, we cannot locate a formula that will solve the following problem.

On an $85,000 loan at 12% simple annual interest, payable monthly, what monthly payment would reduce the loan balance to 64,999.91% after 60 months?

Richard R. Gardiner
Gardiner Macy Companies
Modesto, Calif.

The model on the top of the next page will solve your problem:

	A	B
1	princ	$85,000.00
2	int	12.00%
3	term	60
4	bal	$64,999.91
5		
6		$1,094.89

To assign the labels in column A as range names for the adjacent cells in column B, press slash (MENU, in Symphony*), select* Range Name Labels Right, *and indicate range A1..A4. Cell B6 contains the following formula:*

@PMT(princ – (bal/(1 + int/12)^term),int/12,term)

The underlined component represents the principal minus the present value of the desired ending balance at a given time (60 months, in this example).

CALCULATING CANADIAN MORTGAGES — I

Canadian mortgages are compounded semiannually, not monthly as are American mortgages, so American financial software is a constant frustration for Canadian users. *1-2-3*'s @PMT doesn't work for Canadian mortgages.

Here is the formula that calculates monthly payment for Canadian mortgages, where *loan* is the mortgage principal, *rate* is the annual interest rate, *term* is the term in months, and *payments* is the number of payments made to date:

+ loan * 1/(1 – 1/(1 + rate/2)^(1/6)^term)*((1 + rate/2)^(1/6) – 1)

The following formula calculates the mortgage's remaining balance (not including interest):

@PV(loan * 1/(1 – 1/(1 + rate/2)^(1/6)^term)*((1 + rate/2)^(1/6) – 1),
   (1 + rate/2)^(1/6) – 1,term – payments)

Sean Pfeffer
Montreal, Quebec

CALCULATING CANADIAN MORTGAGES — II

In response to Sean Pfeffer's letter, I'd like to point out that the @PMT function can be made to calculate Canadian mortgages. Here's a briefer version of Pfeffer's formula:

@PMT(*loan*,(1 + *rate*/2)^(1/6) – 1,*term*)

Loan is the mortgage principal, *rate* is the annual interest rate, and *term* is the term in months.

Gordon E. Witte
Torrance, Calif.

2

Lump Sums, Future Values, and Rates of Return

COMPUTING NPV AT START OF PERIOD

The net present value (@NPV) formula in *1-2-3* and *Symphony* computes the net present value of a sum based on payments at the end of the period. Some financial calculators compute the net present value using payments at the beginning of the term.

I ran across this difference and found a formula that allows *1-2-3* and *Symphony* to consider payments at the beginning of the term. To do this I simply multiply the results of the @NPV formula by 1 plus the interest rate. For example:

@NPV(.11,A1..A10)*(1 + .11)

Brad Davis
Del Ray Beach, Fla.

*To use the formula with cell references to data elsewhere on your worksheet, rewrite it as @NPV(*int,pmt*)*(1 +* int*), where* int *is the cell containing an interest rate and* pmt *is a range containing a series of payments. Either could also be expressed as range names.*

CALCULATING SINKING FUNDS

I have discovered how to calculate a sinking fund, that is, how to determine the amount of money I need to deposit each period (each month, for example) into an interest-bearing account in order to accumulate a particular sum. If *future* is the amount I want to amass, *rate* is the periodic interest rate I will earn on the deposits, and *term* is the number of periods over which I will deposit the money, the amount I need to deposit each period is:

@PMT(*future,rate,term*) − *rate*future*

For example, say I want to amass $5,000 in two years by making monthly deposits into a bank account that earns 7 percent annually. Here, *future* is 5000, *rate* is the monthly interest rate, or 7%/12, and *term* is the number of months, or 2*12. So monthly deposits would be calculated by the following formula, which equals about $195:

@PMT(5000,7%/12,2*12) – 7%/12*5000

Molly Simmons
Baton Rouge, La.

CALCULATING PRESENT AND FUTURE VALUE OF LUMP SUM

Two of the most useful financial functions in *1-2-3* and *Symphony* are the @PV and @FV functions. These functions calculate the present and future value of an annuity (a steady stream of payments), given the payment per period, interest rate, and term. However, there are no functions that calculate the present or future value of a lump-sum payment.

The following formulas makes these calculations possible:

Value	Cell
Yearly interest rate	A1
Number of years	A2
Compounding periods per year	A3
Lump-sum payment	A4

Present value: +A4/(1+(A1/A3))^(A2*A3)
Future value: +A4*(1+(A1/A3))^(A2*A3)

For example, assuming 8 percent interest compounded quarterly, a $5,000 sum due in two years is today worth +5000/(1+(8%/4))^(2*4), or about $4,267. Likewise, $5,000 invested under the same terms for two years is worth +5000*(1+(8%/4))^(2*4), or about $5,858.

Brad Heffler, CPA
Heffler & Co.
Philadelphia, Pa.

QUARTERLY COMPOUNDING FACTOR

I want to show the annual rate of growth by quarters for the various categories of our balance sheet. Although I can easily determine a total annual rate of growth by using last year's year-end figure and our projected next year-end figure, I cannot determine the quarterly compounding factor that will provide me with a proper total annual growth at the end of the four quarters.

Lucille Brandner
State Bank of Medford
Medford, Wisc.

In your case, the rate of return can also be discribed as the interest rate theoretically needed to increase your capital from its starting level to its final level. When the number of compounding periods is greater than one, the general equation you use to calculate the interest rate necessary to reach a specific future value over a known number of compounding periods is as follows:

$$((FV/PV)^{\wedge}(1 - N) - 1) = i\%$$

In this formula FV represents future value and PV represents present value.

For example, if you had a beginning balance of $1,800 on January 1, 1985 and anticipate an ending balance of $2,038 on January 31, 1985, you would calculate the quarterly compounding rate that will equate the present value to the future value in four quarters with this formula:

$$((2038/1800)^{\wedge}(1/4) - 1) = i\%$$
$$3.15\% = i$$

1-2-3 Release 2/2.01 and Symphony Release 1.1/1.2 have a built-in function called @RATE that performs this calculation for you.

CALCULATING RATE OF RETURN

Here's how you can calculate the rate of return for an investment: If *initial* is the amount you invested, *end* is the amount you received, and *periods* is the number of time periods of the investment, then the investment's periodic rate of return is:

$$(end/initial)^{\wedge}(1/periods) - 1$$

For example, I bought 100 shares of stock for $3,200. Two years later I sold the stock for $4,570. My annual rate of return was $(4570/3200)^{\wedge}(1/2) - 1$, or 19.5 percent.

Remember, the result is the periodic rate of return. To calculate monthly rate, enter the number of months as *periods*.

Ron and John Pokornowski
Winfield, Ill.

In 1-2-3 Release 2/2.01 and Symphony Release 1.1/1.2, the function @RATE (end,initial,periods) automates this.

HOW @RATE WORKS

It appears that the *1-2-3* Release 2 @RATE function truncates the term at the decimal, thus causing inaccuracies unless the term is an integer.

Andrew Jones
Energy Development Associates
Itasca, Ill.

1-2-3 Release 2 does truncate the term at the decimal point. 1-2-3 Release 2.01 will accept fractional terms.

@IRR WITHOUT GUESSING

Instead of guessing the internal rate of return, as the @IRR function requires you to do, I calculate @IRR for each period from the beginning to the end of the payment flow. I set up my worksheet in two rows. For example, I place the series of cash payments in the top row, cells A1..G1. In the second row I enter a zero in A2 and the following formula in B2:

@IRR(@IF(@ISERR(A2),∅,@IF(A2 < ∅,∅,A2)),A1..B1)

I copy this formula across the row so that a copy appears under every payment. This method hasn't failed me yet.

Feng Hui Lin
Glen Ellyn, Ill.

@IRR ERROR

According to the *1-2-3* Release 1A manual, you should never encounter a formula computation error unless a problem with either the computer or the System Disk exists.

However, if you manipulate the range within the @IRR function so that an error such as @IRR (.1,ERR) occurs in the arguments, then a *Formula computation error* message will appear.

In my case, the ERR appeared because I erased a cell in the @IRR range and then used the Move command to move the contents of another cell into the previously erased cell.

The problem can be corrected simply by editing the @IRR function and reentering the range. Despite the manual's dire warning, there is no need to panic.

Todd W. Orr
Charlottesville, Va.

Because you are obliterating the corner of a range, this situation still produces an ERR in the formula cell when it occurs in 1-2-3 *Release 2/2.01 and in* Symphony. *However, the dramatic error message no longer appears.*

FINANCIAL FUNCTIONS IN SYMPHONY RELEASE 1

Symphony Releases 1 and 1.01 do not have the functions @CTERM or @RATE, which were added in Release 1.1. These calculations are of particular interest to investors in financial instruments such as "stripped" bonds, which pay no periodic interest but have a lump sum payout at the end of the term. It is, however, possible to perform the same calculations in Release 1 by making use of natural logarithms.

The terms are defined as follows: FV means future value; PV means present value; I is the interest rate (annual compounded, expressed in decimals); n, term (years); $ID, investment date; FD means future date.

The calculation of effective interest rate, given FV and PV, becomes:

I = @EXP(1)^((@LN(FV/PV)/n)/ − 1)

For the typical situation, where ID and FD as well as FV and PV are known, *Symphony*'s date arithmetic can be used to advantage, as in the following expression:

I = @EXP((@LN(FV/PV))/((@DATEVALUE(FD) − @DATEVALUE(ID))/365.25)) − 1

Note that the divisor 365.25 is used to place *n* in numbers of years.
Similarly, given I, FV, and PV, the term *n* can be calculated as:

n = @LN(FV/PV)/@LN(I + 1)

F. Byron Birch
Calgary, Alberta

A slightly simpler version of the effective interest rate formula is:

((FV/PV)^(1/n)) − 1

This is, in fact, the formula used by 1-2-3 *Release 2/2.01 and* Symphony *Release 1.1/1.2 to calculate the @RATE function. The formula you give for calculating the term is also the same as that used by these programs for calculating the @CTERM function.*

3

Depreciation, Payback, Tax, and Discount

@DDB AND THE ENDING BALANCE

I tried using the @DDB function to calculate depreciation on my assets by the double-declining balance method. When I double-checked my ending balance on a Hewlett-Packard financial calculator, I got an answer different from the one *1-2-3 Release 2* gave me. Where do I go from here?

Martin Turner
Fort Collins, Colo.

The @DDB function used by 1-2-3 *Releases 2/2.01 and* Symphony *Releases 1.1/1.2 does not fully depreciate an asset in the last period of its life. The HP calculator takes this into account, which is why the number evaluates correctly on the HP calculator. The way around this in* 1-2-3 *and* Symphony *is to subtract the salvage value from the second-to-last-year's ending balance.*

To use the example shown on the next page, you buy a copier for $10,000 and decide that the useful life of the copier is five years and that at the end of five years you can sell the copier for $500 (which the HP calculator calls the salvage value). Enter the labels in rows 1 through 5, 12, and 16 and in column A. In range A6..A11 enter the values Ø through 5. In cell B6 enter the cost of the asset ($10,000). The format of the @DDB function is @DDB (cost,salvage,life,period). In cell C7 enter the formula @DDB(B6,500,5,A7) and copy it to range C8..C11. In cell B7 enter the formula +B6−C7 and copy it to range B8..B11. Cell C15 contains the formula @SUM(C7..C11).

According to the HP calculator, the copier's net cost (price less salvage value) is $9,500. But with 1-2-3 *(and* Symphony*), the copier's net cost is $9,222.40 because the ending balance (salvage value) is $777.60, not $500. This is because cell C11 contains the formula @DDB(B6,500,5,5). To get* 1-2-3 *and* Symphony *to calculate the last-year figure correctly, subtract the salvage value ($500) from the ending* *balance in the next-to-last year (cell B10). Enter the value 500 in cell B11 and in cell C11 enter +B10 – B11.*

```
        Manual HP Solution
        -------------------
  Year        End. Bal      Rate of
                            Deprec.
    0        $10,000.00
    1         $6,000.00    $4,000.00
    2         $3,600.00    $2,400.00
    3         $2,160.00    $1,440.00
    4         $1,296.00      $864.00
    5           $500.00      $796.00
                          ----------
 Total
 Amount
 Depreciated               $9,500.00
                          ==========
```

	A	B	C
1	1-2-3/Symphony Solution @DDB		
2	----------------------------		
3		End. Bal	Rate of
4			Deprec.
5	Year		
6	0	$10,000.00	
7	1	$6,000.00	$4,000.00
8	2	$3,600.00	$2,400.00
9	3	$2,160.00	$1,440.00
10	4	$1,296.00	$864.00
11	5	$777.60	$518.40
12		----------	
13	Total		
14	Amount		
15	Depreciated		$9,222.40
16		==========	

FINDING PAYBACK PERIOD

You can calculate the time it takes for an investment to recover its initial costs, called the payback period, with the following spreadsheet. The key is to use the @IF function to detect when the cumulative cash flow turns from negative to positive.

Assume that the years, starting with 0, are across row 2 in columns B through F. The annual cash flows, starting with two years of net loss representing the amount needed for the initial investment, are in cells B3..F3. To calculate the cumulative cash flow, enter @SUM(B3..B3) in cell B4, then copy it across row 4 out to column F. Making the first argument of the @SUM range absolute anchors it at the beginning of the annual cash-flow figures. Leaving the second argument as a relative reference lets it move as you copy the formula. Enter the following test formula into cell B5:

@IF(B4<∅#AND#C4> = ∅, + B2 + @ABS(B4)/C3,∅)

Then copy this formula across row 5 from column B to column F. Finally, in B6 enter @SUM(B5..F5), which will calculate the exact payback period.

	A	B	C	D	E	F
1						
2	YEAR	0	1	2	3	4
3	CASH FLOW	-100	-50	25	60	90
4	CUM	-100	-150	-125	-65	25
5	TEST	0.00	0.00	0.00	3.72	0.00
6	PAYBACK	3.72				

Dr. Peter G. Sassone
Georgia Institute of Technology
Atlanta, Ga.

DISCOUNTING PURCHASE ORDERS

When I receive lengthy itemized purchase orders that do not include applicable discounts or tax amounts, I use the following formula to calculate those things for me:

@ROUND(price−@ROUND(price∗disc,2)∗tax,2) + price−@ROUND(price∗disc,2)

In this formula, *price* is the current price entry, *disc* is the discount rate, and *tax* is the tax rate. If the discount amounts or tax rates change, simply edit the formula to reflect the new rates.

Maria Dioguardi
Armonk, N.Y.

MAXIMUM TAX — I

I'd like to respond to the answer you gave regarding a formula that computes a tax on a current salary, but only up to a maximum amount. The formula given to solve the problem has a cell named *ytd*, which contains the year-to-date salary; a cell named *max*, which contains the maximum amount that the employee is taxed on; and a cell named *pay*, which contains the current paycheck.

@IF(ytd> = max#AND#(ytd − max)> = pay,∅,pay∗taxrate)

However, in the period that the year-to-date salary first exceeds the maximum amount, only a portion of the current salary should be taxed, whereas the above formula taxes the entire amount of the current salary.

For example, assume that in a current period an employee is paid $200, bringing his or her year-to-date income up to $500. Assume also that the maximum amount of the employee's income that should be taxed is $400. Using the formula on the previous page, the first condition of the @IF statement isn't met since *ytd – max* = 100 and is not greater than or equal to 200. Therefore, the entire period's pay of $200 is taxed. However, only $100 should be taxed since the current salary exceeds the maximum by $100.

My solution involves calculating how much of the current paycheck is under the maximum: *pay–(ytd–max)*. Here is my complete formula:

@IF(ytd< = max,pay*taxrate,@IF(ytd–pay> = max,∅,
    (pay–(ytd–max))*taxrate))

Jay Estabrook
Peat, Marwick, Mitchell & Co.
Burlington, Mass.

Thank you for improving our solution.

MAXIMUM TAX — II

I would like to add to Jay Estabrook's response on a formula that calculates a tax on current salary up to a maximum amount. My solution uses the @MAX and @MIN functions. Both functions act like the @IF function by choosing from a set of values.

The following formula uses the tax rate (*tr*), the year-to-date salary (*ytd*), the current pay (*pay*), and the maximum amount to be taxed (*max*):

+ tr*@MAX(∅,@MIN(max–ytd,pay))

This formula first subtracts the year-to-date salary from the maximum amount an employee is taxed on. When year-to-date earnings are larger than the maximum amount to be taxed, the result will be a negative. Then the @MIN function chooses the lower of the first computation or the current pay. As the value of *ytd* approaches *max*, the @MIN function chooses the result of the first computation rather than the current pay.

The @MAX function then chooses between the value ∅ or the result of the @MIN function. When the @MIN function returns a negative value, *ytd* has exceeded *max*. Finally, the tax rate is multiplied by the result of the @MAX function.

Stephen Y. Suwa
Honolulu, Hawaii

Unfortunately your formula doesn't work when ytd *exceeds* max. *Assume that* ytd *includes current pay and try the following example:*

tr:	*0.1*
ytd:	*32000*
pay:	*3000*
max:	*30000*

Your formula should return 100, since $1,000 of the current pay is not exempt *from being taxed. Instead it returns 0. The following formula submitted by Tom Farrel, of Chevron Research Co. (Richmond Calif.), does return 100:*

$$+ tr * @MIN(pay, @MAX(max-ytd + pay, 0))$$

SECTION

8

DATE AND TIME

The date and time capabilities built into *1-2-3* and *Symphony* are powerful yet frustrating. Their power lies in the ability they give you to perform complex date and time arithmetic, to set up time-sensitive variables, to date-stamp your work, and to increase the sophistication of your macros. Their ability to frustrate lies in the unfamiliarity of the yy-mm-dd syntax, the task of converting date notations into Lotus-required date serial numbers, and the limitations of a serial-number approach to time keeping. None of these hurdles are insurmountable, but they do require some fancy formulas and technical tricks — both of which are abundantly provided by the reader submissions contained in this section. The number of submissions is testimony to the importance of this topic to *1-2-3* and *Symphony* users.

Some other problems are built into the irregularities of our calendar system. For example, with months varying in length from 28 to 31 days it is sometimes hard to figure out end-of-month calculations. The pattern of leap years adds another complication, which was compounded when some early releases of *1-2-3* didn't know that 1900 was not a leap year (to find out why it was not a leap year, even though it is divisible by four, read "The Calendar Caper" in this section).

Finally, the biggest source of problems with date and time calculations is your computer's clock. It must be accurate for the calculations to work. It is all too easy to quickly slip by the DATE and TIME prompts when starting a computer, even though this shortcut is bound to cause problems in the long run. If this is your problem, be sure to read the first couple of items in this section.

Once you've got the correct date and time in your system, you can then proceed to incorporate date-stamping, version numbering, and this section's other helpful hints.

1

Using Dates

SETTING YOUR CLOCK

How can I change the time displayed at the bottom of my screen? It is still an hour off from daylight savings time.

Peter Peurreung
Kansas City, Mo.

The time displayed at the bottom of your worksheet is not generated by 1-2-3 but by a memory board in your computer that has a built-in, battery-operated clock. There are many on the market. Find out which board you have and consult the documentation provided by the manufacturer.

FORCING INPUT OF CURRENT DATE

Entering the current date and time into your computer upon startup allows files to be "stamped" with the time of their creation and revision and allows all time and date functions in the worksheet to function properly.

If other people use your spreadsheets, use @IF to remind them to enter the date and time. In cell A1, or whatever cell is first visible upon retrieval of the file, enter: @IF(@YEAR(@NOW)<88, "The date in the PC is not correct; return to DOS and enter the proper date.","")

This formula remains invisible if a current date has been entered. But if the DOS default date has not been changed, the message appears as a gentle reminder.

Stephen Hall
Arlington, Virginia

You can go a step further: write an autoexecuting macro that tests whether @YEAR(@NOW) is less than 88 (or 89, or whatever the year is). If it is, the macro invokes DOS and runs DATE and TIME.

DATE AND TIME FUNCTIONS

How do the date and time functions work?

Ralph Harper
Newington, Connecticut

Because computers deal only with numbers, you must translate all dates and times into numbers before you enter them.

In both 1-2-3 and Symphony, *the date serial number 1 represents the date January 1, 1900; number 2 represents January 2, 1900, and so on. The number of each day is one higher than the number of the previous day up to a maximum of 73050 (December 31, 2099). The @DATE (year, month, day) function returns the serial number of a specified date. For example, @DATE (85,11,5) returns the serial number 31356. Each of the year, month, and date arguments in the function can be either a number or a reference to a cell containing a number.*

Time is handled in a similar manner by using decimal fractions rather than integers. Midnight is zero (0.0), while noon is 0.5. The number 0.99999 is just before midnight. The time functions can calculate hours, minutes, and seconds. The @TIME (hour-number, minute-number, second-number) function returns the serial value of the specified time based on a 24-hour clock. For example, @TIME (15,0,0) returns the serial value of 0.625 for 3 P.M.

The @NOW function in 1-2-3 Release 2/2.01 and Symphony *returns the combined serial number for the current date and time. The function uses the figures that you entered, or that were automatically entered for you, in response to the DATE and TIME prompts that appeared when you turned on your computer.*

You may display time and date in many different formats. For complete descriptions of format options, see your Reference Manual.

Date and time arithmetic involves adding, subtracting, or comparing the serial numbers of two dates or times. You can then display the result or use it in additional calculations. Date arithmetic is vital to time-sensitive analyses.

THE CALENDAR CAPER

A Renaissance pope may be responsible for a minor error in *1-2-3*'s calendar. The original version of the Julian calendar, promulgated in 45 B.C., had a quadrennial extra day in February based on the assumption that the solar year is precisely 365 1/4 days long. However, the earth actually takes a few additional hours to get fully around the sun. So by 1582 the calendar was out of sync by about 10 days.

As a result, Pope Gregory XIII devised the version of the calendar now in use. He decreed that only the centennial years divisible by 400 would be leap years. This meant that 1700, 1800, and 1900 were without an extra day in February. However, *1-2-3* accepts @DATE (00,2,29), which is February 29, 1900 as a valid date. I realize that this has little significance in real-world computing, but it's nice to know that the Lotus software engineers didn't think of everything!

Laurence Glavin
Wang Laboratories
Lowell, Massachusetts

All releases of 1-2-3 and Symphony *incorrectly treat the year 1900 as a leap year.*

Thanks to Pope Gregory XIII, the year 2000 is a leap year. 1-2-3 Release 1.0 couldn't handle dates beyond this century, so the year 2000 wasn't an issue. Release 1A doesn't treat 2000 as a leap year. However, Release 1A*, 2, 2.01 and all releases of Symphony correctly consider 2000 a leap year.

CONCATENATING DATES WITH STRINGS

How can I have my worksheets display the current date in one of the following styles in one cell?

Today is 9/1/87   Today is 9-1-87

David Otis
Chevy Chase, Md.

In 1-2-3 *Release 2/2.01 and* Symphony, *enter the following formula in one cell:*

+ *"Today is "&@STRING(@MONTH(@NOW),0)&"/"&@STRING (@DAY(@NOW),0)&"/"&@STRING(@YEAR(@NOW),0)*

Replace the slashes with dashes to display Today is 9-1-87.

CONVERTING MILITARY TIME TO STANDARD TIME

I need a *1-2-3* or *Symphony* formula that will convert military time (based on a 24-hour clock) to standard time.

Dennis Kean
Anaheim, Calif.

Use the following to convert military time to standard time:

	A	B	C
1	Military Time:		1523
2			
3	Standard Time:		323
4	Hours:		3
5	Minutes:		23

Cell C3 contains the formula +C1 − (C1> = 1300)*1200. *Cell C4 contains the formula* (C3−C5) /100. *Cell C5 contains the formula* @MOD(C3,100).

CONVERTING DOWNLOAD FORMAT TO @DATE

I have frequently downloaded a file from my IBM System 36 only to find that the date fields, included as six-digit mm-dd-yy — that is, 120185 — are useless in my *1-2-3* and *Symphony* calculations. I finally devised a formula to translate the useless numbers into the appropriate @DATE(yy,mm,dd) format. Assuming that the mm-dd-yy number is in cell A1, my formula is:

@DATE((A1 − (@INT(A1/10000)∗10000)) − (@INT((A1 − (@INT(A1/10000)∗10000))/100)100),@INT(A1/10000),@INT((A1 − (@INT(A1/10000)∗10000))/100))

You could also write a macro to perform the {EDIT}{CALC} process on each of these formula cells to convert the formula to a hard number. Hard numbers use less memory than formulas.

Jeffrey Stevens
Tollie Freightways
Kansas City, Kansas

We had trouble getting your formula to work, so here is a more compact formula that will accomplish the same task:

@DATE(@MOD(A1,100), @INT(A1/10000), @INT(@MOD(A1,10000)/100))

INSTANT CALENDAR

Symphony and *1-2-3* can quickly generate the dates needed for calendars, schedules, and other documents that require lists of dates. The trick is to enter appropriate date and time @functions in the /Data Fill (*1-2-3*) or MENU Range Fill (*Symphony*) commands as your Start and Stop values and to vary the Step value using 1 for successive days, 7 for weekly intervals, and 14 for biweekly periods. Doing so produces date serial numbers that you can format.

For example, the following provides all dates in July 1985:

Start: *@DATE(85,7,1)*; Step: *1*; Stop: *@DATE(85,7,31)*

This provides dates for all of the Thursdays in July and August of 1985:

Start: *@DATE(85,7,4)*; Step: 7; Stop: *@DATE(85,8,31)*

I used this technique to answer a question posed by a coworker doing budget planning who needed to know which years would have 26 biweekly paydays and which would have 27.

I used @DATE of the first payday of this year as the Start value, a Step value of 14, and @DATE of the last day of the year 1999 as the Stop value. The Fill range started downward from cell J3. I put the field name Date in cell J2 just above the column of date numbers and gave the entire list the range name *db*. The Criterion range (L2..L3) contained the field name and, underneath it, the formula criterion @YEAR(J3)=85. Finally, I entered the database statistical function @DCOUNT(db,0,L2..L3) into cell N2. By using the EDIT function key to change the year designation in the criterion formula in cell L3 and watching the numbers in cell N2, I quickly discovered that 1988 will be the next year with 27 paydays.

Paul Nance
Indianapolis, Indiana

*You could automate the final editing process by using the /Data Table 1 (1-2-3) or MENU Range What-If 1-Way (*Symphony*) commands. Change the formula criterion to reference a cell using an absolute address — for example, cell M1. The formula would read @YEAR(J3) = M1, where cell J3 contains the first record of your database. Place the @DCOUNT function at the top of a clear area, and then use the /Data Fill command to list every year from the present to as far into the future as you wish to test. Use a Start value of 85, Step of 1, and the Stop of your choice. Now invoke the Table command and designate cell M1 as the Input cell.*

```
                    Input Cell
              ┌─────────────
          L       M     N         O
      ┌────────────────────────────────────────────
   1  │              85
   2  │  Date              @DCOUNT...
   3  │  @YEAR...    85
   4  │              86
   5  │
```

2

Months

INCREASING DATES BY ONE MONTH

When I calculate monthly payment schedules or any other monthly event, I like to display the due date of each payment rather than the month number. With a payment due on the 15th of each month for a 30-year mortgage, I needed a quicker method than typing 360 dates.

Adding one to each month number won't work past month 12, and I couldn't just add 30 days to the prior month's date, so I devised the following method. After using the @DATE function to enter the date of my first payment in cell A1, I enter separate formulas in cells A2 and B2 and copy them down 359 rows. The formula in column B returns 1 if the current month is January, 0 if it is not. The formula in column A uses that result to determine the month's date. The formula in column B doesn't have to be separate from the one in column A, but I prefer it that way because it allows me to keep the formula in column A short and simple. I assign a date format to the entries in column A and hide the formulas in column B using the Range Format Hidden command (in *Symphony*, MENU Format Other Hidden).

Enter the following formula in cell A2:

@DATE(@YEAR(A1) + B2,@MONTH(A1) + 1 − 12*B2,@DAY(A1))

Enter the following formula in cell B2:

((@ABS(@MONTH(A1) − 11)) + @MONTH(A1) − 11)/2

	A	B
1	15−Nov−86	
2	15−Dec−86	0
3	15−Jan−87	1
4	15−Feb−87	0

L. Lee Brodie
Marietta, Ga.

If you format cells A2 and B2 before you copy them, you won't have to format the whole column — 1-2-3 will do it for you as you copy the formula down.

The following formula offers an alternative to the preceding two. It first determines if the current month is December. If so, the formula then adds 1 to the year, uses 1 as the month, and uses the same day. If not, the formula uses the same year, adds 1 to the month, and uses the same day. Enter this formula in cell A2:

@IF(@MONTH(A1) = 12, @DATE(@YEAR(A1) + 1, 1, @DAY(A1)),
 @DATE(@YEAR(A1), @MONTH(A1) + 1, @DAY(A1)))

Neither approach works when the payment date is the last day of the month and the last day of the next month does not fall on the same numbered day. Adding one month to August 31 will produce an error since September 31 is an invalid date. In such cases refer to the item, ''@CHOOSE the End of the Month'' for a formula to determine the last day of each month.

@CHOOSE THE END OF MONTH

Here is a formula for determining the last day of each month.

+ A1 + @CHOOSE(@MONTH(A1),0, @IF(@MOD(@YEAR(A1),4) =
 0,29,28),31,30,31,30,31,31,30,31,30,31,31)

Cell A1 contains the last day of the preceding month. The formula combines a single @IF statement with an @CHOOSE function that uses the previous month number to determine the last day of the following month. The list of numbers contains the last day of each month. The @MOD function adjusts the days in February for a leap year.

Note that this formula cannot calculate the same day of each month over a column of dates.

Brian G. McNiven
McNiven & Co.
Sydney, Australia

Here is an even simpler formula:

+ A1 + 32 − @DAY(A1 + 32)

Cell A1 contains the serial number of the last day of any month. The formula adds 32 to this serial number, which moves the date up into the second following month. The difference between the sum of (A1 + 32) and the day number of this sum is the last day of the next month.

CALCULATING NUMBER OF MONTHS

I need to calculate the number of months between two dates in order to determine the monthly rate of return of some of my investments. I use the following formula, which assumes that the cell named *end* contains the *1-2-3* (or *Symphony*) serial number corresponding to the ending date and *begin* contains the serial number for the beginning date:

$$(@YEAR(end) - @YEAR(begin))*12 + @MONTH(end) - @MONTH(begin)$$

Clancy O'Grady
Dublin, N.H.

CONVERTING DATE LABELS TO VALUES — I

One of the enhancements made in Release 2 of *1-2-3* is the ability to take labels that look like values and turn them into real values for use in calculations (use @VALUE).

I found label-to-value conversion particularly helpful after downloading some stock information from an information service. The dates appeared as labels, such as '3/4/86 for March 4, 1986. These dates ran down column A, starting in A10. With *1-2-3* Release 1A, I had to laboriously reenter each date as a value — for example, @DATE(86,3,4) — in order to use the dates when sorting or querying my database. With Release 2/2.01 (and with *Symphony*), I simply insert a column to the right of column A and enter @DATEVALUE(A10) in cell B10. I copy that formula down column B and now have a column of date serial numbers, which I can use in date arithmetic.

Steven Quimby
Tuscaloosa, Ala.

After finishing the label-to-value conversion, use /Range Value (in Symphony, *MENU Range Values) to copy the @DATEVALUE formulas onto themselves as values to save memory.*

CONVERTING DATE LABELS TO VALUES — II

Here's an alternative to the previously published Good Idea on converting date labels into values. That approach used two cells per date and this macro-driven approach requires one. Move the cell pointer to the first cell in the column of dates you want to translate. Name that cell *start*. Hold down the MACRO key and press D to run this macro:

```
        A         B
1    \d    {GOTO}start~
2          {EDIT}{HOME}{DELETE}
3          @DATEVALUE("{END}")~
4          /RFD1~/RV~~
5          {DOWN}
6          /RNDstart~
7          /RNCstart~~
8          {BRANCH \d}
```

The second and third lines convert the entry from a label to a date value. Range Format Date 1 formats the cell, and Range Value converts the entry from a formula to a value. Line five moves the cell pointer down one row, line six deletes the range name, and line seven re-creates it on the current row. Line eight restarts the macro and the conversion begins again (use Control-Break to stop the macro when it finishes processing your list of dates).

Pam Breach
Boston, Mass.

For use with Symphony, *revise line 4 to read:* {MENU}FD1 ~ {MENU}RV ~ ~ . *The macro would be faster if it performed the edit functions in lines 2 and 3, but put off formatting the column or converting it to a hard number until it was possible to do the entire column at one time.*

3

Days and Weeks

ENTERING A SERIES OF DATES

Is there a fast way to enter a series of consecutive dates in one column of a worksheet?

Richard Schindiel
Electronic Data Systems
Arlington, Va.

You can enter a series of dates with help from the Data Fill command and your computer's internal clock function. For example, if you want to enter the dates for a two-week period in range A1..A14, press slash and select /Data Fill (press MENU and select Range Fill in Symphony). Specify A1..A14 as the Fill range. When you are prompted for a Start value, enter @INT(@NOW). Enter a Step value of 1 if you want consecutive dates. Then enter @INT(@NOW)+14 for the Stop value.

If you use 1-2-3 Release 1A, enter @TODAY in place of @INT(@NOW). To display the serial dates in date format, select /Range Format Date (MENU Format Date in Symphony), choose the format you want, specify range A1..A14, and press Return. Asterisks will appear if the column isn't wide enough. In that case, select /Worksheet Column Set-Width (MENU Width Set in Symphony) and widen the column to display the dates.

DATE ARITHMETIC WORKDAYS AND WEEKENDS

I am making a scheduling worksheet. If I know the starting date of a project and the number of workdays needed to finish the job, how can I find the exact finish date? My problem is to figure out how many weekend days to add.

Edward Sumptner
Palo Alto, California

Assuming that at least one weekend lies between the start and finish dates, enter the following formulas:

Cell	Formula
A1	TotalWrkdaysNeeded
A2	@DATE(startdate)
A3	@MOD(A2,7)
A4	+ A1–(7–A3)
A5	@INT((A4–1)/5)
A6	2 + 2＊A5
A7	+ A2 + A1 + A6 – 1

Cell A1 contains the total number of workdays needed to complete the task. Cell A2 contains the start date, entered with the @DATE(yy,mm,dd) function.

The formula in cell A3 calculates the start date's day of the week. The value of @MOD is the remainder left over when the serial number of the start date is divided by 7, the number of days in the week. If the result is 2, the start day is a Monday; a result of 6 represents Friday.

For example, if the start day is a Wednesday, cell A3 will display a value of 4. Subtracting 4 from 7 gives you the number of workdays in the first week of your schedule. Then subtracting this from the total number of workdays needed for the project gives you the number of workdays yet to go. The formula in cell A4 performs this double subtraction.

Now jump over the first weekend, but remember that you must later add the weekend's two days to the total. Starting with the next Monday, you will have an intervening weekend for every five additional days needed to complete the task. This means that dividing the remaining number of workdays (the number in cell A4) by 5 tells you the number of intervening weekends. Actually, you need the integer value of the result. For example, if six days are left, you divide 6 by 5 and get a result of 1.2. The @INT function drops the decimal and leaves you with the correct answer of 1 intervening weekend.

Dividing by 5 seems to work, but what if the remaining number of days is exactly divisible by 5. If there are 15 remaining days, the division produces a result of 3 intervening weekends. However, counting the first Monday as day 1 and counting forward 14 additional workdays brings you to Friday, just before the third weekend, which means there will actually only be two intervening weekends. To protect yourself against this situation, subtract 1 from the remaining number of workdays before dividing by 5. The formula in cell A5 summarizes this process.

Now you are ready to figure the total number of weekend days by multiplying the number of weekends by 2 and then adding those initial two weekend days that you ignored several paragraphs ago.

Now for the grand finale. In cell A7 you add the serial number of the start date (A2) plus the total number of workdays needed (A1) plus the total number of weekend days (A6), and then you subtract 1. Why this last subtraction? The start date is also the first day of work: when you add the total number of working days needed, you are counting that first day twice. The subtraction corrects for that double counting.

The whole calculation looks better if you give cells A2 and A7 your favorite date format.

ACCOUNTING FOR WEEKENDS

Every day we must update our work schedule for the following day. We have *1-2-3* (Release 1A) do the work of changing the date on the worksheet. The formula @TODAY + 1 returns tomorrow's serial number. We use one of *1-2-3*'s date formats to display the value. However, the formula will return Saturday's date rather than Monday's. The following formula gets around that difficulty:

@IF(@MOD(@TODAY,7) = 6,@TODAY + 3,@TODAY + 1)

@MOD(@TODAY,7) divides today's date (serial number) by 7 and returns the remainder. If today is a Monday, that expression returns 2; if it is Tuesday, the result is 3; and so on. The entire expression compares the remainder to 6 (which corresponds to a Friday). If the remainder is 6, the formula returns @TODAY + 3, or next Monday; if the remainder is not 6, it returns @TODAY + 1, or tomorrow.

Douglas L. Andrews
Washington State Dept. of Transportation
Hoquiam, Wash.

1-2-3 Release 2/2.01 and Symphony users should substitute @INT(@NOW) for the first @TODAY in the formula and @NOW for the second and third @TODAYs: @IF(@MOD(@INT(@NOW), 7) = 6, @NOW + 3, @NOW + 1).

FROM DATE NUMBER TO DAY NAME

Is it possible to convert a date into the day of the week?

Paul Lewis
New Orleans, Louisiana

The @DATE function returns the date serial number of the chosen date. The date serial number is the number of days since the start of this century. For dates after March 1, 1900, the remainder after dividing this number by 7 indicates the date's day of the week. A remainder of 0 indicates Saturday, a remainder of 1 indicates Sunday, and so forth up to a Friday, which has a remainder of 6. The @MOD function, which stands for the mathematical term modulus, returns the remainder of a division. The following formula returns the day indicator number:

@MOD(@DATE(yy, mm, dd), 7)

If you have Symphony *or Release 2/2.01 of* 1-2-3 *you can convert these indicator numbers into the day name by using an @VLOOKUP table. (If you have Release 1A of* 1-2-3, *you must write a macro to perform a label lookup.) For example, fill a column of seven cells with the numbers from Ø through 6. To the right of this column, enter the days of the week so that Saturday is next to Ø, Sunday is next to 1, and so on. Into the cell in which you want the day name to be displayed enter:*

@VLOOKUP(@MOD(@DATE (yy,mm,dd), 7), tablerange,1)

Another solution, using the @CHOOSE function, would be:

@CHOOSE(@MOD(@DATE(yy,mm,dd)), "SAT", "SUN", "MON", "TUE", "WED", "THU", "FRI")

4

Time

PRINTING SPREADSHEET VERSION NUMBERS

When you have to retrieve, update, and print out the same spreadsheet several times in the same day, keeping track of which is the latest version can be difficult. If you have *Symphony* or *1-2-3* Release 2/2.01, you can use the @TIME function to time-stamp each printout. But with *1-2-3* Release 1A, you need a macro. (This macro will also work in all other versions of *1-2-3* and *Symphony*.) Give cell B1 the name *counter*, then enter this macro in an out-of-the-way cell on the worksheet:

{GOTO}counter ~ {EDIT} + 1{CALC} ~

Name this macro \∅ to make it autoexecute. (In *Symphony* select SERVICES Settings Auto-Execute Set Starting-Cell and point to the cell containing the macro.) Enter the label *Version* in cell A1. Upon retrieval of the worksheet, the top line will automatically be updated to read *Version 1, Version 2,* and so on.

Mike Craig
Rockville, Maryland

But what if you're printing different versions of the spreadsheet without saving and retrieving between printouts? The solution is to make this macro part of your print macro. Calling the print macro would first update the formula and then print the worksheet (or vice versa).

TIME ARITHMETIC

Many of my *1-2-3* calculations involve the time of day. I use a 24-hour clock for the hours, but I have had to convert the minutes to a decimal format manually. Is there a way to avoid this time-consuming and burdensome conversion process?

Frank J. Deluca
Continental Bank
Norristown, Pennsylvania

To avoid doing manual conversion in either 1-2-3 *and* Symphony, *place the number of hours in one cell and the number of minutes in another cell. Then use a formula to automatically convert the minutes to a decimal and to add the decimal to the hours. For example, if the number of hours is in cell A1 and the number of minutes is in cell B1, enter the following formula in cell C1: +A1+B1/60.*

CONVERTING TIME LABELS TO SERIAL NUMBERS

Is it possible in *1-2-3* Release 2/2.01 and *Symphony* to use a label representing time (for example 4:00 P.M.) in math calculations?

Katherine Sanders
Corvallis, Oreg.

You can use the @TIMEVALUE function to convert a label representing time into a time serial number. If cell A1 contains the label '4:00, then the formula @TIMEVALUE(A1) entered into another cell will return the time serial number of 4:00 A.M., which is 0.166666 (the sixes will continue to the width of the cell). This new entry can be used in calculations. Select /Range Format Date Time (MENU Format Time in Symphony) to choose a display format for your time. If you select the second time format (HH:MM AM/PM), the cell will display 04:00 A.M. To get 04:00 P.M., the original label must be '16:00 or '4:00 PM (with no periods). If the cell you want to change contains 4:00 P.M., the formula @TIMEVALUE (cell) will evaluate to ERR — the periods in P.M. are not accepted.

CONVERTING SECONDS TO MINUTES

In one of my worksheets I need to convert seconds to minutes, for example 75.39 seconds. I cannot devise a formula that accomplishes this.

Ed Vilandrie
Foxboro Company
Foxboro, Massachusetts

You need to use the @INT and @MOD functions. @INT returns the integer value of the argument and ignores any fractional excess. Dividing the total number of seconds by 60 gives you the number of minutes plus a fraction, which @INT can strip away. @MOD returns the modulus of the argument: the remainder of a division. If the number of seconds is in a cell named cell, @INT(cell/60) returns the number of minutes and @MOD(cell/60) returns the number of remaining seconds.

CALCULATING ELAPSED TIME

As a management engineer, I must often calculate the time elapsed between two events. I have devised a method that allows me to enter times as HHMM and subtract ending time from beginning time to calculate elapsed time in hours or minutes. The beginning and ending times must fall in the same day.

If you enter beginning time in cell A3 (the figure below shows the entry 1205, which represents 12:05 P.M.) and enter ending time in cell B3 (1322 for 1:22 P.M.), the following formula entered in cell C3 calculates elapsed time in hours:

(B3 – @MOD(B3,100))/100 + (@MOD(B3,100)/60) – ((A3 –
  @MOD(A3,100))/100 + (@MOD(A3,100)/60))

To calculate elapsed minutes, simply multiply the above formula by 60 in D3.

	A	B	C	D
1	Begin	End	Elapsed	Elapsed
2	time	time	hours	minutes
3	1205	1322	1.283333	77

Joel Roth
University of Chicago Medical Center
Chicago, Ill.

Your formula can be simplified to read:

@INT((B3-A3)/100) + @MOD(B3-A3,100)/60

In addition, 1-2-3 Release 2/2.01 and Symphony have an @TIME function that simplifies this procedure. @TIME converts numbers entered as hours, minutes, and seconds into serial numbers that you can use directly in formulas. First, enter the times in two cells, one for the hour and one for the minutes, as shown in cells A2 through B3 below. Cell A4 contains the formula that converts the entered numbers into times and calculates the difference:

@TIME(B2,B3,∅) – @TIME(A2,A3,∅)

C2 calculates the elapsed time in hours as +A4*24. C3 calculates elapsed time in minutes as +C2*60.

	A	B	C	D
1	Begin	End	Elapsed	
2	12	13	1.283333	hours
3	5	22	77	minutes
4	0.0534			

5

Date Formats

WHY NOT MM/DD/YY?

Is there any way to change the displayed date format from the European dd/mm/yy to the American mm/dd/yy?

Dominic Songco
Jackson Heights, New York

Issue the /Range Format Date command in 1-2-3 *Release 2/2.01 (in Symphony MENU Format Date) command and select the Full International date format, which is choice number 4.*

MONTH/DAY/YEAR FORMAT

You can't usually display dates in a Month dd,yyyy format, such as January 23, 1986. However, since this is the format most often used in formal correspondence, I have developed a macro that allows me to choose either the current date or any other date and display it in this format. The macro (shown in the figure below) uses a menu to allow you to do this. (Since I have *Symphony*, Release 1.1, I place the macro in the Macro Library Manager so that I can get to it from any worksheet.)

```
          A          B                      C
1    \d         {MENUBRANCH begin}
2
3    begin      Today                  Other date
4               Use today's date       Use other than today's date
5               {LET holder,@NOW:value}  {GETLABEL "Enter date as mm/dd/yy: ",temp}
6               /RVdateform~~          {LET holder,@DATEVALUE(temp)}
7                                      /RVdateform~~
8
9    dateform   July 15, 1986
10   temp       7/15/86
11   holder                   31608
```

The heart of the macro is the following formula, which you enter into the

DATEFORM cell, the name given to cell A9:

> @CHOOSE(@MONTH(holder) – 1,"January","February","March","April",
> "May","June","July","August","September","October","November",
> "December")&" "&@STRING(@DAY(holder),∅)&","@STRING
> (@YEAR(holder) + 1900,∅)

After entering everything, I select MENU Range Name Labels Right and highlight that range with *begin* at the top and *holder* at the bottom. To use the macro, I place my cursor where I want the formatted date to appear, then type Alt-D and answer the prompts.

Ronnie J. Bouchon
South Bend, Ind.

SECTION
9

GRAPHS

A picture is worth a thousand numbers. The subtle movement of lines or bars quickly reveals trends that would be hard to catch in a purely numerical printout. *1-2-3* and *Symphony* are designed to create analytic graphs — graphs whose primary purpose is to help you, your associates, and your customers analyze worksheet data. To create printed versions of your graphs, both *1-2-3* and *Symphony* have a PrintGraph program that enables you to further enhance your images, and while there are other products on the market that specialize in the creation of presentation-quality graphics, the graphing power provided by PrintGraph is often all you'll need.

For most computer users, *1-2-3* and *Symphony* provided their original introduction to graphics. For many people, those two products are still the only graphics software they use. In fact, recent surveys show that more people use *1-2-3* for graphics, both analytic and presentation, than any other product. If you are one of them, this section will be a cornucopia of good ideas. And even if your use of *1-2-3* or *Symphony* graphics is limited to quick and dirty analysis, this section will help you make your graphs clearer, more revealing, and more useful.

Probably the biggest problem with *1-2-3* graphics is the confusion between naming a graph, which gives it "permanent status" within a specific worksheet, and saving a graph, which turns it into a separate file ready for printing. To complicate the matter further, the graph you most recently created in the worksheet doesn't need to be named — it is automatically included as part of the worksheet. Names are only required if you want to keep more than one graph within a worksheet.

The most exciting tips in this section show you how to create "floating" legends and titles, how to graph more than six ranges, how to include discontinuous ranges in the same graph, and how to get better performance from PrintGraph.

1

Improved Graph Display

DRAW PICTURES

You might create a presentation that consists of worksheet displays and graphs of worksheet data. Or you might create a presentation entirely of graphs. But have you ever considered including in your presentation drawings that serve only to embellish the presentation without providing additional information?

For example, how about beginning a presentation with a screen that depicts your company's logo? Or perhaps you'd like to interject into a sequence of graphs a line drawing that represents the subject of one of the graphs. With a little effort you can produce simple drawings within *1-2-3* or *Symphony* and spice up your business presentations. And with time and patience, you can create surprisingly detailed graphics.

Simple Line Drawings   The trick to "drawing" with *1-2-3* and *Symphony* is to generate data pairs that represent coordinates on a graph. With these pairs in the correct order, when you assign them as the X and A ranges of an XY graph, *1-2-3* or *Symphony* will "connect the dots" and produce whatever image you have the patience to design.

For example, start with a blank worksheet and enter data as shown in the following illustration:

	A	B	C	D
1	1	2		
2	2.5	3		
3	3.5	3		
4	3.5	2		
5	2	1		
6	1	1		
7	1	2		
8	2	2		
9	3.5	3		
10	2	2		
11	2	1		

Create an XY graph as follows: In *1-2-3* press slash, select Graph Type XY X, indicate the range A1..A11, and press Return. Then select A, indicate B1..B11, and press Return. Select Options Scale Y-Scale Manual Upper, and enter 4. Then select Quit Scale X-Scale Manual Upper, and enter 4. Select Quit Quit View.

In *Symphony* press MENU, select Graph 1st-Settings Type XY Range X, indicate the range A1..A11, and press Return. Then select A, indicate B1..B11, and press Return and then Quit. Select Switch Y-Scale Type Manual-Linear, press Return, then enter 4 and select Quit. Select X-Scale Type Manual-Linear, press Return, enter 4, and select Quit Quit Preview.

Whichever product you're using, it should present you with a drawing of a rectangular prism. *Symphony* users can eliminate the X and Y axes of the graph by returning to the graph menu (press any key), and selecting 2nd-Settings Other Hide Yes Quit. Then select Preview to once again view the graph.

This isn't a sophisticated example of your software's drawing capability. But the method of planning this illustration can apply to almost any drawing effort. To plan a drawing, use straight line segments and sketch on a piece of graph paper the image you wish to produce. Try to make key points of the drawing fall into intersections of the grid. Number axes on the graph paper and place the origin (0,0) below and to the left of your sketch. Now place dots on the lines of your sketch wherever there is a corner.

Try to connect the dots in your drawing with one continuous line, retracing segments if you must to finish without lifting your pen or pencil from the paper. Enter data sets into the worksheet in the order that you trace them. Assign graph ranges and view the results; then tinker with your data pairs as needed to sharpen the image. I set scaling to manual to ensure that none of the image I create falls on an axis or border of the graph. For this to be effective, select a maximum scaling value that is close to but greater than the highest values of your ordered pairs. Also, make sure that none of your ordered pairs contains a value of zero.

Circles   To approximate circles in your drawings, generate data as follows: press slash and select Data Fill (MENU Range Fill in *Symphony*). Indicate the range C13..C30 as the range to fill, then enter 0 as the start value, 2*@PI/9 as the step value, and 2*@PI as the stop value. In cell A13, enter the formula @SIN(C13)+1, and in cell B13, enter the formula @COS(C13)+3. Copy from A13..B13 to A13..A23. Then extend the graph's X and A ranges to include the new data in columns A and B. An octagon appears in the top-left corner of this modified graph. Note that the gap in the graph ranges causes your software to ''lift the pencil'' as it connects the dots of your drawing. Without the gap, there would be a line in your drawing running from one corner of the box to a point on the octagon.

You control the placement of the octagon in your line drawing by changing the values used in the sine and cosine formulas in range A13..B23. For example, to move the octagon down, modify the formula in cell B13 to read @COS(C13) + 2 and copy the new formula to the range B13..B23. To change the size of the octagon, uniformly multiply or divide every value in the range A13..A23.

Free Form You don't have to plan out a drawing in advance. When I use XY graphs to create line drawings I often start with a single element (a circle, a square, or whatever) on-screen, and add to it. Use an approach that suits your working style.

I've seen this technique used to create such images as a map of the United States of America and a line drawing of a personal computer. You'll be limited only by the amount of time you're willing to expend fiddling with numbers until your desired sketch emerges.

Daniel Gasteiger
from Lotus Retail News

MAKING GRAPHS MORE ATTRACTIVE
I include an empty cell at both ends of the data range in nearly every graph I print. This moves the graphed information away from the edges, providing a more attractive graph.

Walt Spindler
Owatana, Minn.

This suggestion works well for line, XY, bar, and stacked-bar graphs, but will not affect pie charts.

MAXIMUM NUMBER OF DATA POINTS
How many data points can I plot along the X axis of my graph?

Mark Bittman
New Haven, Connecticut

You can plot as many as you want. The only limitation is the amount of memory in your computer. If necessary, points will be plotted on top of each other to fit the graph onto the screen or paper.

REDUCING GRAPH CLUTTER
Do your X range graph labels run together on-screen? If the problem is that you have too many to fit, try using the /Graph Options Scale Skip command with a skip factor of 2 or more.

Karen Washburn
Manchester, Missouri

The Symphony *commands for your idea are MENU Graph 2nd-Settings Other Skip, with a factor of 2 or more.*

EXPLODING PIE GRAPHS

How do I explode a section of a pie chart in *1-2-3* Release 2/2.01 and *Symphony*, and how do I print the pie slices in different colors?

James Boyd
Hartford, Conn.

Use the A range to plot the data you want to graph and the B range to specify shading, coloring, and exploding the wedges of the pie. Use the following worksheet as an example:

	A	B	C
1	X-range	A-range	B-range
2	1979	1250	0
3	1980	1300	1
4	1981	1700	102
5	1982	1400	3

Enter B-range codes Ø through 7 to indicate the desired coloring or shading for each corresponding pie wedge. The code Ø indicates an unshaded wedge. To explode a pie wedge, add 100 to the B-range shading value. For example, a B-range code of 102 explodes the pie slice associated with it and gives the slice the type 2 shading pattern of color. If you select /Graph Options Color (in Symphony, MENU Graph 2nd-Settings Other Color Yes), the pie wedges appear with colors that correspond to the seven hue settings. Your ability to view and print the colors, however, depends on the monitor and printing device you are using. If you choose /Graph Options B&W (in Symphony, MENU Graph 2nd-Settings Other Color No), the pie graph's wedges appear with a variety of shading patterns.

Two things determine the color of a wedge in a printed version of the graph: the values in the B range when you saved the graph into a PIC file (in 1-2-3, /Graph Save; in Symphony, MENU Graph Image-Save), and the colors you assigned in PrintGraph using the Range-Colors command. If you saved your graph with a B-range value of 2 or 102, PrintGraph prints the wedge in the color you assigned for range A. See the following table for the relationship between B-range values and Range-Colors.

B-Range Value in 1-2-3/Symphony	Range in PrintGraph
1	X
2	A
3	B
4	C
5	D
6	E
7	F

2

Bar and Stacked-Bar Graphs

REDUCING BAR WIDTH IN GRAPHS

You can reduce the width of the bars in a bar or stacked-bar graph when using fewer than six data ranges by specifying empty cells as additional data ranges. For example, if you are graphing two ranges (A and B), select data ranges C, D, E, and F and enter empty ranges for them. You may find the reduced bar widths more effective and pleasing.

Robert Basile
Alexandria, Va.

STACKED-BAR GRAPH MORE THAN 100%

I am having a problem in *1-2-3* Release 2 creating stacked-bar graphs that depict the percentage of units still in backlog. The values graphed add up to 100, yet when the graph prints, the bars go over the top of the graph boundary, indicating that the total exceeds 100%. When I set the scale to manual and specify 110 as the upper limit, the graph prints out correctly totaling 100%. The problem occurs when I set the upper limit to 100. Please give me any suggestions for remedying this situation.

Lorrie Johnson
Bendix Air Transport
Tukwila, Wash.

The situation you describe exists in all releases of 1-2-3. There are several possible solutions, one of which may work for your application.

Even though the numbers displayed are whole numbers and appear to evaluate to 100, there may be trailing decimal places in the 14th or 15th decimal place. Widen your column to allow for the display of 15 decimal places by selecting /Worksheet Column Set-Width and indicating 20 as the column width. Then format the cell to display 15 decimal places by selecting /Range Format Fixed and entering 15. You may see the whole number 100 displayed not as 100.000000000000000, but as 100.000000000000012.

1-2-3 stores values with a precision of 15 decimal places. Microcomputers store numbers using the binary system. When the numbers are translated back into the decimal number system, some numbers do not have an exact binary-to-decimal equivalent. With this in mind, use the @ROUND function to round off numbers to zero decimal places by enclosing them with the @ROUND function. For example, if the number is 3.6453, the formula would be @ROUND(3.6453,0).

If the preceding suggestion doesn't work, try reducing your numbers slightly so that the stacked-bar graphs will display 100% on the graph. You can also continue to adjust the upper limit to 110 since this has worked for you.

BETTER BAR GRAPH TRANSPARENCIES

When I want to produce a bar chart with one bar that stands out, I select the stacked-bar type of graph. I enter the values to be graphed in the A data range, except that I enter a zero instead of the value whose bar I want to stand out. I then enter zeros for all values in the B data range, except that I enter the stand-out value in its appropriate place. The result appears to be a bar graph with one distinctively colored bar.

When I want to produce a set of transparencies that overlay each other with complementary data, I plot the entire graph using an empty penholder for all but one variable. Then I place another blank transparency on the plotter and redraw the same graph while moving the pen to the holder for a different variable. I do this until I've drawn all the variables. The result is a stack of transparencies, each of which has one variable with the appropriate data legend nicely spaced across the bottom.

Edward Townsend
News and Sun-Sentinel Co.
Fort Lauderdale, Fla.

LOWER LIMIT ON BAR GRAPHS

I am having trouble obtaining the desired results when setting up a bar graph in *1-2-3*. The numeric values of the graphed range represent quality percentages that are always between 85 and 100. The graph is used to show the relevant differences between monthly results, not the amount above zero.

1-2-3 allows me to specify manually the lower limit by using the command /Graph Options Scale Y Scale Manual Lower, but when I create a bar graph, it ignores my setting and substitutes a lower limit of zero.

How can I get *1-2-3* to accept the change to the lower limit when I create a bar graph? Incidentally, if I change the graph type to Line, the lower limit constraint I specified is used.

Charles W. Price
American National Rubber
Huntington, W.Va.

No matter what commands you select, 1-2-3 ignores a positive lower limit or a negative upper limit on the Y axis to ensure that the scale includes zero.

You can get around this limitation by using a baseline of 85. Create a section of the worksheet, which is used as the graph range, containing formulas that subtract 85 from each month's figure. You can control the Y axis in bar graphs with Symphony. *Select MENU Graph 2nd-Settings Other Origin and specify the origin of the graph. The Origin option specifies a value used in bar graphs to separate numbers above and below a median line on the Y axis. The default setting for Origin is zero. Make sure that the Origin setting falls between the upper and lower limits of the Y axis, in your case, 85 and 100.*

3

Graph Ranges

GRAPHING MORE THAN SIX RANGES IN XY GRAPH

I have often lamented *1-2-3*'s (and *Symphony*'s) limit of six data ranges in graphing. Happily, I've discovered how to create a *1-2-3* graph with virtually an unlimited number of lines.

In a conventional six-range graph, range X might be A2..A12, with range A as B2..B12, B as C2..C12, and so on, as shown in the top part of the worksheet on the next page. To set up a graph with more than six lines, simply repeat the X-range values, leaving a blank cell between each set, and enter the new corresponding values as a continuation of the other ranges. In the example shown, the X range has been extended to A2..A24, the A range extended to B2..B24, and the other ranges left unchanged. Specify the graph type as XY.

The graph that appears below shows the result, with the A-range extension plotted at the top as the seventh line. You may want to add data labels to the graph

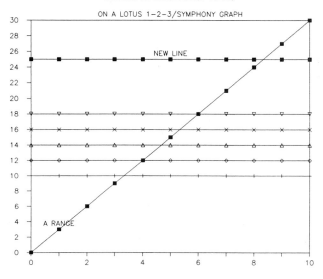

UNLIMITED NUMBER OF LINES

	A	B	C	D	E	F	G
1	X range	A	B	C	D	E	F
2	0	0	10	12	14	16	18
3	1	3	10	12	14	16	18
4	2	6	10	12	14	16	18
5	3	9	10	12	14	16	18
6	4	12	10	12	14	16	18
7	5	15	10	12	14	16	18
8	6	18	10	12	14	16	18
9	7	21	10	12	14	16	18
10	8	24	10	12	14	16	18
11	9	27	10	12	14	16	18
12	10	30	10	12	14	16	18
13							
14	0	25					
15	1	25					
16	2	25					
17	3	25					
18	4	25					
19	5	25					
20	6	25					
21	7	25					
22	8	25					
23	9	25					
24	10	25					

(as I have), since both the original A line and the new line will be printed in the same color and use the same symbol.

You may create additional lines by extending ranges B through F in the same way range A was extended or by again repeating the X-range values.

Mike Craig
Rockville, Md.

GRAPHING MULTIPLE DATA SETS — I

In plotting multiple data sets on an XY graph, you must use the same X values for each set of Y values. However, you may have data sets with different X values. Here's how to do it:

Enter the data so that all X values go down one column, with the X values for the first data set in the first group of cells (e.g., B3..B6), skip a row, then place the X values for the second data range just below (e.g., B8..B10), and so forth (see the figure on the next page). Then enter the Y value associated with each X value for each data set. The values for the first data set go in the first column to the right of the X value column, in this case column C; the Y values for the second data set go in the second column to the right (D), and so on. In the settings of a Graph sheet, the first Y data range is defined as range A, the second as range B, and so on. These ranges must start in the same row as the first X value, even if they have to start with blank cells.

	A	B	C	D	E		
1	RANGES->	X	Y1	Y2	Y3		
2	DATA SET 1						
3		1.0	2.5				
4		2.0	3.5				
5		3.0	6.5				
6		4.0	7.5				
7	DATA SET 2						
8		1.5		2.0			
9		2.5		5.0			
10		3.5		8.0			
11	REGRESSION LINE						
12		0.5			1.0		
13		4.5			9.0		

The Symbol command in the Graph menu allows the data sets representing variable data, A and B, to be shown with symbols only while the regression line is graphed as a line. The resulting graph is shown below.

GRAPH SETTINGS

Range	Format
X B3..B13	
A C3..C6	symbols
B D3..D10	symbols
C E3..E13	line

R.P. Nordgren
Houston, Texas

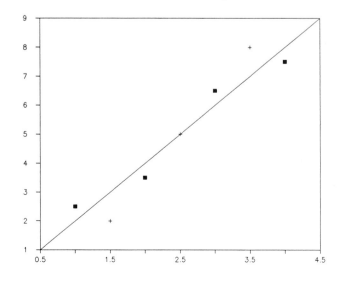

EXAMPLE – TWO DATA SETS, ONE LINE

GRAPHING MULTIPLE DATA SETS — II

1-2-3 and *Symphony* let you overlay scatter graphs with different Y-axis values; they do not ordinarily permit you to plot two entirely different pairs of variables, say (X1,Y) and (X2,Z), on the same graph.

I've found an alternative solution to R.P. Nordgren's suggestion in the previous good idea: I concatenate the ranges I want to plot and create a Data Labels range that contains the symbols for the overlayed plots.

Suppose you want to plot the values in range A1..A30 against those in range B1..B30. Further, you want to overlay that plot with a graph of the values in range C1..C25 against those in D1..D25. First copy range C1..C25 to A31..A55 and range D1..D25 to B31..B55. Range E1..E55 will contain data labels for the overlay. Denote the plot of A1..A30 against B1.. B30 by copying a plus sign (+) into range E1..E30. For the plot of A31..A55 against B1..B55, enter the letter *o* into range E31..E55.

TWO OVERLAID DATA SETS

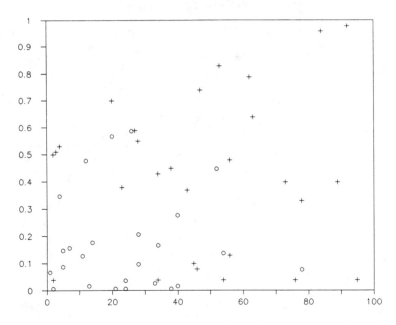

Now select /Graph Type XY (SERVICES Graph 1st-Settings Type XY in *Symphony*). Designate A1..A55 as the X range and B1..B55 as the A range. Select Options Data-Labels A (Data-Labels A in *Symphony*), and enter E1..E55 as the Data-Labels range. Choose Center to position the data labels on each data point. Finally, select Options Format Graph (Format A in *Symphony*) and choose Neither. This prevents *1-2-3* from using the same symbol for all data points, so your data labels become the new plotting symbols. Now you are ready to select View (Preview in *Symphony*) to see the overlayed XY scatter plots.

The only limit to this technique is the number of overlays you can use before the plot becomes unreadable.

David L. Greene
Fargut, Tenn.

GRAPHING DISCONTINUOUS DATA

I was recently asked to prepare a line graph using a data range that contained data in every other cell. I set up X and A ranges as shown below, and I selected both Lines and Symbols for my display option. But when I viewed the graph, all I saw were symbols, no lines. Apparently, data points are not connected unless they are in contiguous cells.

To remedy the situation, I copied the A range into the adjacent column as shown below, and in the first empty cell I inserted a formula that returned the average of the cells above and below it: @AVG(*cellabove,cellbelow*)

I copied this formula into each of the remaining empty cells, then designated this column of figures as the B data range. I selected the Lines display option for the B range and changed the A display option to Symbols. Now, when I view the graph, it appears as symbols in every other month connected by lines, even though it is actually two superimposed data ranges.

Richard Cranford
LOTUS Magazine

	A	B	C
1	X range	A range	B range
2	JAN	61	61
3	FEB		70
4	MAR	79	79
5	APR		72
6	MAY	65	65

C3 and C5 contain @AVG(cellabove,cellbelow)

GRAPHING NONCONTINUOUS RANGES

Symphony does not normally allow you to graph noncontinuous ranges. If you want to graph a historical trend that is in a row or column interrupted on the worksheet by subtotals, blank cells, headings, and so on, you must transfer the data to be graphed, range by range, to another location on the sheet as a continuous range. This is difficult and confusing. Hiding columns does not help.

I have found another method, which is much easier. Create a window called NEW (I am assuming you are working in a window called MAIN), and restrict it to a range outside of your working area. While in NEW, copy the upper-left cell from

MAIN to the upper-left cell in NEW by typing + (plus sign), pressing the WINDOW key, then the Home key, then Return.

Now copy all the other cell entries from the MAIN window to the NEW window by using the Copy command from the upper-left cell in NEW. You can now delete the gaps in the data you wish to graph by deleting surplus rows and columns in NEW. This won't affect the data in MAIN because NEW's Restrict range doesn't overlap MAIN's. Set up your graph in NEW and return to MAIN to continue your work. All subsequent changes to data you make in MAIN will be reflected in NEW and, therefore, in the graphs you generate.

This method of eliminating unwanted data and labels from graph ranges is quick and easy. The only significant drawback is that your worksheet uses almost twice the memory.

George B. Kaiser
Kaiser-Francis Oil Co.
Tulsa, Okla.

This technique of copying the data to an unused part of the worksheet works in 1-2-3 *as well, but because* 1-2-3 *doesn't have Restrict ranges to limit the effect of deletions, be careful when revising the graph ranges. It is safer to use the techniques described in the previous Good Idea if you have* 1-2-3.

MACRO TO UPDATE GRAPHS

With any data series you expand and graph regularly, such as a monthly revision of your year-to-date budget report, changing the graph to include new data is time-consuming and error-prone. Here's an alternative: After you've entered the next period's data in the next empty cell or series of cells on the same row as the old data, use the following macro. Assuming your data are arranged by rows, it expands the graph data ranges by one or more cells, displays the graph, saves it for later printing, and saves the file.

```
/GNUgraph ~ X{END}{RIGHT} ~ A{END}{RIGHT} ~ VNCgraph
    ~ Sgraph ~ RQ/FS ~ R
```

Charles S. Kafka
Eastern Stainless Steel Company
Baltimore, Maryland

To use this macro, you must first create a graph, name it GRAPH, and save it both as a PIC file and as a worksheet file. If you don't follow these steps, the final /File Save command of the macro will overwrite the graph whose name appears at the top-left of your Save menu. In any case, the macro will stop during execution each time the graph displays, requiring the user to manually press a key before it will continue.

4

Titles, Legends, and Data Labels

USING CELL CONTENTS AS GRAPH TITLES

When creating a *1-2-3* or *Symphony* graph, you can use cell contents as your titles. When selecting the title (in *1-2-3*, /Graph Options Titles; in *Symphony*, MENU Graph 2nd-Settings Titles), instead of typing in the title, type a backslash (\) followed by the address of the cell containing the label you want as the graph's title.

This technique has several advantages. It is easier to remember to update titles when they are on the worksheet. Plus, using cell contents overcomes *1-2-3*'s and *Symphony*'s limit of 30 characters for titles typed in during a Graph command. If you use cell contents as your titles, they can be as long as will fit in a cell (the practical limitation is how many characters will display on-screen or when printed).

Carol Gay
Willoughby Hills, Ohio

It is safer to use range names than to use cell addresses. For example, enter \head to specify the upper-left cell of the range head *as the graph's title. The trouble with cell addresses is that* 1-2-3 *and* Symphony *don't adjust the titles when you relocate the cell entry with the Move, Insert, or Delete commands. If you use range names, the reference will adjust.*

You can use the same technique to specify cell contents as graph legends.

SCALING THE Y-AXIS LABEL

I create and print graphs in *1-2-3* Release 1A that contain data representing millions of dollars, but I enter the data rounded off to the nearest thousand. How do I get the vertical scale to display *(millions)* instead of *(thousands)* without adding the unnecessary zeros?

Doreen J. Theiss
Simmonds Precision Products
Vergennes, Vt.

1-2-3 Release 1A automatically scales the data and places the Y-axis label (thousands) *or* (millions), *depending on the number of zeros attached to the numbers you are graphing. The only way to get around this is to scale down your data to values below 990, select /Graph Options Titles Y-Axis, enter (millions), and select Quit. Your graph will display the Y-axis title (millions). Unfortunately, you won't be able to display values 991 through 999 without displaying (thousands) with this method, unless you use only numbers 990 through 999. You can override the Y-axis scale indicator in 1-2-3 Release 2/2.01. Select /Graph Options Scale Y-Scale Indicator No. Then create your own indicator by selecting (from Ready mode) /Graph Options Titles Y-Axis and entering (millions). In Symphony you can override the scale indicator by selecting (in a SHEET window) MENU Graph 2nd-Settings Y-scale Exponent Manual and entering 6. The scale indicator will then read (millions) instead of (thousands).*

FLOATING GRAPH LEGENDS AND TITLES

When plotting an XY graph, it's nice to print legends for each data range in an empty region of the graph rather than at the bottom, which is the only location allowed by the Legend command. You do this by designating the desired descriptive text as a data label rather than as a legend.

EXAMPLE – FLOATING LEGENDS

First, add a new data point at the beginning of each set of XY coordinates in the graph. Give the new data points X and Y values that would place the data labels within the graph where you want them to appear. For example, a data point with an X value near zero, a relatively high Y value, and a Data-Label Right setting causes the label to appear near the top-left corner of the graph. Specify the Symbols format for the data ranges that will contain the floating legends. Expand the data ranges to include the new values. Enter the desired descriptive text in a cell, using one cell for each set of XY data ranges, then use the Data-Label command to designate each cell as the data label for the appropriate XY set.

For graphs that display several data ranges, you can align the data labels vertically by giving each a slightly different Y value. You can also put a similar "floating title" above the legend/labels by using a single data point with a Neither format. See the graph on the previous page.

R.P. Nordgren
Houston, Tex.

Regarding the last point, in 1-2-3 all ranges used for this purpose must contain at least two cells. Leaving the second cell blank solves this problem.

LONGER DATA LABELS

A previous good idea described a technique of using data labels instead of legends in graphs. If your data label is so long that it runs off the edge of the graph, you can extend one data range (A to F, not X), which lengthens the X axis and allows you to fit longer labels inside the frame.

Mark Moritz
Phoenix, Ariz.

DATA LABELS FOR PIE GRAPHS

Whenever I try to use data labels with a pie graph, the graph will not accept them. What is wrong?

Wendy Draeger
Philadelphia, Pennsylvania

Nothing is wrong. There is no place for data labels in a pie chart. However, you can place labels next to each slice of the pie by specifying a range containing the labels you want for your pie slices as the X data range. Designating the same cells for both the X and A ranges labels each slice with the numeric quantity it represents.

RELOCATING PRINTED GRAPH LEGENDS

I find it difficult to connect the legends that appear at the bottom of a graph with the appropriate data range in a six-range line graph. The graph is easier to interpret if the explanatory text appears on the right side of the graph, next to the appropriate data line.

To accomplish this, cancel existing legends and select the Data-Label option. Point to a Data-Label range, either a row or column, that contains as many cells as you have data items in your data range. But leave all the cells blank except the last cell, which should contain the characters you wish to appear on the right side of the graph. Select Right from the final menu in the series to position the data label to the right of the associated data value. The last value in the line is located on the right edge of the graph, so the data label will be printed just to the right of the graph.

Although there may not be enough room on your screen to display the new labels, they will appear in the printed version of the graph.

David Wolf
Toledo, Ohio

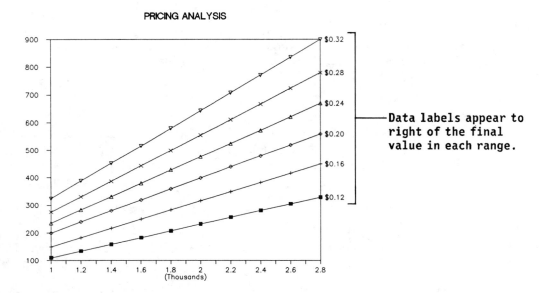

5

Naming and Saving

NAMING AND SAVING GRAPHS

I am having trouble naming graphs and calling them back to make changes. Please describe how to retrieve a graph into the worksheet so that I can make changes to it and how to print a graph using PrintGraph.

Leon Gray
Celanese Chemical Co.
Dallas, Tex.

You are confusing two processes. When you NAME a graph, you attach the graph's settings to the associated 1-2-3 or Symphony worksheet. The graph's specifications will be saved and retrieved along with the worksheet. Named graphs can be viewed, changed, and viewed again. On the other hand, when you SAVE a graph, you capture the worksheet image and send it to a separate file that has a PIC (picture) file name extension. Once in a PIC file, the graph data cannot be viewed or changed in the worksheet. However, it can be previewed and printed, but not revised, using PrintGraph.

For each worksheet, you can create and name as many associated graphs as your computer memory allows. To name a graph, issue the /Graph Name Create command (1-2-3) or the MENU Graph 1st-Settings Name Create command (Symphony). To revise an already named graph, in 1-2-3 select /Graph Name Use, select the name of the desired graph, change the settings you want to revise, then select /Graph Name Create to keep those settings. The new settings will replace the old ones. In Symphony, first select the named graph settings sheet, then make your revisions. Unlike 1-2-3, you do not have to reselect Name Create for the new settings to replace the former ones.

The next time you issue the File Save command, the named graphs will be sent to the disk storage along with the worksheet. If you neglect to save the file after naming or revising the graph, the new graphs will not be there when you retrieve the worksheet file. Although a worksheet can have numerous named graphs, only one graph at a time can be current, meaning it will be displayed when you select the

View command (Preview in Symphony*). The current graph is the last one that you created or the last one that you selected with the Graph Name Use command. However,* Symphony *users can simultaneously display multiple graphs by attaching them to separate GRAPH windows.*

To print a graph using PrintGraph, save the image in a separate PIC file by issuing the /Graph Save command (1-2-3) *or the MENU Graph Image-Save command* (Symphony)*. You cannot retrieve PIC file graph settings back into a worksheet for revision.*

To both preserve a graph's settings in association with a worksheet for later use and revision and to print the current version of a graph, you must both name and save the graph.

DELETING GRAPH FILES

Within the Graph menu, I selected Name Create to connect the current graph's settings with the worksheet and then selected Save to create a separate graph (PIC) file for use with PrintGraph. I used the same name for both the graph and PIC files. When I loaded PrintGraph, the file name appeared under the Select menu, but the graph didn't print. I went back to the worksheet and saved the graph under a slightly different name. This file printed with no problem. Now I want to delete the nonfunctioning graph (PIC) files. But when I select Graph Name Delete, I'm presented with only the list of names associated with the worksheet, not the names of the separate PIC files.

Bill Conan
Atlantic States Bankcard Association
Raleigh, N.C.

You can use the same name for both the graph and the PIC files; that wasn't the problem. The graph that didn't print could have become corrupt for any number of reasons, including a bad sector on your data disk.

Because the PIC file is totally separate from the original worksheet file, in Symphony *you must select SERVICES File Erase Graph (in* 1-2-3, */File Erase Graph), point to the name of the unwanted file, press Return, and then select Yes to confirm the deletion.*

6

PrintGraph

CONFIGURING PRINTGRAPH

Each time I use PrintGraph in *1-2-3* Release 1A, the menu tells me I have an Epson FX 80 printer. The problem is that I do not have an Epson. Consequently, I must reconfigure the program for my printer. But when I start up the program again, my revised configuration has been forgotten. Is this a case of software amnesia?

Anne Fishman
Newton, Massachusetts

Unless you tell it otherwise, Lotus software contains certain assumptions, or default settings. As you have discovered, an Epson FX 80 is the default PrintGraph device setting in 1-2-3 Release 1A. You are correctly using the Configure command to enter a new device setting. However, entering this information merely places it in computer memory. Like all information in your machine's temporary memory (RAM), this information is lost when you turn the machine off. The next time you start PrintGraph, you will be back to the default. The solution is to save the new configuration on your disk. This creates a permanent change in your default setting. With 1-2-3 Release 1A, selecting Configure Save Replace does the trick. In 1-2-3 Release 2/2.01 and in Symphony select Settings Save to save your new PrintGraph defaults.

RECONFIGURING PRINTGRAPH

I produce a lot of graphs on a dot-matrix parallel printer and a six-pen serial plotter. When I tired of reconfiguring my PrintGraph specifications to change from printer to plotter and back again, I created two batch files from DOS to allow both configuration files to remain on the disk at the same time.

Here's how I did it: First I entered PrintGraph and set up the Device configuration for the printer. Then I saved the printer specifications, quit the PrintGraph program, and exited to DOS. PrintGraph automatically created the file GRAPH.CNF, which I renamed GRAFPRIN.CNF. I reentered PrintGraph and specified the Device configuration for my plotter, saved this configuration, and returned to DOS again. PrintGraph created another GRAPH.CNF file, which I renamed GRAFPLOT.CNF. Finally, I entered the following to create the DOS batch files PRINTER.BAT and PLOTTER.BAT:

```
copy con:printer.bat
copy grafprin.cnf graph.cnf
lotus
^z

copy con:plotter.bat
copy grafplot.cnf graph.cnf
lotus
^z
```

Each file copies the appropriate version of the PrintGraph configuration file to the file name GRAPH.CNF, which is the file PrintGraph will take its information from, then runs *1-2-3*. The Control-z command (represented as ^z) marks the end of each file (press Control and z, do not type a caret and a z). When you issue Control-z and press Return, DOS automatically saves the file to disk.

Now when I want to print graphs, I need only enter the word *printer* or *plotter*, and I'm on my way.

John B. Ford
Glen Allen, Va.

If you use 1-2-3 *Release 2/2.01 or* Symphony*, substitute the file name PGRAPH.CNF for GRAPH.CNF.*

GRAPH ON THE SCREEN LOOKS DIFFERENT ON PAPER

Why is the image of a graph that I view on-screen different from the printed version of the same graph?

George Muro
Queens, New York

Before you print a graph with PrintGraph, in 1-2-3 you must first save the graph in a picture (PIC) file. In Symphony you would use the Image-Save command. A PIC file provides greater precision than does your monitor screen. This may at times result in a slightly altered appearance.

ERROR MESSAGE USING PRINTGRAPH

I have *1-2-3* Release 1A, PrintGraph, and File Manager stored on my hard disk. I am trying to print a graph file from my A drive. The PrintGraph program recognizes the picture file that I want to print named REGRODD. I select the file REGRODD by pressing the Spacebar. But when I select Go to print the graph, the error message *File does not exist* appears as shown on the bottom of my screen, as shown on the next page.

What's going on?

Robert H. Parrish
Elkhart, Ind.

The solution to your problem lies in changing the default directories where the

PrintGraph program looks to find pictures (graphs) and fonts. On the copy of your screen shown below, PrintGraph is looking for pictures in B:\. This works because hard-disk computers can refer to the floppy-disk drive as either A or B. When you select Go to print the graph, PrintGraph loads the fonts that are specified (BLOCK1). Here's where the process fails. On this screen, PrintGraph is looking for fonts in A:\. Your PrintGraph program, including the font files, is actually located on the hard disk, identified as C:\, which means that the program can't find BLOCK1.FON, generating the error message File does not exist.

To change the directory that PrintGraph looks in to find the fonts, in 1-2-3 *Release 1A select Configure Files Fonts and specify C:\subdir, where subdir is the subdirectory in which you have placed the PrintGraph program files, then select Quit Save Replace. In* 1-2-3 *Release 2/2.01 and* Symphony, *select Settings Hardware Fonts-Directory, specify C:\subdir, and select Quit Save.*

```
Copyright 1982, 1983 Lotus Development Corp.  All Rights Reserved.  ERROR
Insert diskette for drive A: and strike--------------------------------
Loading Font: A:\ BLOCK1


================================================================================
  SELECTED GRAPHS     COLORS            SIZE      HALF        DIRECTORIES

     REGRODD          Grid:    Black  Left Margin:  .750       Pictures
                      A Range: Black  Top Margin:   .395       B:\
                      B Range: Black  Width:       6.500       Fonts
                      C Range: Black  Height:      4.691       A:\
                      D Range: Black  Rotation:     .000
                      E Range: Black                           GRAPHICS DEVICE
                      F Range: Black  MODES
                                                               Epson FX80/1
                      FONTS           Eject: No                Parallel
                                      Pause: No
                      1: BLOCK1                                PAGE SIZE
                      2: BLOCK2
                                                               Length    11.000
                                                               Width      8.000


File does not exist
```

NO FILES OF SPECIFIED TYPE ON DISK IN 1A

Why do I get the error message *No files of specified type on disk* in PrintGraph when I know they exist?

John Krieger
Warwick, Mass.

You will get this error message in the PrintGraph that comes with 1-2-3 *Release 1A and* Symphony *Release 1/1.01 when the picture directory is incorrectly specified. To correct this, select Configure Files Pictures on the PrintGraph menu. Specify the directory or subdirectory that contains the PIC files and select Save on the Configure menu to save these settings.*

The error message displayed in a similar situation when using the PrintGraph that comes with 1-2-3 Release 2/2.01 and Symphony 1.1/1.2 is more descriptive.

NUMBER OF GRAPHS IN RELEASE 1.1 DIRECTORY

I tried to print a graph using PrintGraph in *Symphony* Release 1.1, but when I selected Image-Select from the menu, nothing happened. There was no error message, and the menu remained. What's up?

Marc Carter
Provo, Utah

When using PrintGraph in Symphony *Release 1.1, the total number of PIC (picture or graph) files that can be in the graphs directory plus the number of .PIC files queued for printing cannot exceed 52. You probably have too many PIC files; copy some of them to another disk or subdirectory. This limitation was eliminated in* Symphony *Releases 1.2.*

PRINTGRAPH SETTINGS

I have numerous PIC files saved on numerous disks. Many of these graphs use different PrintGraph Font, Size, and Rotation settings. Since my PrintGraph disk starts with my most recently saved options, I often have to reset them to suit a particular graph.

The problem is that I find it confusing to remember which settings go with which graph. So I print a copy of the settings for each graph and file the hard copy with a copy of the graph. After selecting the graph to be printed and entering all my settings, I simultaneously press the Shift and PrintScreen keys, which prints an exact copy of whatever is on my screen.

Paul F. Kimball
Lilburn, Georgia

You can simplify this process by giving each graph a title, then filing the screen dumps alphabetically.

TRUNCATED LEGENDS

I have a problem using PrintGraph. Whenever I print more than two long legends the printed version chops off the left and right legends. However, the graph displayed on the monitor has all the legends in the proper place. PrintGraph works fine if only two legends are shown or if each legend is fairly short. What's up?

David W. Wille
Herget and Co.
Baltimore, Md.

Depending on the type of graph, font selection, and total number of legends, there is a limit to the total number of characters you can print. For example, if you are making a bar graph that has six ranges, you will probably want to have six legends. With all releases of 1-2-3 *and* Symphony *Release 1.0/1.01 you have 15 characters to use when naming the six legends. In this case, you could have three legends each with three-character names, and three legends each with two-character names. Follow these guidelines to keep legends from truncating.*

BAR AND STACKED-BAR GRAPHS

Number of legends	Total characters
6	15
5	21
4	27
3	33
2	38
1	19

LINE AND XY GRAPHS

Number of legends	Total characters
6	18
5	24
4	30
3	36
2	38
1	19

Symphony *Release 1.1/1.2 will allow up to 19 characters in each legend, even if you have up to six legends. It accomplishes this by splitting the legends into two rows on the printed graph.*

TO AND FROM PRINTGRAPH QUICKLY

If you have at least 512K of memory, the *1-2-3* Release 2/2.01 System command lets you use PrintGraph without having to exit from *1-2-3* and reload your worksheet file. At Ready mode, select /System to return to DOS. Enter *pgraph* to start

PrintGraph (if necessary, put the PrintGraph disk in Drive A). After you print the graphs, return to DOS and type *exit* to return to where you left off in *1-2-3*.

You can do the same thing in *Symphony*, if you have 640K RAM, by attaching the DOS add-in (SERVICES Application Attach DOS) and selecting SERVICES DOS anytime later. (If you use a floppy-disk system, you must insert your Help and Tutorial Disk in drive A before attaching DOS, and you must have a disk containing the DOS file COMMAND.COM in drive A when selecting SERVICES DOS.)

Donald Taylor
St. Petersburg, Fla.

SAVING TIME WITH PRINTGRAPH

A printer takes longer to draw a graph than to print text or numbers. Save time by saving all your graph printing until right before lunch break, or the end of the day, or some other time when you will not need your computer.

PrintGraph prints both *1-2-3* and *Symphony* PIC files. These are the files created when you save a graph. Use the Graph menu Save command in *1-2-3* and Image-Save in *Symphony*. Remember, saving a worksheet that contains a graph does not save the graph in the special PIC file that PrintGraph requires.

PrintGraph allows you to print a series of graphs automatically. To start, copy all the PIC files you want to print into a single disk or directory. Start PrintGraph. If you are using a hard disk, enter the name of the PIC directory in the Graphs-Directory setting. Make any other desired adjustments to the settings sheet.

Use the Image-Select command to select the graphs you wish to print. The UpArrow and DownArrow keys move you through the list of graphs. Press the Spacebar to mark or unmark desired graphs.

Adjust the printer paper, then select Align and Go. All the marked graphs will be printed according to the current settings.

If you want each graph to be printed on a separate page, remember to set Action Eject to Yes.

FASTER GRAPH PRINTING

I sometimes have to print 20 or 30 graphs at once. Printing one graph to a page takes about six minutes for each graph. But if I use half-size, I can print two per page, one on the left and one on the right side of each page — a process that takes about three minutes per graph. I go a step further and print six graphs per page, which only takes about one minute per graph. First I select those graphs I want to appear on the left side and enter the following settings:

Left margin: 0.00   Height: 2.707
Top margin: 0.395   Rotation: 0
Width: 3.750

After printing the first set of graphs, I feed the paper into the printer/plotter so that the first sheet is ready to be printed again. Leaving a blank page at the top of the fanfold simplifies this process. Then I set the left margin to 4.00 and select the graphs I want printed on the right side of the page.

You can print even more graphs per page. I've been able to get 28 on a page. The lettering wasn't readable, but the major trends of the graphs were easy to see and understand.

Finally, changing the rotation to 270 moves the top of the graphs to the right side of the paper. With a top margin of 0.25 for the first group of graphs and 5.5 for the second group, you can fit four graphs on each page.

Michael C. Provost
Monaca, Pa.

ELIMINATING GRAPH SCALE WHEN PLOTTING

I use a plotter to generate my graphs from PrintGraph. When I don't want the graph scale to appear in the printout, I place a capped or empty pen in place of the one set to print the scale.

H.J. Koenigsaecker
CompuProfit
Panorama City, Calif.

This also suppresses the printing of titles, axes, and grids.

WIDE GRAPHS ON THE EPSON FX100

To print *1-2-3* graphs wider than 8½ inches on an Epson FX100 printer, you must have a special FX100 PrintGraph driver, found in the Graphics Printer Library I or II and available from Lotus dealers. *1-2-3* Release 2 does not have drivers that print graphs larger than 8½ inches by 11 inches. To overcome this limitation, use the *1-2-3* Release 1A PrintGraph program with your PIC (picture) files that you created using *1-2-3* Release 2.

To change PrintGraph to produce the widest possible graph on the Epson FX100, load the PrintGraph program. From the main menu select Options Size Manual Left and enter 0.000. Select Top and enter 0.000. Next, select Width and enter 12.898; select Height and enter 19.000. Set rotation to 0.000 or 90.000. Select Quit three times to return to the main PrintGraph menu. Select Configure Page Length and enter 20.000; select Width and enter 14.000. Press Quit twice to return to the main menu. Select Go to start printing.

Jennifer Lester
Old Town, Maine

1-2-3 Release 2.01 does have drivers that allow larger graphs in Epson FX printers.

PRINTING GRAPHS WITHOUT PRINTGRAPH

If you have a graphics printer, you can create a quick printed version of a *Symphony* graph without the hassle of PrintGraph. First, load the GRAPHICS.COM program from your DOS disk into memory before loading *Symphony*. (I include this in my AUTOEXEC.BAT file.) The program uses only about 800 bytes of RAM. Second, when a graph appears on the screen, press the Shift and PrintScreen keys. Your graph will be ready within three minutes. I have tested this with both an Epson FX-80 and an HP ThinkJet and have had no problems. Third, you can turn the window border off by selecting SERVICES Window Settings Border None Quit Quit. I created a macro to make this a one-key process.

In my opinion, the printed graph is more legible than a similar half-size graph from PrintGraph. You also get a printout of exactly what you see on the screen. Of course, for multiple graphs or for plotter output, PrintGraph is far better.

R. G. Schafermeyer
Cincinnati, Ohio.

This tip works with certain graphics boards including the IBM color card, Plantronics Color Plus card in shared mode, and EGA cards. It does not work with a Hercules card and a monochrome monitor.

7

PrintGraph Fonts

BETTER DENSITY CONTROL WITH 1A's PRINTGRAPH

One of the penalties that came with the *1-2-3* upgrade to Release 2 was the loss of some of the print-density options with PrintGraph. For example, Release 1A for the Epson FX-80 printer offered four densities, ranging from fast/poor quality (FX80/1) to slow/excellent quality (FX80/4). Release 2/2.01 offers only the two extremes. I do a lot of printing and had decided that FX80/2 is the best compromise between time and quality. So I was upset that Release 2/2.01 deprived me of this option.

One day I was inspired to try to print a Release 2 PIC file using Release 1A's PrintGraph. It worked! I can now use the FX80/2 density to print my Release 2 graphs — even using Release 2's graphics enhancements, like exploded pie charts.

Ed Fine
Stoughton, Mass.

You might also try using Symphony *PrintGraph. You can print any PIC file using the PrintGraph that comes with any Release of* 1-2-3 *or* Symphony.

USING 1A PRINTGRAPH FONTS WITH RELEASE 2

I don't think the fonts that come with *1-2-3* Release 2's PrintGraph are as clear as those that came with *1-2-3* Release 1A. I found, however, that I can use 1A's fonts with Release 2's PrintGraph disk by copying the old fonts I want onto my Release 2 PrintGraph disk and changing the file extensions from FON to FNT.

Steve Medved
Pittsburg, Kan.

PRINTGRAPH'S BLOCK 1.FON

Our facility intermittently experiences an unusual problem using *1-2-3* Release 1A. Occasionally the file called BLOCK1.FON on the PrintGraph disk becomes damaged in some way. When I use the DOS command DIR (directory) to check the file sizes, BLOCK1.FON seems to occupy more than three megabytes, a neat trick on a 360K floppy disk. If I run the program with the font file in this condition, I get the error message *Divide Overflow*.

We can correct this problem by deleting the offending font file and copying the identical file from another of our *1-2-3* packages. Is there a way to prevent this error rather than continually fix it?

John D. Hopkins
University of Georgia
Athens, Ga.

Another error message that may appear in this situation is Memory Full. In either case, there isn't a way to fix this problem other than copying another BLOCK1.FON file onto the damaged one. Erasing the file before copying isn't necessary, so you can skip that step. 1-2-3 Release 2/2.01 and Symphony do not have this bug.

SECTION
10

DATABASE AND SORTING

The great beauty of an integrated, worksheet approach to data analysis is that the same row and column structure can serve both as a spreadsheet and as a database. Each row can serve as a record, meaning a series of related data items, and each column can serve as a field, meaning a particular type of data. For example, the first cell — meaning the first column — of each row might contain a part number, the second cell might contain the part name, the third cell might contain the current inventory level, and so on.

Once your database is set up, you can then use the same data for computational purposes by referencing the cells in the database in formulas. In this way your information can serve a double purpose. And the best part is that you use the same set of skills to achieve both goals. You enter data into cells, insert rows, move the pointer, and build formulas the same way in both database and spreadsheet applications. Since learning how to use a product takes a significant amount of time, which adds up to a significant cost, this ability to leverage your skills is one of the big advantages of integrated products such as *1-2-3* and *Symphony*.

A spreadsheet does have some limitations when being used as a database, however. In *1-2-3*, you have to create your own error-checking procedures, and you have to devise your own report-generation facilities. But there are add-in products that simplify this task and turn *1-2-3* into the front end of a full-powered database system by providing the advanced capabilities that *1-2-3* lacks.

Most of the tips in this section will help you accurately enter data, analyze that data, and find and pull out or modify specific information. In addition, there are tips on sorting columnar data, whether in a database or just in a spreadsheet. The last half of this section deals specifically with *Symphony* databases, which incorporate much more powerful forms-entry, error-checking, and report-generating capabilities.

1

Entering and Analyzing Data

DUPLICATE FIELD NAMES NOT ALLOWED

Can I use the same field headings for more than one column when I create a database?

Dan Hill
Keene, New Hampshire

Every database field name in a worksheet must be unique. This is true whether the worksheet contains one or multiple databases.

COPY FIELD NAMES TO CRITERION RANGE

My office-mate and I spent hours trying to debug a worksheet. It turned out that when we typed a field name into a Criterion range, we accidentally included an extra blank space at the end of the word. The solution was to use the Copy command to get an exact copy of each needed field name in the Criterion range.

Scott Tolzmann
Clovis, Calif.

DATE FIELDS IN A DATABASE

When I enter a date into the date field of my entry form, it appears with the DD-MM-YY format. When I switch to a SHEET window, I see a date serial number in the Database range. Why?

Lisa Kagami
Division of Public Works
Honolulu, Hawaii

If you use Symphony *Release 1, columns in the Database range associated with formatted fields won't be formatted for you automatically. You must assign the format using the Format commands.* Symphony *Releases 1.1 and 1.2 will automatically format columns in the Database range as you enter records through the form.*

QUERY UNIQUE PROBLEM

I created a *1-2-3* database containing several numeric fields relevant to a given sales location. As the number of locations increase, I want to count how many there are. However, when I use the command /Data Query Unique, the records copied into the

Output range contain duplicate sales locations. Does the Unique command copy unique records based on only those fields specified in the Criterion range or does *1-2-3* compare all of the fields within a record when checking for duplicate information?

Lou Geibel
Pittsburgh, Pa.

Selecting /Data Query Unique copies all relevant fields of records that match the Criterion range to the Output range, eliminating duplicates. In your case, include only the sales location field name in a one column-wide Output range, and use a Criterion range with no criteria specified. The list of unique sales locations will be copied into the Output range.

If you still have problems getting a list of unique locations, check the duplicate sales records in the Output range to make sure that spellings and capitalizations match, otherwise 1-2-3 doesn't consider the records unique. Also make sure that you haven't accidentally added blank spaces at the end of each location name, since blank spaces are considered characters. To check, place the cursor on the cell in question and press the EDIT key. If the blinking cursor on the edit line is two places away from the last character in the entry, there is an extra blank space. To delete it, press the Backspace key. This also applies to Symphony.

FINDING AND EDITING RECORDS

The /Data Query Find command in Release 1A locates records but does not let you edit them. The following technique compensates for this limitation. One field in each record of our database is a unique sales number. Since range names must be labels, I use a macro to insert a label prefix before each sales number and convert the existing sales numbers into labels. I position the cursor in the sales number column and select /Range Name Label Right, which creates a unique range name for each record. I then use the /XL macro command to make sure that all future sales numbers were entered as labels. Now, I can press the GOTO function key followed by any desired sales number to both find and edit the desired record.

Daniel P. Panosian
Panosian's Inc.
Elmira, New York

You might want to first select /Data Query Extract to obtain a list of all the sale numbers whose records meet certain criteria. Tying the process together with macros and split windows could make for a very efficient system. Release 2/2.01 of 1-2-3 lets you both find and edit records.

FINDING AND EDITING DATA

If you press the End key during a Data Query Find command in *1-2-3* Release 2/2.01, *1-2-3* highlights the last record of the database, even if it does not meet the criterion.

You can edit it as if it were a found record. Similarly, pressing the Home key causes *1-2-3* to highlight the top record in the range. Is this part of the design of the Data Query Find command or is this a problem with *1-2-3*?

Mary Levesque
Omaha, Nebr.

This is a bug in 1-2-3. *The MENU Query Find command works correctly in* Symphony.

FINDING LABELS IN ANY FIELD IN A DATABASE

Sometimes I need to search for an entry in a large database, but I don't know what field it's in. I developed a way to search all the label fields at once, no matter how many there are. This works in *1-2-3* Release 2/2.01 and in the SHEET environment of *Symphony*.

1. Enter a new field name in the column directly to the right of your current database. Copy that field name to the cell directly to the right of your current Criterion range. To reset the Database ranges, select /Data Query Input, press RightArrow Return, select Criterion, press RightArrow Return, and select Quit (in *Symphony*, press MENU, select Query Settings Basic Database, press RightArrow Return, select Criterion, press RightArrow Return, and select Quit Quit Quit). In either program also create and define an Output range, including any fields you want to appear in your report.

2. Press slash (in *Symphony*, MENU), select Range Name Labels Down, indicate all the field names across the top row of the database, and press Return.

3. In the first cell beneath the new field name in the database, enter a formula that concatenates (combines) all of the nonnumeric fields that could contain the entries you are looking for (the fields need not be consecutive). If the possible fields were named *fieldname1, fieldname3, fieldname4,* and *fieldname7,* the formula should be:

   + fieldname1&fieldname3&fieldname4&fieldname7

4. Copy the formula down the column to the row corresponding to your last database entry.

5. Press slash (in *Symphony*, MENU), select Range Values, and indicate the range containing the formula and all its copies. When the program prompts you for the range to copy to, press Return. This converts the underlying formulas to their calculated values.

6. If you are looking for the entry that contains the name Jones, enter the following formula below the new field name in the Criterion range (where *fieldname* is the name of the new field):

   @FIND("Jones", *fieldname*,0) + 1

You may get an ERR in your Criterion Range, but that won't affect the process and can be ignored.

7. Select /Data Query Extract Quit (in *Symphony*, MENU Query Extract Quit).

Diane Robinson
Quincy, Mass.

Keep in mind that there are some limitations to this technique. Because you are concatenating fields in your formula, you are creating new strings that may generate unexpected results. For example, if two fields beside one another contain the entry BCA, *then a search for* ABC *would produce a find for that record* (ABC *is a substring of* BCABCA). *The technique is foolproof only if your database consists exclusively of single-character labels (such as you might use for codes). Also, as step 3 implies, you cannot include any numeric fields in your formula.*

DELETING UNWANTED SPACES IN DATABASES

Another way to detect unwanted spaces in a database is to create a three-row Criterion range. For the first criterion under each field name, enter a space followed by an asterisk. This criterion will match all records preceded by a space character. Enter the formula @IF(@RIGHT(*firstrecord*,1) = " ",1,0) as the second criterion, where *firstrecord* is the cell address of the first record in the database. The formula will locate all records that end with the space character. With both criteria entered, it is a simple matter of using /Data Query Find (MENU Query Find in *Symphony*) to search for all records that contain preceding or trailing spaces or that consist of one or more spaces.

Richard A. Swanberg
Fort Worth, Tex.

MODULARIZED DATABASE ANALYSIS

If you have a database that you use for a variety of independent analyses, you can speed up calculations and simplify the job of database maintenance by saving the database in one file named DATABASE and creating separate worksheets for each of the individual analyses. This way, you have to update only one file to keep the database current, no matter how many different ways you use that database.

Each of the analysis files should contain prenamed Criterion and Output ranges. When you wish to conduct a particular analysis, retrieve the appropriate file, combine the database into the file in a preselected spot, and run your calculations. The last step is to initialize the analysis worksheet in preparation for its next retrieval by erasing the contents of the various ranges and deleting the Database range name. This keeps you from having multiple copies of your database, some of which would be out-of-date.

This technique also works well when you have multiple spreadsheets that draw upon the same large @LOOKUP table.

I use a set of three macros to automate this process. The first macro, named \Ø, automatically runs when I retrieve the worksheet. Its function is to combine DATABASE into the current analysis worksheet. The second macro guides me through the query process and then runs the analysis. And the third macro erases the Database ranges.

W.E. Frank
Chevron USA
Denver, Colorado

PULLING LAST NAME FROM DATABASE

If a field in your database contains a customer's first and last name, but you only want to pull out the last name, you can use string @functions to accomplish this task in *1-2-3* Release 2/2.01 and *Symphony*.

@RIGHT(*string,number*) pulls the rightmost *number* of characters from the string. If the name *Abigail Adams* is in cell A2, @RIGHT(A2,4) returns *dams*. @LENGTH(*string*) returns the total number of characters in the string. @LENGTH(A2) returns the value 13, which includes both the letters and the space between the words. Finally, @FIND(*search-for-string,search-within-string,offset*) looks through the search-within-string, starting the offset number of characters into the string (with the first character counting as zero), for the search-for-string. @FIND(" ",A2,Ø) looks through *Abigail Adams* for a blank space, starting with the first character in the string.

Because you can nest @functions within each other — using one to produce an argument for another — putting the three functions together gives you:

@RIGHT(A2,@LENGTH(A2) – @FIND (" ",A2,Ø) – 1)

which returns *Adams*.

Dennis Lynch
The Software Connection
DeKalb, Illinois

The process works fine unless the person's name includes a middle initial, a pre-ceding title such as Dr., or a two-part first name such as Mary Jean.

DATABASE STATISTICAL FUNCTIONS SIMPLIFIED

I frequently use *1-2-3*'s database statistical functions to calculate counts and sums of selected database fields. Until recently, I set up multiple Criterion ranges, each containing a different criterion, for my @DCOUNT and @DSUM formulas. However, the many Criterion ranges I needed were tedious to construct. I discovered I can use the Data Table command (Range What-If in *Symphony*) to shorten the task significantly.

To set up a data table to analyze a database field containing state names, I first enter in a column a list of the state names I want to analyze. Elsewhere on the worksheet I create a Criterion range consisting of two cells, one over the other. The top cell contains the name of the database field containing the state names; the bottom cell is blank. This is the criterion range I reference in my @DSUM formula. I enter the @DSUM formula one column to the right and one row above the first item in the list of states to be analyzed.

First I select /Data Table 1 (in *Symphony*, MENU Range What-if 1-Way). When *1-2-3* prompts for it, I designate the Table range as the blank cell above the list of state names, the list itself, and the column to the right headed with the @DSUM formula. (If I want to include additional formulas, for example @DCOUNT and @DAVG, I simply enter them in consecutive cells directly to the right of the @DSUM formula and include those columns in the Table range too.) When *1-2-3* prompts for the Input cell, I designate the blank cell in the Criterion range.

1-2-3 invisibly places the first state name into the Criterion range, calculates the @DSUM formula, and enters the result beneath the @DSUM formula in the cell to the right of that state name. The program proceeds through each remaining state name until it has generated a table containing a statistic for each state name in the list.

Kent Akselsen
Salamanca, N.Y.

LOCATING FIRST BLANK ROW OF DATABASE

I am creating a record of the investments I make on my house. At each new session, I want to begin entering data where I left off the session before. The rows of my database begin in column A, so I press the GOTO key and enter A2048, which is the last row in a *1-2-3* Release 1A worksheet. I press the End key, then the UpArrow key to take the cell pointer up to column A of the last row of the database. When I press the DownArrow key, the cell pointer moves down one row to the first empty row of the worksheet, where I can begin entering new data.

Michael Slaton
San Bernardino, Calif.

You can automate this process by linking the above commands together to create a macro:

	AA	AB
1	\0	{GOTO}A2048~
2		{END}{UP}
3		{DOWN}

The macro moves the cell pointer to column A of the first empty worksheet row. This macro is located in AB1..AB3, although you can put the macro anywhere. Name the macro \0 by pointing to cell AA1, pressing slash, selecting Range Name Labels Right, and pressing Return. A macro named \0 runs automatically when you retrieve the worksheet.

2

Criteria

VERIFYING SELECTION CRITERIA

Before using the database commands Data Query Delete, Extract, or Unique, use Data Query Find to verify on-screen that you have correctly specified the selection criteria. Data Query Find highlights only those records meeting the current criteria. This can save you time and effort, particularly when working with large databases; you won't mistakenly delete records or waste time generating data extracts using the wrong criteria.

James Copeland
Saxon Oil Co.
Dallas, Tex.

Symphony *users can also use this technique before printing a database report based on selected criteria.*

BOOLEAN EXPRESSIONS AS CRITERIA

I ran into trouble when I used a Boolean expression containing a range name as the criterion for a database.

However, when I substituted the range name's value for the range name itself, the trouble disappeared. I discovered that when I refer to a range name outside the database in a formula criterion, the reference to the range must be absolute.

For example, consider a formula criterion to find database records containing a date earlier than May 5, 1987. Assume that the range named *inputdate* is a single cell containing the date 05-May-87, and the range named *date* is the cell directly below the field name in the database. Therefore, the reference to *inputdate* in the criterion formula must be absolute: + date < $inputdate.

Christopher Beck
Natel & Co.
Carlsbad, Calif.

USING DATES AS CRITERIA

Many of our databases contain date fields. We often need to extract data according to date criteria — for example, all records pertaining to the transactions between May 1 and May 31, 1985. How can I do this?

Kenneth G. Fulton
Republic Bank
Carrollton, Texas

As you create the database, use the @DATE function to enter dates. This function returns a serial number of the date. The serial number of any date is equivalent to the number of days that date is away from December 31, 1899. For example, @DATE(85,5,1) returns the serial number 31168.

You must also use the @DATE functions to enter your database criteria. For example, if the date field were named Day and the first entry is located in cell A2, you could enter the following formula criteria:

+A2>@DATE(85,5,1)#AND#A2<@DATE(85,5,31)

Symphony *users can designate the Day field as type Date, which would allow them to enter the date in standard mm/dd/yy format.*

DATABASE TEXT SEARCH

In a *1-2-3* or *Symphony* database, you can search for label entries that start with particular characters by specifying *text*∗ in a criterion record. For example, I have a database of magazine articles containing a field named *Title*. By specifying *tax*∗ in the *Title* field in the Criterion range, I find articles whose titles begin with *tax* such as *Taxes, Tax amendments,* and *Taxing alternatives*. This technique won't work for articles that contain the word *tax* elsewhere in the title — the title has to begin with *tax* to be found using that criterion.

To search for embedded text, use the @FIND function in the criterion record. @FIND returns an integer that indicates where in the entry the specified text appears. When the string is found, the @FIND formula returns a positive number, which is interpreted as TRUE, so the record is selected. If the string is not in the entry, the @FIND formula evaluates to ERR, so the record is not selected. However, if the string you're searching for happens to start the entry, the @FIND function returns 0, because *1-2-3* and *Symphony* consider the first position to be numbered 0. A zero is interpreted as FALSE in a criterion record, so the record is not selected.

For example, to find articles about tax laws, I first used the following formula in the Criterion range in the *Title* field (the cell containing the article's title in the first record is named *title*):

@FIND("Tax",title,0)

The entries *Federal Tax Guidelines* and *State Tax Proposal* are found, but *Tax Amendments* is not. To circumvent this problem, I rewrote the formula to read as follows:

@FIND("Tax",title,∅) + 1

Now if the entry begins with *Tax*, the result is ∅+ 1, which is TRUE. For entries not containing *Tax*, the result is ERR + 1, which still evaluates to ERR.

George FitzGerald
Medford, Mass.

Because @FIND is case-sensitive, the above formula would find Guide to Taxes, *but not* Guide to taxes. *If you have entries with different combinations of uppercase and lowercase, convert the second argument in the @FIND formula to uppercase using @UPPER and search for uppercase strings. For example, convert the above formula to read as follows:*

@FIND("TAX", @UPPER(title),∅) + 1

PUTTING @IF IN CRITERION RANGE

I needed an easy way to print out all my data records that contained an even number in column B. Entering @IF(@INT(B2/2) = B2/2,B2,∅) into the Criterion range did the trick. When I selected /Data Query Extract, the desired records were copied to the Output range. Dividing by a 3 or 4 instead of a 2 pulls out all the records whose B field is divisible by 3 or 4 respectively.

Michael Miller
North East, Pennsylvania

A slightly more compact formula is @IF(@MOD(B2,2) = ∅,B2,∅).

3

Sorting

SORT KEYS

In the following example, I want *1-2-3* to sort all names alphabetically. When I specify Primary-Key as A1..B3, the database sorts only column A alphabetically. Why won't column B sort when I've specified both columns in the range?

	A	B
1	Carla	Jeff
2	John	Connie
3	Lynda	Alice

Lynnette Archie
Pacific Bell
Sacramento, Calif.

You must place all the names in one column. You can place data associated with each person in the same row as the person's name. If you designate the entire range of filled cells as the Data range, all rows will remain intact during the sort.

The sort keys are the columns the program uses as the basis of the sort. Select Primary-Key and point to any cell in the Names column, then type A to select ascending order to create an alphabetized list.

THREE-KEY SORTS

You can sort based on three keys if you use the following double-sort method. First decide which fields should be the first, second, and third columns used as the basis of the sort. Then do the first sort by selecting the second column as the primary sort key and the third column as the secondary key. Create a new column of numbers, starting with 1 at the top of the column being sorted and going down to the bottom of the column. The /Data Fill command does this quickly. Now sort again, selecting

213

the first column as the primary sort key and the number column as the secondary key. Don't forget to expand the sort range to include the number column.

Thomas P. Craven
Raytheon Co.
Portsmouth, R.I.

Symphony provides sorting on up to three keys at a time.

MORE THAN THREE SORT KEYS — I

By combining fields with string arithmetic, you can sort using an almost unlimited number of key fields. For example, suppose you have string (label) data starting in row 2 of columns A, B, C, D, E, and F. You can create a new field in column G by entering the formula + A2&B2&C2&D2&E2&F2 in cell G2, then copying it down as many rows as you have in your database. Using this new field as your primary sort key gives you the same result as using a six-key sort.

Lyle K. Watkins
Kendall Co.
Pelzer, S.C.

The @STRING function lets you also include numeric values as part of the new field.

MORE THAN THREE SORT KEYS — II

A previous good idea noted that a database can be sorted on label fields in columns A, B, C, D, E, and F if the Primary-Key field is an additional field containing the formula + A2&B2&C2&D2&E2&F2. However, in *1-2-3* Release 2/2.01, this works only if the new field is converted from the formula to a value, by selecting /Range Value. Even then, the sort only gives correct results when all strings in a given column are the same length. For example, if columns A and B contain last and first names, then sorting on the primary field + A2&B2&C2&D2&E2&F2 in ascending order would put *Smithson, John* before *Smith, Vincent* because the sorting values would be *SmithsonJohn* and *SmithVincent*, the spacing being ignored in the formulas.

To get around this problem, you must use a formula that makes all strings the same length before concatenating them. To sort a database with three columns, for example, use this formula in column D:

```
+ A2&@REPEAT(" ",(20 – @LENGTH(A2)))
  &B2&@REPEAT(" ",(20 – @LENGTH(B2)))&C2
```

The number 20 is the maximum width of the corresponding field. Copy this formula down column D, convert the formulas to values with the Range Value command, and sort.

Bob Dougherty
Fort Collins, Colo.

The technique also works in Symphony, *except that you don't need to convert the formulas into values. In either case, the technique fails if there are blank cells in the columns used in the sorting, which causes the string formulas to return ERR.*

KEEP TRACK OF DATABASE RECORD ORDER

When you develop a database, include a column of sequential numbers to record the order in which you originally entered your data. This lets you reorder the database after sorting it by another field. In addition, since data is often read in from a variety of sources in no particular numeric or alphabetical order and only sorted after data entry is finished, re-sorting by the sequential number field facilitates proofreading against the source materials.

You can use the /Data Fill (*1-2-3*) or MENU Range Fill (*Symphony*) command to enter the sequencing numbers. Be sure to include this column in the Input (*1-2-3*) or Database (*Symphony*) range specification. Finally, since this column is typically excluded from printouts, place it on the extreme left or right side of the database.

David G. Potter
Littleton, Colorado

RETAINING DOUBLE-SPACING AFTER RECORD-SORT

Symphony's Record-Sort process moves all blank lines to the top of the Database range. Entries that were originally double-spaced then become single-spaced. By issuing the SERVICES Print Settings Spacing 2 command, I can still print double-spaced. However, the column headings that I created with the Top-Label command also print out double-spaced. Is there any way to solve this besides manually reinserting empty lines?

Betty Banister
Peoria, Illinois

First, erase the blank lines that clutter your database. You need not enter them anymore. Then set the Print Settings to single-spacing. In the SHEET window of your database, issue the MENU Query Settings Report Main command and press the DownArrow key once. This will create a two-line Report range. The first line should contain the regular range name references to the first line in your database, and the second line should be blank. Now connect the database with the print command by selecting SERVICES Print Settings Source Database and entering the name of your database. When the report prints out, it will be double-spaced.

SORTING IN SYMPHONY

1-2-3 veterans will need to learn a few new tricks to sort in *Symphony*. *1-2-3*'s Data Sort command sorts a column of data, but *Symphony*'s Query Record-Sort command expects the column to have a field name at the top. For this reason, the sort won't include the top line of the specified sort range. Instead, the field name remains at the top, where it belongs. To get around this, insert a blank row as the first row of the sort range.

Anthony Ciaramella
Glen Rock, N.J.

4

Creating Symphony Databases

SYMPHONY FORM TO 1-2-3 DATABASE

How can I translate my *Symphony* database files into *1-2-3*?

Paul C. Hartnett
American Maize Products Co.
Stanford, Conn.

Retrieve your Symphony *database in* Symphony. *Move the cell pointer to the first field name in your Database range, and select SERVICES File Xtract Formulas. Enter a new file name with a WK1 extension, and indicate the entire Database range, including field names, as the range you want to extract. Save your database file. Then select SERVICES New Yes. Then Retrieve the new file and save it. Select SERVICES Exit to leave the* Symphony *program. Next, load* 1-2-3 *and retrieve the file.*

You don't have to translate Symphony *files if you're using them with* 1-2-3 *Release 2/2.01. To retrieve the file, select /File Retrieve in* 1-2-3 *Release 2/2.01, press Escape and enter *.*, and select a file name.*

You do have to translate (import) a Symphony *file into a* 1-2-3 *Release 1A file.* Symphony *Release 1 does not have a Translate utility that allows you to translate* Symphony *files to* 1-2-3 *Release 1A. If you use* Symphony *Release 1/1.01, you must create an ASCII (print) file and read it in* 1-2-3 *Release 1A. However, the Translate utility in subsequent releases of* 1-2-3 *can translate* Symphony *files into* 1-2-3 *Release 1A files.*

Enter trans *at the DOS prompt with your Install and Utility Disk (*Symphony *Release 1.1) or your Utility Disk (*Symphony *Release 1.2) in the drive. On a hard-disk system make sure that you are in the subdirectory where your* Symphony *program files reside. You can also select File-Translate at the Access menu. Then follow the menu instructions to translate your file.*

If you are going to use your Symphony *database with* 1-2-3 *Release 1A, you need to remember a few items concerning the effect of translation on your database:*

- Symphony *database range names are discarded during translation. After you retrieve the file in 1-2-3, select /Data Query Input to specify your database as your 1-2-3 Input range.*

- *Formulas that contain @functions not included in 1-2-3 Release 1A are converted to labels.*

- *Any data beyond row 2,048 is lost. (1-2-3 Release 1A has 2,048 rows:* Symphony *and 1-2-3 Release 2/2.01 have 8,192 rows.)*

- *You won't be able to translate password-protected* Symphony *Release 1.1/1.2 files.*

- Symphony *Release 1.1/1.2 allocates RAM differently from 1-2-3 Release 1A. Consequently, a file that can be retrieved by* Symphony *may be too big for 1-2-3 Release 1A. If this is the case, use the File Xtract command to break up your database into two or more files.*

1-2-3 DATABASE TO SYMPHONY FORM

My office uses both *1-2-3* Release 1A and *Symphony* on an IBM AT. How can we translate our *1-2-3* database files into *Symphony* files to use in a FORM window?

William Gibson
Citizens Bank
Providence, R.I.

If you are using Symphony *Release 1.1/1.2 or higher, you can easily read 1-2-3 files into* Symphony. *Select SERVICES File Retrieve. When you see the prompt* Name of file to retrieve: A:*.WR? *press Escape. Then type* *.WK? *and press Return. All of the 1-2-3 worksheet files in the current directory will be listed. (If your 1-2-3 files are not in the current directory, issue the SERVICES File Directory command to change the current directory before following the previous instructions.) Retrieve the 1-2-3 file as you would a* Symphony *file. When you save the worksheet,* Symphony *will append a .WR1 extension on the new file. The original 1-2-3 file will remain intact.*

If you are using Symphony *Release 1, you can retrieve 1-2-3 Release 1A worksheet files just by changing the file extension in the prompt* Name of file to retrieve: *as described above. If you want to use 1-2-3 Release 2/2.01 files, you must translate them into the* Symphony *Release 1 worksheet file format with the 1-2-3 Release 2/2.01 Translate utility.*

Given the preceding instructions, here is a method you can use to create a Symphony *database from a 1-2-3 database: Retrieve your 1-2-3 database in 1-2-3. Write down the name of each field and the width of each column. Create a temporary file by selecting /File Xtract Formulas; specify the database records excluding the field names as the range to be extracted. This new file will be the file to bring over to* Symphony. *Next exit from 1-2-3 and load* Symphony, *where you will create a simple database form. Enter the database field names starting in cell*

A1. These are the names that you used in your 1-2-3 database. For example, enter Part no, Item, Qty, *and* Cost *in cells A1 through A4. Edit each field name to include codes for the type of field it should be (numeric, label, etc.) and the width of the field. For example, if cost is a numeric field six characters wide, you'd enter COST:N:6.*

Press the TYPE key and switch to a FORM window. The message No Definition range defined *will appear in the upper-left corner of your monitor. Ignore it, press MENU, then select Generate, then Label. Press Return twice more. Now you will be prompted to specify the range of field names. In this example, specify range A1..A4 and press Return. You now have a form that you can later use to enter new records into your database. When you switch to a SHEET window, your worksheet will look like this:*

```
        A          B        C         D        E         F          G        H
 1  │ Part no
 2  │ Item
 3  │ Qty:n
 4  │ Cost:n
 5  │
 6  │ Part no _____
 7  │ Item _____
 8  │ Qty _____
 9  │ Cost _____
10  │
11  │ Name      Value      Type        Default   Formula    Validity    Input    Prompt
12  │ Part no               L:9                                                  Enter Part no
13  │ Item                  L:9                                                  Enter Item
14  │ Qty                   N:9                                                  Enter Qty
15  │ Cost                  N:9                                                  Enter Cost
16  │
17  │ Part no   Item       Qty         Cost
18  │      0         0           0          0
19  │
20  │ Part no   Item       Qty         Cost
21  │
22  │
23  │
24  │
25  │ Part no   Item       Qty         Cost
26  │
```

Move your cell pointer to cell A26, which is the upper-left corner of the Database range where you should place the records. Select SERVICES File Combine Copy Entire-File Ignore Formulas, and choose the new temporary file that contains the 1-2-3 database records. Your 1-2-3 records are now in your Symphony *database. Next, select MENU Range Name Create and select* MAIN_DB. *Expand the range named* MAIN_DB *to include the records you have just combined into your* Symphony *database. Now switch back to a FORM window. You are now ready to enter your new records.*

SPREADSHEET TO DATABASE

I created a mailing list database by entering all the names and addresses into the rows and columns of a SHEET window, but now I want to switch to a FORM window database. Is this possible, or must I retype everything?

B. J. Jochim
Memphis, Tennessee

No retyping is necessary. Start with a new worksheet, then, in a FORM window, generate a database system that contains the same fields in the same order as your spreadsheet mailing list. (Consult the documentation for complete instructions.) For example, make the first field Names, the second Address, and so on. Then switch to a SHEET window and use the SERVICES File Combine command to bring in your existing mailing list, starting in the row under the field names in the database range. Make sure that the only thing being combined is the mailing list — don't include any field names or other data. Finally, select MENU Range Name Create, point to the database range (the one that ends with __DB), and expand the highlighted area to cover all your records. The result is a fully functioning database system, FORM window and all.

STARTING A NEW DATABASE IN OLD FORM

We start new databases by making sure that the Criterion range contains no criteria so that all records are selected. Then we select MENU Query Delete Yes.

Nicholas J. Santoro
Federal Home Loan Bank of Des Moines
Kansas City, Mo.

ADDING A FIELD TO A FORM

How can I add a field to a form after using the form for a while?

G.F. Herron
St. Louis, Mo.

Follow these steps to add a new field:

1. *Insert a row in both the Entry and Definition ranges, wherever the field is to go. Enter the new field name in those rows. In the appropriate columns in the definition range, include the field type, the prompt you want, and any other relevant information. Be sure to enter underscores after the field names in the Entry range; otherwise, you get an error message. The order of the fields in the Entry and Definition ranges must match.*

2. *Copy the new field names from the Definition range to the Report, Criterion, and Database ranges. In cases where the new field is positioned in the middle of the other field names, use the Move command to move the other field names and database columns over one column to create space for the new field name.*

3. *Give the new field a range name by moving to the new name at the top of the database range and selecting MENU Range Name Labels Down Return.*
4. *Update the Main Report range by typing +FIELDNAME under the new field name in the Above Report range.*
5. *Check each range to make sure that you've expanded the range to include all of the fields in your database. Switch to a FORM window to see the new form layout.*

In the example below, the field name ZIP has been added. In the Above Report range, cell E20 contains +ZIP, and in the Database range, cell E28 has been named ZIP with the command MENU Range Name Labels Down.

Symphony Release 2 has a built-in Field command that handles this whole process for you.

	A	B	C	D	E	F	G	H
1	Name:L:20							
2	Address:L:20							
3	City:L:15							
4	State:L:2							
5								
6	Name _____							
7	Address _____							
8	City _____							
9	State __							
10	Zip _____							
11								
12	Name	Value	Type	Default	Formula	Valid	Input	Prompt
13	Name	Sue Lane	L:20					Enter Name
14	Address	1 Main St	L:20					Enter Address
15	City	Denver	L:15					Enter City
16	State	CO	L:2					Enter State
17	Zip	78654	L:9					Enter Zip
18								
19	Name	Address	City	State	Zip			
20	Joe Lu	9 Mill St	Salem	NH	19876			
21								
22	Name	Address	City	State	Zip			
23								
24								
25								
26								
27	Name	Address	City	State	Zip			
28	Joe Lu	9 Mill St	Salem	NH	19876			
29	Jack Lee	4 Will St	Lynn	MA	01765			
30	Sue Lane	1 Main St	Denver	CO	78654			

DATABASE RANGE MISMATCH

I just created a database using *Symphony*'s Form Generate command. When I try to use my new database in the FORM environment, the error message *Entry/Definition Ranges mismatched* appears. I have checked that all the field names match and that the ranges are the correct size, but I still cannot solve this problem.

Ejaz Saeed
Detroit, Michigan

Check whether you have a field name that contains an underscore, such as FIRST__NAME. Because underscores are reserved for use in the Entry form, Symphony cannot interpret those that appear within database field names. It is also suggested that you not use the following characters when creating database field names:

*$ @ ? ! __ : " ' , < > . + − / ***

5

Data Entry
in a Symphony Database

ENTERING NUMBERS INTO FORM WINDOW

I am having trouble entering zip codes that begin with zero into my database FORM window. Whenever I try to enter a zip that begins with a zero, *Symphony* drops the zero and displays only the last four digits. Am I doing something wrong?

Cynthia L. Watts
Bowling Green, Ohio

When you first set up your form, you entered a list of field names to be used by the Generate command to create your database. Symphony *required you to specify how it should treat the data that you intended to enter into each field — that is, as a label, number, date, or time — and how many characters each field could contain. You could have specified this information in two ways. First, you could have followed one or more field names with codes that affected only that particular field For example, if you entered the field name and code City:L:15,* Symphony *would interpret this to mean that data you enter into the* City *field should be considered labels and that you can enter a maximum of 15 characters.*

The second method is to make menu choices as part of the Generate command that specify the data type and character number for all fields that did not have specially entered codes. Symphony *automatically places the appropriate code letter and number for each field name in the* type *column of the Definition range.*

Your problem is that your Zip *field treats data as if it is numeric. Since leading zeros have no numeric value,* Symphony *drops them. The solution is to recode the* Zip *field to treat the data as a label. Go to the Definition range, look down the* Name *column until you find* Zip, *then look two cells to the right. This should be the* Type *column. Change the N to L. All zip codes entered after this change will be entered as labels. You will have to manually change the zip codes already entered into your database.*

USE FORMULAS IN DATABASE DEFINITION RANGE

The *Formula* column in the Definition range of a database enables you to expedite and simplify data entry. Formulas entered in this column can take that field's Input data, which you enter via the FORM window, and transform it according to the instructions contained in each formula. For example, if you enter 35 in the *Mileage* field using the FORM window, *Symphony* places the 35 in the appropriate row of the Definition range under the *Input* column heading. Next, the data is passed through the formula, for example G15*.35, and the result is temporarily placed in the *Value* column just to the right of the *mileage* field name. When you press the Insert key, *Symphony* takes everything in the *Value* column and inserts it into the current record of the Database range.

Database formulas can also contain @functions, such as @VLOOKUP, which allows you to enter a customer name and have the lookup table locate the person's purchase order number and automatically place it in the form. Or you can enter a number and have the table return the person's name.

Deborah J. Burris
Ernst and Whinney
San Antonio, Texas

FORM-WINDOW MACRO

When entering numbers into a database through a FORM window, it can be cumbersome to turn the NumberLock key off each time you need to press the Insert key to insert the completed record into the database. An easier way is to use a macro. For example, if your record has four fields, the macro, named \x in this example, would look like this:

{?} ~ {?} ~ {?} ~ {?} ~ {INSERT}{BRANCH \x}

Once this macro is invoked, you only need to use the numeric keypad and the Return key.

Rick McMasters
Riverside Markets
DuBois, Pennsylvania

You get this macro's increased simplicity at the expense of error checking. If you make a typing error, you have to break out of the macro, finish entering data into the record manually, then reinvoke the macro when you start the next record.

PROTECTING DATABASE FIELDS

Once you enter data in a database, you may want to protect the data so inadvertent changing or erasing is difficult or impossible in a FORM window. By changing a field's type (specified in the Definition range) to Computed, you prevent someone from being able to move the cursor to that field, thereby protecting the contents from being altered. For example, to protect the entered names and addresses in a database from being altered, change the entry in the Type column in the Definition range corresponding to the fields from Label (L) to Computed (C); leave the lengths of the fields the same. If you need to add more names and addresses, temporarily change the Type back to Label.

Mark H. Gruner
Electronic Data Systems
Dallas, Tex.

INSERTING AND DELETING ROWS IN NAMED RANGES

In a previous tip you said that deleting rows in the middle of the range would not change the named Database range. However, in *Symphony* if you delete the second row of the database, the one located underneath the field names, the Main Report range formulas evaluate to ERR.

Roger Nord
Prudential-Bache Securities
Fresno, Calif.

You're right. If the Main Report range formulas evaluate to ERR, enter +name *in the Main Report range, where* name *is the first field name in the database, then copy the formula across the width of the Main Report range.*

6

Reports from Symphony Databases

PRINTING SELECTED DATABASE RECORDS

Is it possible to output database reports of only selected records using *Symphony*?

Marjorie H. Bewsher
Halifax, Nova Scotia

Symphony *gives you a couple of ways to print selected records in a database.*

Assuming you created a database using the Symphony Form Generate command, you can use the MENU Criteria Edit command to control which records will be printed in the database report. If you then want to print all records once again, you must delete all criteria. The Criteria Ignore command doesn't affect report printing.

Also, you can use the spreadsheet row number of the first record in the database range you want to print a series of consecutive records. Enter the following formula in the Criterion range:

$$@CELL(``row", !fieldname) > = rownumber1 \#AND\# @CELL$$
$$(``row", !fieldname) < = rownumber2$$

where rownumber1 is the row number of the first record desired and rownumber2 is the row number of the last record desired.

PRINT REMAINING RECORDS ONLY

When my printer runs out of paper in the middle of a long database report, before I resume printing, I enter a formula to cause *Symphony* to print only the unprinted records. In a blank cell in the row directly below any field name in the Criterion range, I enter the following formula, where *fieldname* is the name of the field in which I entered the formula and *last* is the row number of the last record that was printed:

$$@CELL(``row", !fieldname) > last$$

The formula returns Ø because my first database record does not meet the selection criteria.

Robert Francis
Dedham, Mass.

PRINTING DATABASE SUBTOTALS ONLY

I have been working with *Symphony*'s database report ranges for about a year. I really appreciate the flexibility that the multiple-pass reports give me. However, sometimes I want to print a summary list; that is, I want to print only my Above or Below Report ranges, which contain a database statistical function, without printing the Main Report range, which contains the detail. Here's how I do it:

In the leftmost cell of the Main Report range, I enter the split vertical bar character (¦), found on the same key as the backslash on an IBM PC, and nothing else. This character causes the data to its right (that is, the Main Report range) to be ignored when printing. It also keeps the printer from advancing one line for each record matched. My printed report now consists of a series of Above or Below Report ranges with no detail between the totals.

If my Main Report range is more than one line, I "hide" each with the split bar.

Daniel Volitich
Smithy Braedon Co.
Washington D.C.

You don't need a Main Report range at all if you always want summary reports and never want to see the detail. Cancel your report ranges (from a SHEET window, MENU Query Settings Cancel Report) and then specify your Above and Below Report ranges containing the database statistical functions.

CRITERIA AND DATABASE REPORT PRINTOUTS

You can use database report ranges for several purposes, including printing a list of records in the database and producing form letters. To connect the database to the Print command, select SERVICES Print Settings Source Database, then enter the name of your database.

Any criteria entered into the database Criterion range limit the records that are used in the printing process to those that meet the criteria. Issuing the Criteria Ignore command does not affect printing operations. To eliminate the effect of criteria, you must erase the criteria. In a SHEET Window, go to the Criterion range and erase the contents. In a FORM window, select MENU Criterion Edit, press the Delete key, and enter Y (yes).

STRING FUNCTIONS IN REPORT RANGE

I enter names in a database last name first, comma, then a space and the first name. This lets me sort the *Name* field according to last name. However, when preparing form letters, I usually want the name to appear as first name, then last name. The following formula transposes the names when I use it as part of a *Symphony* Main Report range in which *name* is the field containing the names.

@MID(*name*,@FIND("," ,*name*,0) + 2,@LENGTH(*name*) —
   @FIND("," ,*name*,0))&" "&@LEFT(*name*,@FIND("," ,*name*,0))

Sandie O'Toole
D'Arcy MacManus Masius
St. Louis, Missouri

This formula uses @FIND to locate the comma, which is then used as the marker between the first and last names. Another approach is to put the first and last names in separate fields, which would allow a much simpler formula: + FIRST&" "&LAST.

MULTIPLE-PASS REPORT

How does *Symphony*'s multiple report feature work?

Bob Klein
Videojet
Aurora, Colo.

Symphony's multiple-pass report feature lets you print reports that group the database records by a common characteristic. For instance, assume you have a national sales database like the one shown on the next page and you want to print reports of records in the same city; that is, you want to group together everyone in Newark, then everyone in Atlanta, and so on. The process works by sequentially moving criteria from an Entry list into the Criterion range, printing all records that meet this and any other existing criteria, then repeating the process with the next item in the Entry list. The following example illustrates how to accomplish this task.

Start by creating an Entry list. To do this, switch to a SHEET window and copy the field name from the field by which you are going to group the reports. For this example, use the field name City *and copy it to cell E19.*

Next, type the city names Newark, Boston, and Atlanta in cells E20..E22 respectively. These names will be used as the Entry list.

Now, specify the report type as a multiple-pass report with MENU Query Settings Report Type Multiple. At this point, Symphony *prompts you for the Entry list (E20..E22). Don't include the field name* City. *Symphony now prompts you for an Input cell. The Input cell is the cell in the Criterion range into which* Symphony *sequentially places each item from the Entry list. The Input cell in the example is B18.*

Make sure that the Main Report range is specified as A15..C15, and extend the Above Report range to A13..C14 so that a blank line will appear between reports. Assign the Print Settings Source Database, then use the SERVICES Print Align Go command. Symphony *prints a report similar to that shown below the spreadsheet on the next page.*

```
      A         B         C
1  NAME:L:10
2  CITY:L:20
3  PRODUCT:L:15
4
5  NAME _____
6  CITY _____
7  PRODUCT _____
8
9  Name      Value     Type...
10 NAME      Smith     L:10
11 CITY      Newark    L:18
12 PRODUCT   tires     L:15
13
14 NAME      CITY      PRODUCT
15 Smith     Newark    tires
16
17 NAME      CITY      PRODUCT
18
19 NAME      CITY      PRODUCT
20 Smith     Newark    tires
21 Wass      Boston    autos
22 Laird     Atlanta   autos
23 Toma      Newark    buses
24 Jones     Atlanta   tires
```

NAME	CITY	PRODUCT
Smith	Newark	tires
Toma	Newark	buses
NAME	CITY	PRODUCT
Wass	Boston	autos
NAME	CITY	PRODUCT
Laird	Atlanta	autos
Jones	Atlanta	tires

The report printed above includes the Above Report range (NAME, CITY, PRODUCT) and the database records grouped together by city. You can also include a Below Report range. One of the Below Report range's most useful purposes is to produce summary statistics such as how many records are in a particular city. To add this to the example, place the word Total in cell F19 and the formula @DCOUNT(MAIN__DB,0,MAIN__CR) in cell G19, and specify F19..G19 as the Below Report range using the MENU Query Settings Report Below command. The formula in G19 evaluates to a value of 5 since the database contains five records. The Below Report Range looks like the following:

	F	G	
19	Total	5	

Now your report will print like this:

NAME	CITY	PRODUCT
Smith	Newark	tires
Toma	Newark	buses
Total 2		

NAME	CITY	PRODUCT
Wass	Boston	autos
Total 1		

NAME	CITY	PRODUCT
Laird	Atlanta	autos
Jones	Atlanta	tires
Total 2		

You can get fancy by adding more cells to the Above Report, Below Report and Main Report ranges.

SECTION
11

LABELS AND
WORD PROCESSING

There are a surprising number of people who use *1-2-3* as a word processor. Rather than learn a complicated word-processing program, they rely on *1-2-3* labels and the Range Justify command to write quick memos and letters. One person even used *1-2-3* to write an entire book!

1-2-3 Release 2 greatly expanded the label-processing capabilities of Release 1A. You could concatenate and manipulate labels in new ways, concatenating, splitting, and referencing them in formulas. Unfortunately, since labels were no longer computationally inert, they no longer evaluated to zero when included in numeric formulas. All of a sudden, formulas that included labels as well as numbers were invalid. Not surprisingly, this caused great consternation among *1-2-3* users.

To correct the label-in-formula and other problems, Lotus Development quickly prepared Release 2.01, which once again gave labels the computational value of zero by distinguishing between simple labels and "strings" that were the result of "string arithmetic." Simple labels, the kind that are preceded by a label prefix, will not affect formulas. However, strings will affect numeric formulas and must be dealt with more carefully.

For all its string-handling capabilities, *1-2-3* does not contain a word processor. *Symphony* does. So most of this section deals with the *Symphony* DOC window environment. *Symphony* is one of the easiest introductions to word processing available, and although most of the commands and functions are straightforward, there are some less obvious areas, such as the relationship between DOC format lines and Print setting sheets.

Of course, *Symphony* doesn't have all the bells and whistles of a newly released, full-featured word-processing program. But it does have plenty of power for most day-to-day office needs.

231

1

Using Labels

CENTERING LABELS

While creating a *1-2-3* worksheet, I needed to center an entire column of label entries. I know how to accomplish this one cell at a time by editing each entry to begin with a caret (∧), but is there a command to center-align an entire range of cells?

Nancy Bromhead
Warner Electric Brake & Clutch Co.
South Beloit, Ill.

Symphony and 1-2-3 contain two commands that affect alignment. The commands /Range Label-Prefix (1-2-3 Release 1A), /Range Label (1-2-3 Release 2/2.01), and MENU Range Label-Alignment (Symphony) only change the alignment of a particular range of labels that are already in the worksheet. The commands /Worksheet Global Label-Prefix (1-2-3) and MENU Settings Label-Prefix (Symphony) affect the entire worksheet, but only for labels you subsequently enter. However, the two global commands do not affect cells previously formatted with the /Range Format (1-2-3) and MENU Settings Format (Symphony) commands, even if labels are subsequently entered in those cells, because these localized commands take precedence.

UPPERCASE TO LOWERCASE

I recently created a 250-record database of names and addresses. By mistake, I entered everything in uppercase letters. How can I change my records from uppercase to lowercase letters without retyping everything?

C. I. Parsons
Nashville, Tenn.

1-2-3 Release 2/2.01 and Symphony contain string functions that can help you. The @LOWER function converts all letters in a referenced string to lowercase letters. The @PROPER function converts the letters in a string to proper capitalization, meaning that the first letter of each word will be uppercase and all other letters will be lowercase.

232

SPLITTING APART CELL ENTRIES — I

Using *1-2-3* Release 1A, our secretary entered names of the company's employees in one column, first and last name in the same cell. This had one major drawback: it allowed sorting only by first name. I needed to find a way to separate the first and last names into adjoining cells in a row. Here's my solution:

First, narrow the column containing the names to one character. Then, with the cell pointer in this column, select /Range Justify and specify the entire column as the range. What results is a long column of single names, which alternates between the associated first and last names. Insert a column to the right of the names. The following looping macro, named \s, moves one person's last name to the cell to the right of that person's first name:

/M ~ {RIGHT}{UP} ~ {DOWN}{DOWN}/XG\s ~

Place the cell pointer in the cell containing the first last name (the second entry in the column) and invoke the \s macro. Once the entire database has been rearranged, press Control-Break to stop the macro and then reset the column width. You now have the desired result, except that every other line is blank. To eliminate the blank lines, use the Data Sort command and select all the names as the Data range, specify the last names as the Primary Key, and sort in ascending order. This brings all the blank lines together at the top of the database. Now just move the records up.

Tom Wagner
Culpepper, Va.

In 1-2-3 Release 2/2.01 and Symphony, you can accomplish this splitting by using string functions. If the column of names starts in cell A1 and columns B and C are blank, enter the following formula in B1:

@LEFT(A1,@FIND('' '',A1,∅))

In C1, enter:

@RIGHT(A1,@LENGTH(A1)–@LENGTH(B1)–1)

Copy these formulas down columns B and C. Then select /Range Value (in Symphony, *MENU Range Values) to convert these string formulas into labels.*

SPLITTING APART CELL ENTRIES — II

A user once created a mailing list I could sort only by first name. He had entered the first name, then the last name, in the same cell. In some instances, he had also included a middle initial. The middle initials created problems when I tried to use the formulas suggested in the Good Idea column on splitting apart cell entries.

I got around the middle initial this way: Assume the column of names begins in cell A1 and that columns B and C are blank. Place the formula @LEFT(A1,@FIND

(" ",A1,∅)) in cell B1, then copy it down column B. This formula starts from the leftmost end of the string containing the full name, searches for the space between the first name and the last name or middle initial, then displays the first name. Now enter the following formula in cell C1 and copy it down column C:

@IF(@ISERR(@FIND(".",A1,∅)),@RIGHT(A1,@LENGTH(A1) –
    @LENGTH(B1)–1),@RIGHT(A1,@LENGTH(A1)–@LENGTH(B1)–4))

This formula first searches for the period that punctuates a middle initial. If it does not find a period, the formula subtracts the length of the first name from the length of the entire string and displays the contents of the remainder (the last name) in column C. If it finds a period, it subtracts the length of the first name plus the spaces and the middle initial from the length of the entire string and displays the last name in column C. If you use the Range Value command on the entries containing formulas, you will then be able to sort the database by last names.

Richard J. Schaeffer
St. Clair Hospital
Pittsburgh, Pa.

These formulas also work in Symphony. *However, this method deletes the middle initials. Enter the following formula in column D to display the middle initial:*

@IF(@ISERR(@FIND(".",A1,∅)), "", @MID(A1,@FIND(".",A1,∅)–1,2))

The formula tests for the period that punctuates a middle initial. It displays a null string if it does not find a period; otherwise, it isolates and displays the middle initial.

SPLITTING APART CELL ENTRIES — III

"Splitting Apart Cell Entries — II" presents a formula for displaying the middle initial of a name. However, I discovered that when the name in column A includes initials for both the first and middle names, the formula returns the first initial rather than the middle initial. I corrected the problem by changing the start number for the @FIND functions from ∅ to 2. Enter the following formula in cell D1:

@IF(@ISERR(@FIND(".",A1,2)),"",@MID(A1,@FIND(".",A1,2)–1,2))

William Cox
Waco, Tex.

DISPLAYING LABELS WITH @IF

Unlike *1-2-3* Release 2/2.01, Release 1A of *1-2-3* does not permit the use of labels in the result clauses of @IF functions. For instance, @IF(A1>A2,5,6) is all right, but @IF(A1>A2,"Buy","Sell") is not.

Macro \a at cell B8 in the following figure provides a means of producing labels from the result clauses of @IF formulas. This allows you to generate the appropriate labels for the spreadsheet itself.

```
         A           B
1              25
2              30
3    Strategy:
4
5    Buy
6    Sell
7
8    \a           {GOTO}b12~
9                 @IF(A1>A2,5,6)~
10                {EDIT}{CALC}
11                {LEFT}{/Ca{RIGHT}~
12
13               ~b3~/REb12~/XQ
```

You wish to display the labels *Buy* or *Sell* at cell B3. Base the argument of the conditional statement on a comparison of the values in cells A1 and A2. If cell A1 is greater than cell A2, *Buy* will appear in cell B3; otherwise, cell B3 will read *Sell*.

The macro begins by moving the cell pointer to the fourth line of the macro, which is blank, and enters a formula based on an @IF function. Cell A1 is not greater than cell A2, so the formula returns the value 6 in cell B12. {EDIT}{CALC}, executed by the next line of the macro, converts the formula in cell B12 to a simple number. Still in Edit mode, the cursor moves to the left of the value, where it enters /Ca, then moves to the right of the string and enters a tilde. The statements at cell B12 and the beginning of cell B13 now mean, "copy the contents of cell A6 to cell B3." The result of that operation with the data set shown will be to place the word *Sell* to the right of the prompt *Strategy*. The final line of the macro erases the contents of cell B12 and stops the macro.

F. Eugene Halaburt
Dallas, Tex.

The following macro is simpler and achieves the same result:

```
         A           B
1              25
2              30
3    Strategy:
4
5    \a           {GOTO}b3~
6                 /XIa1>a2~Buy~/XQ
7                 Sell~
```

/XI, the macro corollary to @IF, can be accompanied by a macro command to enter text into a cell. In this case, the cell pointer first moves to the cell where the text will be entered, then the /XI statement tests to see if the value in cell A1 is greater than the value in cell A2. If it is, the statement directly to the right executes (entering the label Buy *at the current location of the cell pointer and terminating the macro with the /XQ command). If not, the macro skips the statements to the right and begins executing at the next line (entering the label* Sell *at the current location of the cell pointer and terminating the macro).*

RANGE JUSTIFY AS WORD COUNTER

If I import a text file containing fewer than 2,000 words into *1-2-3* Release 1A, set the width of the column containing the text to 1, then select Range Justify, every word ends up on a separate line. This shows me the number of words my manuscript contains. Sorting the list places all similar words together, which allows me to scan for misspellings and overuse of complex terms. I keep the original copy of the justified list so that I can use Query Find to locate the misspellings in the original text file.

This technique can also help you find misspelled variable words in BASIC programs.

John E. Predmore
Fairport, N.Y.

If you increase the column width to 72, you can also use 1-2-3 *as a very simple text processor. Start typing and when you hear a beep indicating that you've reached the 240-character-per-cell maximum, invoke the following macro, which enters the text, selects /Range Justify, moves to the bottom of the current paragraph, and presses the EDIT key to allow you to continue typing.*

~/RJ~{END}{DOWN}{EDIT}

SEARCH AND REPLACE

I have found a simple way to replace all occurrences of a word or number on my *1-2-3* worksheets. First, I print my spreadsheet to a file using the Print File command. This sets up an ASCII file that I can bring into my word processor. I then use the word processor's search-and-replace feature. I bring the file back into *1-2-3* by using the File Import command, and finally, the imported data is put back into its original columns using the Data Parse command.

Robert Schmidt
Los Angeles, Calif.

Lotus HAL, *from Lotus Development Corp.,* Spell-In, *from Turner Hall Publishing, and* Tonto, *from Kimosabe Products, as well as other products, all add the search-and-replace capability to 1-2-3 worksheets, although these products are in other respects markedly different.*

To gain access to Symphony's word-processing search-and-replace feature, you can print the spreadsheet to a range (SERVICES Print Settings Destination Range), then create a DOC window around that range (SERVICES Window Create). Set the Justification to None (MENU Format Settings Justification None). Then use the MENU Replace command.

2

Symphony DOC Format
Lines and Settings

DOC SETTINGS SHEET

I understand the rule and exception system. The Configuration settings sheet provides the rules, and the individual command settings sheets create the exceptions. However, I cannot find the individual settings sheet for the DOC window. Is there one?

Robert Zeigler
Yarmouth, Massachusetts

To find the DOC window settings sheet, select MENU Format Settings. This sets the default format line for that particular DOC window. You can override the default format line by inserting a special format line anywhere in the document with MENU Format Create. If while editing a specially entered format line you select Reset, the default format line will reappear.

PROTECTING NAMED FORMAT LINES

Symphony allows you to create and customize multiple format lines in any section of the document. You can also use the Line-Marker command to name each format line. The MENU Format Use-Named command then allows you to insert exact copies of the named format line in other sections of the document. The original is displayed as a regular format line showing margins and tabs. The copies are displayed as an ''at'' sign followed by the name you gave to the original, such as @FULLWIDTH.

There are several advantages to using named copies of format lines. For example, to edit all copies of a named format line at once, select MENU Format Edit Named to go to the original. Edit the original, then select Quit. All the copies are similarly edited, and you return to your starting location.

You detach a named copy from the original by moving on or just below it, then selecting MENU Format Edit Current. When you finish editing the line, select Quit. The line no longer refers to the original.

238

When using copies of named format lines, be careful not to delete the original. A missing original invalidates all the copies. If you rejustify the text under an invalid format line, it will be rearranged according to the closest preceding valid format line. This could ruin your fancy layout. So it is a good idea to place the original version of each format line at the top of the document. Label the line by placing a copy just beneath the original. By doing so, you will not mistakenly erase the original. See below for an example.

Should an original be erased, you can revitalize the invalid copies by creating a new format line and giving it the same name as the lost one.

If you use the same series of specialized format lines in many documents, you can save them in a separate file and retrieve that file each time you start a new document.

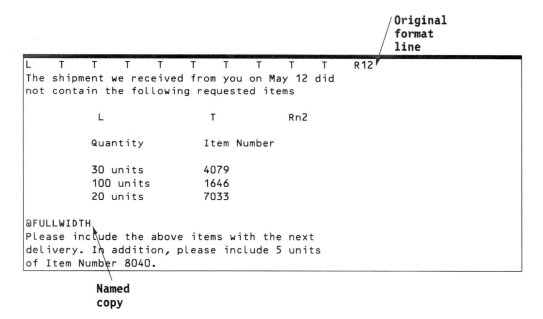

Original format line

Named copy

MOVING BETWEEN FORMAT LINES IN A DOC WINDOW

The MENU Line-Marker command names a particular format line in a document. This is a process similar to assigning range names to cells. You can move around a long document by pressing GOTO MENU MENU, then selecting the name of the desired line.

If you want to move up or down between format lines, press End-JUSTIFY (End-F2) to move to the next format line, or End-WHERE (End-Alt-F2) to move to the previous format line. Repeated pressing of these key combinations eventually moves you to the beginning of the document or to the last inserted format line.

UNDERLINING SPACES IN DOC

How can I get *Symphony* to underline spaces?

T.K. Young
University of Manitoba
Winnipeg, Manitoba

Use the special print attributes ▲S▲U to underline words and the spaces between words, and then use ▼▲Q to turn the attributes off.

In a DOC window, position the cursor wherever you want to begin underlining. Hold down the Control key and press B (a solid triangle will appear on the screen), then press S (this tells Symphony *to apply the next attribute to the spaces between words. Hold down the Control key and press B again, then press U (the code for the underline attribute).*

Now move the cursor one character beyond where you want the underlining to stop. Hold down the Control key and press E (a solid inverted triangle appears), then hold down the Control key again and press B, then press Q. The ▼ tells Symphony *to stop underlining, and the ▲Q tells* Symphony *to stop applying attributes between spaces. If you leave out the ▲Q, the next time you use an attribute such as underline or strikethrough,* Symphony *will apply it to the spaces between words.*

REJUSTIFYING OLD TAB SETTINGS

Is it possible to edit a format line to change the position of a tab and then have the document automatically move to the new tab position when it rejustifies?

Steve Wexler
Medical Arts Press
Minneapolis, Minn.

Since Symphony *Releases 1 through 1.2 don't use a tab character but fill tabs with blank spaces, changes to the tab setting will affect only tabs you enter henceforth. If you are entering columnar information, you should switch the window type to SHEET and enter your data in worksheet cells. Column widths can be changed to modify the spacing between columns — which is much easier than manually changing old tab settings. Switch back to a DOC window when you're ready to resume entry of paragraph-formatted text.*

Symphony Release 2 has a separate tab code.

3

Symphony DOC Window
Justification and Word Wrap

DOC WINDOW WORD WRAP WILL NOT WORK

Why are there times when the DOC window word-wrap feature does not work?

Joel Kahn
New York, New York

You may have accidentally pressed the Insert key. This puts you in Overstrike mode (Ovr is displayed in the bottom-right corner of your screen). In this mode newly typed characters replace rather than displace existing text.

Word wrap is suspended when justification is set to None. You can see the justification setting in the upper-right side of the screen.

To turn off Overstrike mode, press the Insert key. To change justification on the default Format line, press MENU and select Format Settings Justification or edit the current format line by selecting MENU Format Edit Current.

INDENTS AND HANGING INDENTS

Symphony provides several methods for indenting text. To indent the first line of a paragraph, press the Tab key or Spacebar the desired number of times before typing the first character of the paragraph. *Symphony* will maintain the first line's indentation even when the paragraph is rejustified.

To indent all the lines of a paragraph one space from the current left margin, press INDENT, which enters a hard-space indent character before the first character in the paragraph. A hard space appears on your screen as a right arrow, but the arrow does not appear on the printout. When you finish typing the paragraph, press JUSTIFY. The entire paragraph is indented one space.

You can combine these two methods by starting the paragraph with an indent character, then adding additional indent characters or tab stops before the first text character. When rejustified, the first line is indented the desired number of spaces, while subsequent lines are indented one space.

You can also create hanging indents. For example, you may wish to have a number (1.), letter (A,), word (FIRST), asterisk (*), or other character stick out to the left of a line. You must first increase your left margin to allow space for the hanging indent. Then type the hanging characters at the beginning of the line. Make sure to leave a blank space between the hanging characters and the rest of the line. Letters, numbers, and words must be followed by a period(.). Hanging words can be as long as your left margin allows. After you are finished typing the line or paragraph, press JUSTIFY.

If you wish to start a paragraph with 1. or A. but don't want these characters hanging out to the left, decrease your left margin so that there is no room for hanging characters.

DOCUMENT JUSTIFICATION

In a DOC window, *Symphony* doesn't always seem to allow for the standard two spaces between the period at the end of a sentence and the first letter of the next sentence. What are *Symphony*'s justification rules?

Bob Coughlin
East Longmeadow, Mass.

In a DOC window, the justification rules are as follows: If a word or an abbreviation contains no vowels and ends with a period, Symphony *single-spaces to the next word. If a word or abbreviation has at least one vowel and ends with a period,* Symphony *double-spaces to the next word, as long as the next word begins with a capital letter; otherwise, it single-spaces.*

To prevent single-spacing, first delete the blank space between the period and the following letter. Then, for each desired space, select COMPOSE and press the Spacebar twice. The mid-level dots visible on the screen will hold the words together through justification but will not print.

DOCUMENT JUSTIFICATION EXPANDED

In a previous item about *Symphony*'s rules concerning spaces after punctuation, you forgot to mention that *Symphony* adds two spaces after a numeral that has a period unless the following letter is lowercase. The following two lines are examples of this justification rule.

1. Test line.
2. test line.

Claude Delphia
Patterson, Calif.

4

Symphony DOC Window Tricks

DETERMINING WORD COUNT

I create *Symphony* documents that must be a specific length. I use the following technique to get an approximate word count.

First I save my document. Then I erase any format lines I may have inserted in the text. Next I change the right margin to 1 (MENU Format Settings Right Set 1). This causes *Symphony* to break each line after one word, since no more than one word can fit on a line. I then go to the end of my document and see on which line the last word falls. If it falls on line 800, my document is approximately 800 words long. This technique also treats blank lines between paragraphs as ''words.''

I then retrieve the saved worksheet and know where I stand in terms of length.

Lillian Wagner
Butte, Mont.

SPREADSHEET LABELS IN A DOC WINDOW

Why can I gain access to only certain spreadsheet labels through a DOC window?

Molly Fontaine
Boston, Massachusetts

If you switch from a DOC window to a SHEET window, you will notice that each line of text appears as a long left-justified label. You can then edit the text in the SHEET window. The reverse of this is also true. Left-justified labels entered in the leftmost column of a SHEET window appear as lines of text if you switch the window type to DOC.

You cannot gain access to centered or right-aligned labels and all labels not located in the leftmost column of a SHEET window when you switch the window type to DOC.

A MULTIPLE-LETTER FILE

Instead of creating a separate *Symphony* file for each letter or memo you type, keep all your letters in one file. Adding new letters one below the other keeps your data

243

compact and conserves memory. To find an old letter, select the Search command and enter an identifying keyword, such as the name of the person to whom the letter was sent. To print a letter, move to the desired text, then:

- Select SERVICES Print Settings Source Range
- Press Esc
- Move cursor to top or bottom of the letter
- Press the TAB key
- Expand highlight to cover entire height and width of text
- Press Return
- Select Quit Align Go Page Quit

OUTLINER ADD-IN — I

If you are in an OUTLN window when you save a worksheet using *Symphony* Release 1, you must have the *Symphony Text Outliner Add-In* attached when you retrieve the file. Otherwise, after you issue the Retrieve command, your screen will go blank except for an APP indicator in the top-right corner of the control panel. If you've made this mistake, the program will appear to be frozen, but it's not. Just select SERVICES Window Settings Type DOC. Your text will appear and you can process it. Now to attach the *Outliner*, select SERVICES Application Attach, point to Outliner, press Return, then select Quit.

Tony Buckley
Watertown, Massachusetts

When you try to retrieve a file that was saved in an OUTLN window in Symphony *Release 1.1/1.2 the program doesn't freeze. Instead, you receive a message indicating that the Outliner Add-In must be attached.*

OUTLINER ADD-IN — II

After you attach the *Symphony Outliner Add-In* and switch to an OUTLN window, you are not able to use any Application command (Attach, Detach, Invoke, Clear) until you switch to another window type. However, if you select SERVICES New No while in an OUTLN environment, you lose access to the Application commands, regardless of which window type you switch to. This means you will not be able to detach or clear an application or invoke another application until you exit from *Symphony* and then restart the program. Fortunately, there is no problem with selecting SERVICES New Yes.

This bug was corrected in Symphony *Release 1.1/1.2.*

SECTION
12

PRINTING

After you've entered all your data, after you've analyzed it, then comes the time to show your conclusions to other people. Unless your computer monitor is light enough to carry around and big enough for everyone to see, you're probably going to want hard copy, a printed version of the key sections of your worksheet. And you're probably going to want that printout to have a clean, coherent, professional look. The first step is to arrange your worksheet data in an appropriate layout — and ''appropriate'' doesn't necessarily mean crowding everything together in one place. Some of the tips in this section show you how to print non-contiguous ranges into a tight, well-organized report.

Today, the numerous output devices on the market provide a wide range of choices. For most people, dot-matrix printers are good enough. However, the arrival of affordable laser printers has begun to increase our level of expectation of print quality. Soon, 300 dpi resolution will be considered the low end. The following good ideas are almost entirely device independent, meaning that you can apply them no matter what type of printer you use.

We start at the top with multiple-line headers, include the sides with comments about margins, cover the middle with setup strings and embedded attribute control codes, and end at the bottom with page breaks and footers. If that's not enough, you'll find ideas about printing multiple copies, using multiple printers, and printing multiple ranges.

1

Printing

SETTING PRINT BORDERS

I recently realized that I had misunderstood how to use the *1-2-3* command /Print Options Borders to freeze border columns or rows on my printed reports. If the report consists of range A5..H44 and I want it to include column headers residing in range A1..H4, when I select Options Borders Rows, all I have to specify is range A1..A4. *1-2-3* will fill in the remaining columns for me. Furthermore, if I specify another Print range as M50..X65, my printed report will automatically contain the row borders M1..X4 at the top of each page.

Kathryn Sternitzky
De Pere, Wis.

In Symphony, *the command sequence for printing borders is SERVICES Print Settings Other; then you must select Top-Labels, Left-Labels or both.*

CLEANER-LOOKING REPORTS

When dealing with long columns of added numbers in dollar format, you may have difficulty spotting the subtotals and totals. To help highlight these numbers, I use two formats: the comma (,) format for input lines and a currency format for total lines. This eliminates hundreds of dollar signs, uncluttering the spreadsheet and making the numbers with a preceding dollar sign stand out.

Bryan Glenn
Calcasieu Marine National Bank
Lake Charles, La.

In Symphony, *use the Punctuated format for the input lines.*

CONNECTING PRINTOUTS TO DISKS

My worksheets are scattered on 14 disks, and remembering which printout comes from which disk gets rather difficult. Now in every worksheet that I create, I include a header that prints the date, disk number, and report title — for example, *DATE @¦ Disk 2¦ Budget Plans.*

G. J. Osborn
Eli Lilly International
London, England

PRINT FILES

Is there a way to print using the Print File command? The only time I use print files is when I want to use *Sideways*.

Rhoda L. Ware
Dominion Bankshares Corp.
Roanoke, Va.

You can use files created with 1-2-3*'s /Print File command or* Symphony*'s SERVICES Print Settings Destination File command in programs, such as most word processors, that accept ASCII files.*

To create a print (ASCII) file, in 1-2-3 *select Options from the print menu and set the Left, Top, and Bottom margins to 0, Right to 240, and under Other select Unformatted. This will eliminate extra blank lines in the file. In* Symphony*, select SERVICES Print Settings Margins No-Margins. Be sure to select Quit from the print menu, because the final "close file" code may not be sent until this last step.*

You can also print PRN files through DOS by using the DOS TYPE command in conjunction with Control-P. To try this, create a print file from one of your previously saved files. Exit from 1-2-3 *or* Symphony *and get to the DOS A> prompt (on a hard-disk system, C>) and type the following:*

Type filename.prn

Replace filename *with the name of the PRN file that you created. Now press Control-P and then Return. To stop printing, press Control-P again.*

You can also use the following DOS commands to print an ASCII file in DOS:

Copy filename.prn PRN
*   or*
Print filename.prn (then press Return twice)

You can also bring PRN files back into 1-2-3 *and* Symphony *by using the File Import command. Then you can use the standard Lotus print commands to print the files.*

2

Parts of the Page

SEVEN PARTS IN A PAGE

When I have specified a top margin and bottom margin of zero, why does my printout have a blank space at the top and the bottom?

Marguerite Laird
Bethesda, Md.

Thanks to David A. Stuart of Needham, Mass., here is a complete explanation of the seven parts of a printed 1-2-3 or Symphony page.

1. *Depending on the program and release you're using, the top margin can be from zero to 32 lines and starts at the actual top of the page and goes down to the header line. The default setting is two lines.*

2. *One line is reserved for a header whether or not you choose to enter one.*

3. *The top spacer always consists of two blank lines that separate the header from the body.*

4. *The body varies in length and is the content of your print range. The body also includes any borders (1-2-3) or top-labels and left-labels (Symphony) that you may define.*

5. *The bottom spacer always consists of two blank lines that separate the footer from the body.*

6. *One line is reserved for a footer, whether or not you choose to specify characters for it.*

7. *Depending on the program and release you're using, the bottom margin can be from zero to 32 lines and separates the footer from the actual page bottom. The default setting is two lines.*

The page length defines the total number of skipped and printed lines that exist on one page. Although the page length default setting is 66 lines, allowing 6 standard height lines per inch on 11-inch paper, you can adjust it to between 1 and 100 lines.

Since 1-2-3 and Symphony automatically reserve 6 lines on each page for the header, footer and spacers and you can control the number of lines used for the top and bottom margins, you can also control and calculate how many lines of a spreadsheet will fit on one page. Note that if you select /Print Printer Options Other Unformatted (1-2-3) or SERVICES Print Settings Page Breaks No (Symphony), headers, footers, spacers, and page-break margins will be suppressed. Also note that if you insert a page-break code on the worksheet with /Worksheet Page (1-2-3 Release 2/2.01) or MENU Page (Symphony, DOC Window), the printer will move to the top of a new page when it reaches that code no matter how much space is left on the current page.

EXTRA LINES APPEAR IN PRINTOUT

When I print a worksheet and then immediately print it again, large gaps appear at irregular intervals in the printout. This continues for four or five reprints, and then it returns to normal. The only solution I have found is to exit from the program and then reenter after printing the original. What is causing this to happen?

Rodger B. Smith
Scarborough, Maine

Your first worksheet printout probably ended somewhere in the middle of a page, perhaps line 33. Without leaving the Print command menu, you probably manually rolled the printer paper to the top of the next page before printing the second copy. Doing so causes the Lotus program's internal line counter to lose track of the top of the page. The line counter monitors the movement of paper through the printer.

When you first selected Print, the counter started at zero. It counted 66 lines for each page until it got to the last page, where it stopped counting at line 33, the last line of the printout. When you manually advanced the paper, the counter stayed at 33 and began counting lines again, starting with 34, when you selected Go to print the second copy. When the counter reached 66, which is normally the end of the page, it told the printer to begin a new page. In your case, this occurred somewhere in the middle of the page and resulted in the gap. After a few print runs, the printout ends at the bottom of a page, and on the next printout, the line counter is once again in sync with reality.

There are several solutions to this problem. After finishing the first print job, you can select Page (in 1-2-3) or Page-Advance (in Symphony) to move to the top of the next printer page without confusing the line counter. If you want to adjust the paper manually, remember to select Align before selecting Go. This will reset the line counter to zero. You could also select Quit and then reset the Print command.

PAGE LENGTH LIMIT OF 100

When I use the setup string \015\027S\001\0273\015 with an Epson printer, the printout yields 158 lines on an 11-inch page. Can't I get around the page length limit of 100 in *1-2-3* and *Symphony* so that I can take full advantage of this neat trick?

Russ Carr
San Jose, Calif.

By using the /Print Printer Options Other Unformatted command in 1-2-3 *or the SERVICES Print Settings Page Breaks No command in* Symphony, *you can print as many lines as can fit on one page. These commands suppress headers, footers, and page breaks, and the printer will continue to print even on the perforation of the paper.*

DETERMINING THE WIDTH OF YOUR SPREADSHEET

When I'm creating a report, I adjust the width of my worksheet columns to suit the width of the paper I'm using. However, I sometimes find it hard to determine the width of the report. To check it easily, I use an @CELL formula to determine the width of each cell to be printed. By totaling the results of these @CELL formulas using an @SUM formula, I can determine the exact width of my Print range.

For example, suppose I want to print columns A through M. To determine the total number of characters across that range, I would enter the formula @CELL ("width",A1..A1) below my data (let's say I put the formula in cell A150). Then I copy this formula across from column A to columns B through M. I place the formula @SUM(A150..M150) in column N to calculate the width of the Print range.

Since there is a default left margin of 4 spaces, I add 4 to the total to get the number I need to enter as my right print margin. If the total is larger than the number of characters my printer can print across the page, I can either change the Print range, change the margin settings, use compressed print, or use a wider sheet of paper.

Sonia Maverick
Long Beach, Calif.

Be sure to recalculate the spreadsheet after changing a column width. To set your right margin in 1-2-3, select /Print Printer Options Margins Right (in Symphony *select SERVICES Print Settings Margins Right) and enter the number.*

MULTIPLE COPIES

Every once in a while I try to print a range, and instead of getting a single printout, I get multiple printouts. What am I doing that causes this?

Patrick R. Ireland
Plessey Dynamics Corp.
Whippany, N.J.

Multiple copies of the same range are printed when you select Go on the Print menu and hold the key down long enough for the computer's auto repeat function to register several Go's instead of the one intended. It can also result from a faulty keyboard with a loose connection.

Another possibility is that you accidentally set up your print range as a border using /Print Printer Options Borders Rows (or Columns) or in Symphony, *SERVICES Print Settings Other Top-Labels (or Left-Labels). To cancel border settings, select /Print Printer Clear Borders (in* Symphony, *SERVICES Print Settings Other No-Labels).*

Some printers, such as the HP LaserJet Series II, can be set to print multiple copies.

USING THE WORKSHEET PAGE COMMAND

When I use the Worksheet Page command, sometimes it works and sometimes it doesn't. I used the command in seven files at the same location, yet the page break worked in some files and just printed the double colons in the others. Do you have any idea why this happens?

Wendy Nielson
The Church of Jesus Christ of Latter-Day Saints
Salt Lake City, Utah

You must insert a page break into a row of its own or a row that contains data you do not intend to print. Selecting /Worksheet Page (in Symphony *DOC, MENU Page) actually inserts a row. The page break must be in the leftmost column of the Print range.*

To enter the page break manually, insert a row where you would like the page break to occur. In Symphony, *you must be in a SHEET window. Enter a split vertical bar followed by two colons (¦ ::) and include the row in the Print range. If you precede the double colon with any other label prefix (for example, an apostrophe), it will be printed and no page break will occur.*

3

Entering the Print Range

BEING WHERE YOU WANT TO BE

I usually position my cell pointer in the range I want to print before executing the Print command. But the Print command always returns me to the previous print range when asking for a new print range. Unless I remember the cell address of the new range, I have to press Escape, find the new range, and specify it.

I discovered that, when prompted for a range, I can press Backspace instead of Escape, and *1-2-3* or *Symphony* returns me to the cell currently containing the pointer instead of returning me to the previous print range. This technique also works with other commands that remember ranges (Query, Graph, Data Fill, and so on).

James Loveridge
Overland Park, Kan.

RIDING THE RANGE

When you highlight a range, you can use the period (.) to move the active corner, represented by the blinking underline cursor, to each of the four corners of the range. This allows you to expand the range outward from the active corner in any direction.

David A. Martin
Pennsauken, New Jersey

In Symphony, *you can use the Tab key for the same purpose.*

PRINTING TWO RANGES

I would like to print two separate ranges of my worksheet next to each other — that is, range A10..B400 and range I10..J400. How can I do this without moving everything around?

Steven J. Riechers
Channel Lumber Company
Craigmont, Idaho

By specifying one of your ranges as a border and the other range as the print range, you can get the necessary results. In 1-2-3 select /Print Printer Options Borders and

252

specify the first range as the column border and the second range as the print range. In Symphony *select SERVICES Print Settings Other Left-Labels for one of the ranges and specify the other range as the print range. Note that if you specify a group of cells both as the border (Left-Labels or Top-Labels in* Symphony*) and as part of the print range, that range will print twice.*

*Printing two separate ranges can also be accomplished by using the MENU Width Hide command (*Symphony *Release 1.1/1.2) or the /Worksheet Column Hide command (1-2-3 Release 2/2.01). The columns that you hide will not appear in the printout.*

PRINTING DISTANT RANGES

Here is another method for printing noncontiguous rows or columns without the intervening cells. First save your worksheet, set Recalculation to Manual to keep formulas intact, then delete any columns or rows you don't want to appear in the printout. Now print. Simply retrieve the original file when you want to proceed.

Linda Stanley
ComputerEase
New York, N.Y.

1-2-3 Release 2/2.01 and Symphony *Release 1.1/1.2 let you hide the columns you don't want to print.*

WORKSHEET WIDTH

To set my print margins accurately, I find the width of my spreadsheet with a cell that counts 72 spaces. The ruler line in the cell looks like:

1... + ...10... + ...20...   ...70..

I keep this one cell in a special file and use the File Combine command to bring it into my worksheet (in an empty row starting in the first column of the print range) just before I print. I have three other width-measuring cells — each in its own worksheet — that contain 73 through 144, 145 through 216, and 217 through 260.

Joey Robichaux
Baton Rouge, La.

4

Headers and Footers

PAGE NUMBER IN HEADING — I

When I print my worksheet, how can I make the first page number be a number other than 1?

Joseph Amato
Digital Equipment Corp.
Littleton, Mass.

Suppose you want to begin the sequential page numbering at 7. Before you press Go, select Align. The Align command tells 1-2-3 Release 1A that you are starting at page number 1 by setting the line counter to zero. Next, turn your printer off-line and select the Page command six times. Each time you select Page, 1-2-3 increases the sequential page numbering by one. Now, turn your printer back on-line and select Go. The page number on the first page of your printout will be 7. (This technique doesn't work with 1-2-3 Release 2/2.01). In Symphony press SERVICES Print Align Settings Page Number Print-Number, and enter the number to print on the first page. Don't press Align again, since it would reset the Print-Number to 1.

PAGE NUMBER IN HEADING — II

You previously answered a question about page numbering with a technique that didn't work for *1-2-3* Release 2, which is what I own. How can I make the first page number in the header (or footer) be a number other than 1?

Mary K. Tortorici
Illinois Bell
Chicago, Ill.

Set the range to be printed, then select /Print Printer Options Unformatted and specify a page length of 1. Assuming you want your first page number to be 4, select Quit Align Page Page Page (press Page as many times as the number you want on the first page less one). The printer will advance the paper three lines. Roll the paper back to the top of the form (the perforations), reset the page length for a normal page (66 lines for 8½-by-11-inch paper), and select Go. The desired number will now

print in the header or footer. This method must also be used with 1-2-3 *Release 2.01.
Be sure not to select Align again after resetting the page length.*

TOP LABELS

I want to have column headings at the top of each page, but I can't enter a range of
cells to use as the header. Is there a way around this limitation?

Rand Coffman
Weyers Cave,Virginia

Select /Print Printer Options Borders Rows in 1-2-3 *or SERVICES Print Settings
Other Top-Labels in* Symphony, *then point to the row of labels you wish to use as
column headings. The portion of the Top-Label row located in the same columns as
your print range will be printed at the top of each page above the associated
columns of data.*

FOOTER WRAPAROUND

I have a problem with the footer when I print my worksheet using a wide-carriage
printer. When I specify the footer *BTC REPORT⌐ #⌐ @*, the printer properly positions
BTC REPORT flush left and the page number in the middle of the page, but the date
wraps onto the next line. For example, if today's date is 14-Apr-86, the date appears
as *14-* on the first line and *Apr-86* flush left on the next line. I use condensed print,
and I have set the right margin at 240. Can you help?

Kathleen Jackson
Journey Co.
Irvine, Calif.

What you specify as your left print margin is the key to the solution. 1-2-3 *and*
Symphony *use the left margin specification as the starting point for finding the right
margin location and, therefore, the printed layout of the rightmost header and
footer. Using condensed print on 14-inch-wide paper, if the total of the left and right
print margins exceeds the maximum character count of 240 (for example, a left
margin of 4 plus a right margin of 240), the footer will wrap around. Your left
margin must be zero to accommodate a right margin of 240.*

*Some printers, such as the Epson FX 100, print 16.667 characters per inch (cpi)
for condensed print instead of 17.16 cpi. Therefore, to avoid a wrap of approximately six characters, set the right margin to 233 (16.667 cpi times 14-inch-wide
paper equals 233.338).*

In addition, if 1-2-3 *or* Symphony *send a header or footer containing more
characters than can fit on one line, the extra characters will wrap to the next line.*

EJECTING THE LAST PAGE

I have a simple solution for getting the footer to print on the last page of a
multiple-page document. Whenever I complete a *Symphony* document, I insert a

hard page break (MENU Page) below the last line of the document. Then when I print the document, I need only select Go; I don't have to worry about advancing a page. In addition, this practice forces my HP Laserjet printer to automatically eject every document's last page without my having to press the manual form-feed button when the last page does not fill with text.

Margot S. Kruskall, MD
Dover, Mass.

With 1-2-3 Release 2/2.01 you can move to the first column of the first row below your print range, select /Worksheet Page, and include the additional row in your Print range to force a page-advance at the end of the report.

PRINTING ROW NUMBERS AND COLUMN LETTERS

How can I print my worksheet showing the column letters and row numbers? This would be helpful in a big worksheet when I want to refer someone else to a particular cell.

Hank Fisher
Sacramento, California

With the cell pointer in A1, insert a row and then insert a column. Move to cell A2 and select /Data Fill (1-2-3) or MENU Range Fill (Symphony) to number each row down to the bottom of the spreadsheet. Enter a Start value of 1 and a Step value of 1. Move to B1 and enter the column letters as far across as needed. Entering column letters is a tedious but one-time job. Once you have entered the column letters, you can use the File Xtract command to create a special file that contains only the column letters. You can then select /File Combine Copy to pull the prepared column letters into other files.

When printing, select the column of row numbers as a Border column (in Symphony, as left labels), the row of column letters as a Border row (in Symphony, as top labels), and make sure your print Source range includes neither row 1 nor column A.

5

Setup Strings and Attributes

ATTRIBUTE CHARACTERS DON'T COUNT

When I lay out a document that includes attribute characters, everything looks fine on the screen, meaning that all the columns are lined up properly. However, when I print it, everything in the line containing the attributes has been moved to the left. What's going on?

Ron Markvan
Office of Human Resources
Beaver, Pennsylvania

When Symphony prints a line containing attribute codes and symbols, it follows their directions in terms of print style, but they are not printed, and they do not affect the number of characters to be printed on that line. Symphony prints the full number of printable characters that the current margin allows. To get around this situation, arrange your data in columns first and then insert the attribute symbols. Ignore how the alignment appears on-screen.

EMBEDDING SETUP STRINGS

How can I embed setup (initialization) strings so that I can print part of my worksheet with compressed mode on and the rest of the worksheet with compressed mode off?

Larry Wolfe
Ventura, Calif.

You can enter setup (initialization) strings in worksheet cells to switch from one print style to another. Precede the setup string with two split vertical bars: The first one acts as the label-prefix character and will not be displayed in the cell; the second tells 1-2-3 Release 2/2.01 (or Symphony) that the following is a setup (initialization) string.

For example, ⦙⦙\015 will turn compressed mode on with an Epson printer. To turn compressed mode off, enter ⦙⦙\018 in a cell below the range you want printed in compressed type and above the range you want printed with compressed mode off.

Don't place any text, values, or formulas in other cells on the row containing the setup (initialization) string because 1-2-3 *Release 2/2.01 and* Symphony *won't recognize or print that information. Make sure you enter the setup (initialization) string in the leftmost column of your print range.*

MIXING PRINT MODES ON A SINGLE LINE

I have been using *1-2-3* Release 2's capability of assigning different print attributes (boldface, underline, and so forth) to different rows of a spreadsheet. Usually, I use the Worksheet Insert Row command to insert a blank row above and below the range I want to print with a special attribute. In the cell at the intersection of the upper inserted row and the leftmost column of the Print range, I enter two split vertical bars (¦¦), followed by the setup string I wish to use. For example, to make an Epson printer print boldface, I enter ¦¦\027\069 (do not enter a label prefix before the split vertical bars). In the cell at the intersection of the lower blank row and the leftmost column of the Print range, I enter the setup string to turn that feature off — in this case, ¦¦\027\070. If you do not enter the second setup string, the printer will continue to print in that mode until you reset the printer by either turning it off or sending a reset code (for Epson, \027@).

Since this method limits you to changing print modes between lines, I developed a way to change modes on a single line. To do so, you must enter all text for that line into a single cell in the leftmost column of the Print range. The cell entry should begin with two split vertical bars, followed by text. When you want to start a particular print attribute, enter the setup string as part of the text. For example:

¦¦This line contains \027\069emphasized,\027\070 and \015condensed\018 print.

¦¦This line is in \0274italic\0275and\027\045\049underlined\027\045\048 print.

When you print those entries, the setup strings will disappear and the words between them will be printed using the specified attributes. Since the attribute setup string won't print, you must subtract the number of characters it occupies from the length of the string in order to calculate how wide the printed result will be. For example, if your printer has a maximum width of 80 characters, your actual Print range could be 100 characters across and still fit within that space if 20 of those characters compose setup strings.

Douglas M. Horner
Washington, D.C.

The setup strings used in the foregoing examples work with an Epson printer. For information on which setup strings to use with your printer, refer to your printer's manual and the relevant sections of the 1-2-3 *documentation. Check to see if* 1-2-3 *advances the printer to the next line after printing the specially formatted cell. If not, you can either add the setup string for a line-feed to the end of the cell's contents or leave the next row blank.*

CHANGING PRINT STYLES

I've created a file that contains all the printer control strings I use on my Epson printer. Beneath each string I've written a brief description of the printer code. I select /File Combine Copy (SERVICES File Combine Copy in *Symphony*) to transfer the file into a blank area of the worksheet I wish to print. I then copy the control strings to the relevant locations on the worksheet.

Thomas Hart
Dedham, Mass.

1-2-3 Release 1A users can use this technique only to provide a reference of setup strings since Release 1A can issue setup strings only from its menu.

DOUBLE-SPACED PRINTING

I use *1-2-3* to write short memos and letters. I would like my Epson to print them double-spaced. How can I do this?

Jennifer Reiley
Urbana, Illinois

The /Print Options Setup command (SERVICES Print Settings Init-String in Symphony) lets you send your printer control codes that activate special print features such as condensed, emphasized, enlarged, or italic type. You should enter these codes as three-digit numbers preceded by a backslash. For example, \015 is the Epson code for condensed type.

Your Epson manual describes how to use a control code to set the line spacing to any number of seventy-seconds (n/72) of an inch. Single-spaced text is printed with six lines to the inch. Dividing 72 by 6 gives you a spacing of 12 seventy-seconds (12/72) of an inch between each line. Double spacing requires doubling the space between lines to 24 seventy-seconds (24/72) of an inch.

The control code listed in the Epson manual is Esc A n, *where n is the number of seventy-seconds of an inch you want between each line. In the ''Printer Control Code'' appendix of your 1-2-3 manual, the three-digit number for Escape appears as \027, and the code for capital A is \065. You should note that capital and lowercase letters require different codes. Putting a zero in front of 24 converts it to a three-digit number without changing its value. Therefore, the setup string you should enter for Escape A 24 is \027\065\024.*

This setup code moves the paper forward two spaces every time it would normally move forward one space, so you should set your page length to 33. This also doubles the amount of space at the top and bottom of the page, so you should adjust your margins. Remember that this doubles the space between headers or footers and the body of text. If using headers and footers, set top and bottom margins to 0.

REFERENCING PRINTER CONTROL CODES

When you were asked about using formulas to reference a table of printer control codes, you said this couldn't be done because *1-2-3* and *Symphony* won't recognize the code in the format of a formula. I have found a way to accomplish this with an Epson FX printer and *1-2-3* Release 2/2.01.

Enter the printer control code or setup strings (initialization strings in *Symphony*) as labels in your worksheet. To use one of these codes, position the cell pointer where you want the setup string and enter a formula referencing the cell with the desired code. For instance, if the Epson code for condensed print is in cell AA1, enter + AA1. Leave the cell pointer on the formula cell and press EDIT CALC Return. The printer control code is now in the format *1-2-3* or *Symphony* requires. You can also give each control code a range name and use that range name in the formula (for example, + *condensed*).

Mary Levesque
Omaha, Nebr.

Each of the setup strings must be originally entered with a preceding label-prefix character such as an apostrophe (') so that both split vertical bars are displayed.

UNDERLINING ONE WORD IN A CELL

You can use the COMPOSE key to underline selected characters in a cell when printing in *1-2-3* Release 2/2.01. Press EDIT and move the cursor after the character you want to underline. Then press COMPOSE (Alt-F1 on an IBM PC), type *mg* (for merge), and press the underline character (on the same key as the hyphen). What appears on the screen is the letter, followed by an arrow and the underline character. When *1-2-3* prints this, it will print the letter, then back up and print the underline.

The process may seem tedious since you must enter the merge sequence after each letter you want underlined, but it's a great solution when you have a boss who requires underlining. The technique works in *Symphony* as well.

Linda Haefer
Great-West Life Center
Englewood, Colo.

This only works on printers that have backspace capability.

CAN'T EMBED SETUP STRINGS IN 1A

Is there a way to change the print mode within a Release 1A worksheet?

Joan S. Berry
Laurel Fuel Co.
Jackson, Miss.

There is no direct way to embed setup strings in 1-2-3 Release 1A. That feature was added to 1-2-3 Release 2/2.01 and Symphony. *However, you can write a macro.*

You can set up a macro that uses a different setup string for each range of the worksheet. For example, assume that you have three ranges you want to print in three different print styles — the first you want printed in boldface, and the second in italics, and the third in condensed print. You can print the three ranges in different print modes on an Epson FX series printer with the following macro. See the instructions below if you have another printer:

	A	B	C
1	\p	/PPAQ	
2	loop	/C~range~{RIGHT}	
3		/C~setup~	
4		/PPR{BS}	
5	range		
6		~OS1{ESC}\027@	
7	setup		
8		~QGLQ{LEFT}{DOWN}	
9		/XGloop~	
10			
11			
12	Range	Setup	
13	rng1	\027G	
14	rng2	\0274	
15	rng3	\015	

Before using the macro, make sure to align the printer paper so that the perforation is at the printhead. Use the Range Name Create command to name the ranges you want to print. For example, to print range D10..G20, select /Range Name Create, enter the range name (in this example, rng1*), and specify range D10..G20. Then record range names in a column with their associated setup strings in the adjacent cells to the right as shown in range A13..B15. Make sure that cells below the last line of this table are blank; otherwise, the macro will try to use them. Next, to assign the labels in column A as range names for the adjacent cells in column B, select /Range Name Labels Right and indicate range A1..A7. Before invoking the macro, position the pointer in cell A13, the cell containing the range name of the first Print range. The macro will automatically stop when the last range name in the table has been printed. Return 1-2-3 to Ready mode by pressing Escape several times. You can control the spacing between the ranges you print by changing the macro code in cell B8 (each L advances the printer one line).*

For other printers, check the printer manual for a list of appropriate control codes, translate the control codes into setup strings (see your 1-2-3 documentation), and insert them in the list starting in cell A13. For printers other than the Epson FX

series printers, replace the contents of cell B6 with ~OS1{ESC}master reset, where
master reset is your printer's master-reset code (if there is one). Check your printer
manual to make sure the master-reset code will not cause unintended results. (You
can skip the master-reset step in 1-2-3 Release 2/2.01 and Symphony).

To run the macro, place the cell pointer on the first range name to be printed (in
this example, cell A13), then hold down the MACRO key (Alt on most computers) and
press P. (For more details, consult your 1-2-3 documentation on invoking macros).

PRINTER PRINTS ON SAME LINE

When I try to print part of my spreadsheet using *1-2-3*, the printer doesn't advance,
and all of the text is printed on the same line. Can you help?

Jerry Woldman
Children's Hospital
Washington, D.C.

Neither 1-2-3 nor the printer are issuing a line-feed command after each carriage
return. Select /Worksheet Global Default Status and check whether Auto-LF is set to
Yes. Yes means that 1-2-3 assumes the printer is issuing a line-feed command so
1-2-3 will not. Change Auto-LF to No by selecting /Worksheet Global Default Printer
Auto-LF No. 1-2-3 will now send a line-feed after each carriage return.

RESETTING REMOTE PRINTER

If you've ever attempted to print a letter from your word processor after printing a
compressed mode worksheet, you know that printers don't automatically reset to 10
characters per inch. Since *1-2-3* Release 1.A and *Symphony* don't contain a Printer
Reset command, you're forced to turn the printer off and back on again, which resets
it to the default characters per inch. However, this can be a difficult operation if your
printer happens to be located far from your desk.

An alternative is to print your worksheet, then before you quit, print a second
range containing one blank cell using the print setup strings you want the printer to
retain.

Kim A. Heathman
Jenkon Data Systems
Vancouver, Wash.

RESETTING YOUR PRINTER

In a previous tip, one reader suggested resetting a printer by printing a blank cell after
specifying the desired setup string. While this works, it is unnecessary and, worse,
you'll be disappointed when someone else uses the printer but doesn't use the
technique. I have adopted the following as a standard.

In my configuration settings, I specify *Symphony*'s or *1-2-3*'s default setup string
to be my printer's master reset code — the code that initializes the printer to its state
when first turned on. For example, the reset code for Epson FX printers is \027\064.

So in *Symphony* I select SERVICES Configuration Printer Init-String and then enter \027\064 (in *1-2-3*, select /Worksheet Global Default Printer Setup). I select Update to save the specification. Whenever I use the default string, the printer automatically resets before printing. When I change the setup string, I append it to the master reset code, so the printer is first reset, then set for my new settings. I am assured that previous settings have not been retained.

Robert Wierman
Redding, Calif.

Unfortunately, not all printers have a master reset code.

6

Solving Problems

PRINTING FORMULAS

Is it possible to print the formulas of a complex worksheet to trace its logic? Can I print the cell addresses along with the formulas?

Paul Hopkins
Doraville, Ga.

Yes, it is possible to print cell formulas in both 1-2-3 *and* Symphony. *Specify a range and select /Print Printer Options Other Cell-Formulas (1-2-3) or SERVICES Print Settings Other Format Cell-Formulas (Symphony). The cell entries are listed one per line.*

Another approach is to format the cells for Text (1-2-3) or Literal (Symphony). Be sure to widen the columns to display the whole formula. This method won't print cell addresses, but will show formulas in their correct position on the worksheet.

CREATING NONPRINTING ROWS

I have discovered a feature of *1-2-3* Release 2/2.01 and *Symphony* that I cannot find mentioned in the manual. When you enter the split vertical bar (the character sharing the backslash key on an IBM PC keyboard) as the first character in a cell, the entire row to its right will not be printed, provided the cell containing the split vertical bar is in the first column of the print range. You can use this technique to stop rows from printing.

	A	B
1	The answer is yes	
2	The answer is yes	
3	The answer is no	
4	The answer is no	
5	The answer is yes	

Using the column to the left of a database, enter the split vertical bars in rows you don't want to print. This character does not hide the rows on the screen; it only prevents them from being printed. The figure on the previous page shows labels entered in cells B1 through B5. Cells A3 and A4 contain the split vertical bar. The character does not appear in the cells; it appears only in the control panel.

When you print the range A1..B5, the following is the result:

The answer is yes
The answer is yes
The answer is yes

You can use text to the right of the vertical-bar characters as nonprinting internal notes on the worksheet.

Thomas Jarrell
Floyd S. Pike Electrical Contractor
Mount Airy, N.C.

The split vertical bar is usually used to embed printer setup strings in a worksheet. In this example, column A must be included in the print range and no other character can be in the same cell as the vertical bar.

MORE THAN ONE PRINTER DRIVER

I cannot specify the default printer when I install my driver set. No matter which text printer I select first in the *1-2-3* Release 2/2.01 Install Program procedures, the same driver (for the C. Itoh) is the default when I load *1-2-3*. I would like to have the IBM driver as the default, with the C. Itoh available for selection. I can switch to the IBM printer after loading *1-2-3* by selecting /Worksheet Global Default Printer Name, so I've written an autoexecuting macro that selects the desired printer. Is this macro necessary?

J.E. Kirkpatrick
Aeronautical Research & Management
Canyon Lake, Tex.

Select /Worksheet Global Default Printer Name, specify the desired printer, then select Quit Update from the menu. This preserves the new setting as the default printer by modifying the 1-2-3 *configuration file. If you don't update the configuration file, the new setting is lost.* Symphony *users can select SERVICES Configuration Printer Name, specify the printer, then select Quit Update. If you're using a floppy-drive system, be sure the* 1-2-3 *System Disk or* Symphony *Program Disk is in the drive before you select Update.*

GETTING PRINTER ERROR WITH RELEASE 2

If you get the message *Printer error* while trying to print with *1-2-3* Release 2/2.01, try one of the following procedures.

If you have a parallel printer designated as Parallel 1, select /Worksheet Global Default Printer Interface 5 (DOS Device LPT1). If it's designated as Parallel 2, select Interface 6 (DOS Device LPT2).

If you have a serial printer, you may need to use the DOS MODE command to specify your printer's baud rate and interface settings. (Consult your DOS manual for information about MODE.) The baud rate you set with the MODE command must match the baud rate of your printer. (Consult your printer's manual for information on setting the baud rate.) *1-2-3* requires no parity, 8 data bits, and 1 stop bit. You must also select the printer interface that matches the DOS output device you define with MODE. Select /Worksheet Global Default Printer Interface and select 5, 6, 7, or 8, depending on what you selected with MODE.

Katherine Jones
New York, N.Y.

If you get this printer error, first make sure that the correct text printer is current by selecting /Worksheet Global Default Status. If the correct printer isn't listed, refer to your documentation and go through the Install program again to change the default text printer.

Also make sure the printer is turned on, is on-line, and the cable is securely connected to the port specified in the default printer interface.

SLOW PRINTING WITH EPSON LQ-1500 & 1-2-3 RELEASE 2.01

I recently upgraded to *1-2-3* Release 2.01, and I find that my Epson LQ-1500 printer pauses before each line-feed, adding considerable print time. The printer worked fine with Release 2. Am I missing something?

Marvin Berkowitz
Andal Corp.
New York, N.Y.

If you have a Quadram Quadboard, check your CONFIG.SYS file for the following command to load a Quadclock: DEVICE = QUADCLOK.SYS. If you find this command, remove it, either with a text editor (such as DOS's Edlin) or by reentering the CONFIG.SYS commands, omitting DEVICE = QUADCLOK.SYS. This command appears to cause the Epson LQ-1500 to slow down when you print with 1-2-3 Release 2.01.

KEYBOARD LOCKUP

On several occasions I have accidentally pressed the PrintScreen key while holding down the Shift key instead of pressing just the Shift key. If the computer isn't attached to a printer, the computer locks up, and any unsaved work is lost when I restart the computer. Is there any way to unlock the keyboard without restarting the computer?

Theresa C. Benton
Greenbelt, Md.

The only way you can unfreeze the keyboard quickly is to connect a printer (one that works with the software you are using) to the computer and allow it to print the screen. Of course, you can wait for the PrintScreen instruction to run its course, which usually takes longer.

STACK OVERFLOW PROBLEM

I sometimes get an error message that reads *Stack Overflow* or some variation of that. When this happens, the program crashes. Have I discovered a fatal flaw?

Pam Lemtar
Sharon, Massachusetts

You have run across a known problem — but one built into the IBM PC. And this problem can affect any program you run, even DOS. It occurs when you type more keystrokes than the current program can absorb so that the computer's type-ahead buffer fills and the computer starts beeping while you continue to press keys. This situation typically occurs when you try to send a file to an unattached or off-line printer. The printer driver senses something is wrong and takes a 60-second time out — 30 seconds of nothing, then 30 seconds of a flashing WAIT indicator. In the midst of this, you probably tried to get some response by pressing additional keystrokes, which triggered the crash.

To avoid this problem, don't try to print unless your printer is attached and on-line. If you make this mistake, however, don't panic — the computer will come back in about 60 seconds. If the computer doesn't come back, you should check to see if you have a malfunctioning board.

7

Symphony

THE QUICK WAY TO PRINT A DOCUMENT

If you are working in a DOC window and wish to print your entire letter or manuscript, you do not have to enter a Print Settings Source Range. Make sure the Source setting on the Print settings sheet is blank. If it's not, select Source Cancel. Now just press SERVICES and select Print Align Go. *Symphony* will print the whole document. This works no matter how long the document and no matter where your cursor is located within the text.

RECALCULATION AND PRINTING

I am using *Symphony* Release 1 and have Recalculation set to Manual. Yet every time I print, the worksheet is recalculated. Why?

Sandra Stewart
Manis Wholesale Co.
Rome, Ga.

When you use Symphony *Release 1/1.01 and print from a FORM window with the Source setting on the Print settings sheet set to Database,* Symphony *recalculates the worksheet twice — once after you select Print from the SERVICES menu and once after printing. If you print from a SHEET window,* Symphony *recalculates the worksheet only after it finishes printing.*

Symphony Release 1.1/1.2 recalculates the worksheet after it finishes printing only if you are printing from either a FORM or SHEET window and if Source on the Print settings sheet is set to Database.

If Source on the Print settings sheet is set to Range, no release of Symphony *will recalculate as a result of printing, regardless of whether Recalculation is set to Manual or Automatic.*

If printing a multiple-pass report, Symphony *will also recalculate after each pass.*

MIXING SINGLE- AND DOUBLE-SPACING

I wanted to double-space my worksheet (about 200 rows) to make it easier to read, yet restrict my Tob-Labels range (about 6 rows deep) to single-spacing. I found I can switch to a *Symphony* DOC window and insert a format line above and below the Top-Labels range. I set the line spacing to 1 on the upper format line and 2 on the lower. I then expand the Top-Labels range to include both format lines.

To make it easier for those less familiar with DOC windows, I simplified the method. In a SHEET window, enter a split vertical bar (¦) followed by the line spacing value (1, 2, or 3) in the positions described above. Then you need not leave the SHEET window to use this feature. Nothing else in the current Print range should be entered on the rows containing the split vertical bar, as *Symphony* will not print them.

Emily D. Lanin
Minneapolis, Minn.

The page length setting must be modified to account for the new spacing.

LONG LABELS WON'T PRINT

When I print my spreadsheet, the long labels are cut off. I have adjusted the Print and Window settings sheets, but I can't find the problem.

Bob Lange
Peekskill, New York

When you select SERVICES Print Settings Source Range, be sure to expand the highlight to cover the entire width of the long label. Anything not highlighted will not appear in the printout. This is also the case with 1-2-3 Release 2/2.01.

FORMAT LINES VERSUS PRINTER MARGINS

I want to print my text with wide margins on both sides. When I narrow the margins on the Print settings sheet, the left margin is fine, but the right side of each line is truncated. What should I do?

Ben Posner
Bloomington, Illinois

You are changing the wrong settings. You should use a format line to narrow the margins of your document. To do so, insert a format line at the top of the document. Select MENU Format Create, and then press Return. Next select Margins, and enter the desired settings.

Format line margins are calculated by the number of characters from the first potential character location on the left side of the text area. A left margin of 3 means that each line starts with two blanks preceding the first character. A right margin of 66 means that the last character of each line is 66 spaces from the left margin of the document's text area. These margin settings, for example, allow 64 characters on each line, including blanks you create by pressing the Spacebar or Tab key.

Because of the word-wrap feature, each line may contain fewer than the maximum possible number of characters. You can disable word wrap by pressing the Insert key, which turns on Overstrike mode, or by changing the justification setting to None.

In the Print settings sheet, the margin settings control the size of the white-space border that surrounds the text area of the document on each page. The print margin settings are added to any format line margin settings. For example, if the left print margin setting is 10 and the format line left margin setting is 3, the printer first moves 10 spaces in from the left edge of the paper, then leaves two blank spaces and types the first character in the 13th space.

The Print settings sheet right margin determines the rightmost character of each line that is printed. A right print margin of 50 means that the printer prints only the characters that are within 50 spaces of the left edge of the paper.

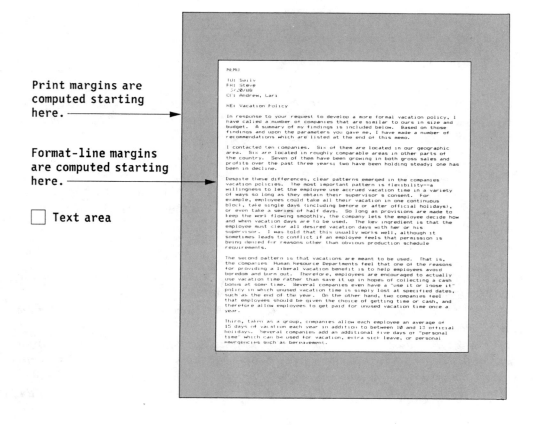

Print margins are computed starting here. ─────────►

Format-line margins are computed starting here. ─────────►

☐ Text area

The cause of your trouble is the difference between the format line, which measures its right margin starting from the left edge of the text area, and the print setting, which measures its right margin from the left edge of the paper. For example, assume the following settings:

	Left	Right
Print	10	50
Format	3	66

The first character of each line will be printed in the 13th space on the page. Each line of the document extends 64 spaces to the 76th space on the page. However, the print margin will truncate each line at the 50th space.

It is easiest to keep your right print margin wide and control the width of your printed text with format lines.

PRINTING INTERMEDIATE PAGES OF A REPORT

Symphony supposedly allows you to print any part of a multipage report with complete control of the page numbering. I specified a source range that covered the entire worksheet and specified 2 as both the print number and the start number. My header correctly contained 2 as the page number, but the material that printed out was from page 1. What is the problem?

Sally Mathes
Holley, New York

This is a problem with Symphony *Release 1/1.01 that was corrected in Release 1.1/1.2. The start number is the page number at which you want* Symphony *to begin printing. For example, if you have a 12-page report and want to print only pages 6 through 8, you would enter 1 for Print-Number, 6 for Start-Page, and 8 for End-Page. The printed pages would be numbered 6 through 8.*

As part of this process, no matter what you enter for Start-Page, Symphony *goes to the top of the source range and counts lines and pages (according to the page length setting you are using — which is usually 66 lines per page) in order to find the first line of your desired starting page. As* Symphony *divides up the source range into pages, it normally considers the first 66 lines to be page 1 of the report. However, this is actually controlled by the Print-Number setting. If you enter a Print-Number of 6,* Symphony *considers the first 66 lines to be the sixth page of the report, not the first page.*

This relationship between Print-Number and Start-Page leads to some interesting results and problems. If you enter a number for Start-Page that is equal to or smaller than the Print-Number, Symphony *starts printing at the very top of your source range but uses the Print-Number to number the pages. On the other hand, if you use a Print-Number of 3 and a Start-Page of 6,* Symphony *considers the first 66 lines to be page number 3 and counts ahead through pages 3, 4, and 5 to the top of what it considers to be page 6, which it then prints and labels as page 6 in your footer or header. However, this is actually the fourth page of your report, not the sixth page.*

One result of this relationship is that there doesn't seem to be any way to tell Symphony *Release 1/1.01 to start printing at the fifth page of the report and give it a page number of 1. Fortunately, this problem has been corrected in later releases of* Symphony.

SECTION
13

COMMUNICATIONS

1*-2-3* does not contain a communications environment. *Symphony* does. So much of this section will be of primary interest to *Symphony* users. However, several of the techniques will be useful to anyone who does telecommunications.

Telecommunications seems relatively straightforward. You connect two computers with a phone line and transmit data. Reality is not quite so simple. For example, both computers must be using the same protocol, which means, among other things, that both computers must be expecting to send and/or receive information at the same speed. Both computers have to use the same kind of error correction systems to compensate for any "noise" or other causes of interference that might garble the transmission. And both computers have to recognize the same codes that indicate when transmission is beginning or ending.

As if that weren't enough, once connection is made, both computers have to be speaking the same language. It does no good to be able to call Athens if you can't speak Greek and the other person doesn't speak English. And even if you both know Greek, you have to be using the same dialect; ancient Greek is not the same as modern Greek.

Despite these complexities, which often turn telecomputing into a lengthy exercise in frustration, the fruits of success are so sweet that the effort is worthwhile. The ability to instantly send inventory updates to hundreds of branch offices or collect budget information from the other side of the world not only increases your ability to do business, but also can change the way your business is done.

The good ideas in this section do not have such grandiose purposes. However, they should help *Symphony* users figure out how to make better use of the COMM environment.

1

Symphony Communications

**CONNECTING COMM SETTINGS SHEETS
WITH SPECIFIC WORKSHEETS**

If you usually communicate with one particular remote computer, your company's mainframe, or an information service, you can save yourself the trouble of constantly creating the needed settings sheet.

Enter the required settings, then select Name Save. The settings sheet will be saved in a special file that will have a CCF file extension.

Next configure *Symphony* to load that file automatically and use it as the initial COMM settings sheet. Select SERVICES Configuration Communications Set, and then put the pointer on or type in the name of the desired CCF file. If typing, make sure to include the disk-drive letter and full path name. Then select Update from the menu to save the new configuration file as your default configuration settings sheet.

You can, of course, create and save additional CCF files and use them when you desire by using the COMM window's Settings Name Retrieve command.

Finally, you can connect any one of these supplementary CCF files to particular worksheets. For example, suppose you mainly communicate with your mainframe but you occasionally dial up Dow Jones. You have prepared a special worksheet that parses incoming stock information and updates your portfolio. To load the DJ.CCF file automatically every time you retrieve the Dow Jones worksheet, first retrieve the spreadsheet. Select SERVICES Settings Communications Set, put the pointer on, or type in, the name of the desired CCF file, including the disk-drive letter and full path name. Select Quit without updating and then save the file under the same name. Every time you retrieve the file, the DJ.CCF file will be made current.

CHANGING INTERFACE SETTINGS

When I try to configure *Symphony*'s Communications Settings sheet, I can't set any of the Interface settings using the command MENU Settings Interface. Why?

Bob Gleason
Weston, Mass.

274

Part of the installation procedure asks "Do you plan to use communications?" If you responded No to this question, Symphony *will not permit you to set any of the Communications Interface settings. Go back into the Install program and respond Yes to this question.*

DOUBLE VISION DURING COMM?

When I am in a COMM window and communicating with another computer, why does my monitor display two characters for every one I strike?

Lynn Schrieboffer
Montclair, New Jersey

Symphony *communicates with remote computers in two ways. The remote computer either echoes the characters you send back to your screen or it doesn't. If every character you type disappears into the blankness of your screen, and you wish to see what you are typing on your own screen, you must turn on* Symphony*'s internal echoing facility by going to the COMM settings sheet and changing Echo to Yes.*

If every character you type appears twice, you probably are transmitting to an echoing system and also have the Echo setting of your COMM window at Yes. To correct this, select MENU Settings Terminal Echo No.

ASCII CODE ALTERNATIVES

I routinely prepare the first draft of my reports and letters using the *Symphony* DOC window. Then I send the text to my secretary's word processor for final editing and publication. I use modems and the Transmit-Range command in the COMM window to transfer the document. However, an end-of-line symbol appears at the end of each line in the text, which my secretary must remove before she can edit the document. This is very time-consuming on large documents.

I solve the problem by replacing the \m code adjacent to the SEND EOL: prompt in the COMM window setting with the ASCII code for space (\032). Failure to enter a space code at the SEND EOL prompt causes the last word of each line to join the first word of the next line. I then transmit the document as one long paragraph.

To solve the justification problem on the word processor, I simply enter two slashes at the beginning of each paragraph as I first type the document. (Actually, any symbol will do, as long as it's not found elsewhere in the text.) After transmission, I search for the symbols and quickly justify the text.

Steve Grigory
San Antonio, Tex.

2

Log-in, Settings, and Capture

VARIABLE RECEIVE STRINGS IN COMM LOG-IN SHEETS

The Log-in settings sheet of a COMM window lets you enter both parts of the "dialogue" you need to go through every time you hook up to an electronic database or mainframe computer. *Symphony* will transmit the Send string, then wait to hear the Receive string before transmitting the next Send string.

Each Send and Receive string you enter can have a maximum of 30 characters. The Receive string must exactly match what is sent to *Symphony*, or else *Symphony* has no way of knowing that it is OK to proceed.

But what if the other computer sends you a string that is more than 30 characters long, or that contains variable information such as the current time and date?

The solution is to enter the last few characters of the string you know will be sent to you. *Symphony* will ignore all the rest of the incoming data, including the variable parts, while it waits for something to arrive that exactly matches the characters you entered.

CONTROLLING LOG-IN SEQUENCE

When using the Phone-and-Login command in the COMM window, I found that the log-in starts before the connection is made. If I wait for the connection and manually start the log-in sequence, it works fine. What am I doing wrong?

James Perry
Bristol, Conn.

It sounds like the OnLine *indicator was already on when you started the Phone-and-Login. The most common cause for this is incorrect switch settings on the modem. On the Hayes 1200 modem, switch 6 must be in the off or open position for* Symphony *to correctly interpret the presence or absence of a connection (carrier). Switch 3 must be off or open on the Hayes 1200B.*

In a Phone-and-Login sequence, Symphony *dials the number, then waits for the* OnLine *indicator to come on. If this indicator is incorrectly on due to the switch settings,* Symphony *prematurely starts the log-in sequence.*

SYMPHONY AND DOW JONES

Can you help me connect to the Dow Jones News/Retrieval service?

Kenneth J. Friedman
Cupertino, Calif.

Assuming you call Dow Jones directly, here are the settings you should enter on the Communications Settings sheet (select MENU Settings in a COMM window).

INTERFACE

Baud:	1200
Parity:	None
Length:	8
Stop bits:	1

TERMINAL

Screen:	Window
Echo:	No
Linefeed:	No
Backspace:	Backspace
Wrap:	Yes
Delay:	20

SEND

EOL:	\013
Delay:	20
Response:	(leave blank)

HANDSHAKING

Inbound:	No
Outbound:	No

Enter the following settings on the Login Settings sheet (select MENU Settings Login). Make sure to use uppercase and lowercase letters as indicated, since Dow Jones is case-sensitive; otherwise, a time-out error will occur. Replace the lowercase x's with your Dow Jones identifier numbers.

	COUNT	SEND (maximum time 20)		RECEIVE (repeat time 5)
A	4	\013	A	TERMINAL =
B	2	d1\013	B	@
C	2	c dow\013	C	PLEASE?
D	2	djns\013	D	\019
E	2	xxxxxxxxx\013	E	DOW JONES

COMM DATA CAPTURE

Why am I having problems capturing data into the correct columns during a COMM session? I've tried to set the column widths to match the size of the data.

John R. Bauer
The Pillsbury Co.
Minneapolis, Minn.

The column widths that you see during a Capture procedure are the column widths in the window being used for the COMM session. Did you set up multiple windows — one for the COMM environment and one for the SHEET environment? Column widths in one window don't affect those in the other window. Make the COMM window current, press TYPE and select SHEET. Adjust the columns to the appropriate widths and then press SWITCH to return to the COMM window. Also, be sure to specify a sufficiently wide multicolumn capture range instead of a single-column capture range.

HAYES SMARTMODEMS

Are you using the Hayes 1200- or 2400-baud Smartmodems? Are you getting an *OnLine* indicator message at the bottom of your monitor every time you load *Symphony*? This *OnLine* message is supposed to indicate that you have established connection with another computer. If you haven't, and the indicator displays otherwise, and you are using a Hayes 1200-baud modem, you may need to change switch 6 from On to Off. If you are using a Hayes 2400-baud modem, you will need to set its switches via software (model 2400 has no DIP switches). To set switch 6 to Off, open a COMM window and enter *AT&C1&S1&W*.

Sonya G. Ruffin
Business Computer Solutions
Washington, D.C.

COMMUNICATING WITH A DIRECT CONNECT

I am unable to get *Symphony* to communicate through a direct-connect 9600-baud link. Can you help?

Mike Donovan
Advance, N.C.

With a direct connect, the computers are hard-wired together. Although you don't have to type in any identifier numbers (passwords), the same rules that apply for other communications apply for the direct connect.

You must be sure that both systems use the same interface settings. For example, the baud rate, parity, word length, and stop bits must match between the sending and receiving computers. Also make sure that Echo is set to Yes on the Communications Settings sheet on both computers.

With Symphony *Release 1/1.01, you must install the driver for the COM port that you'll be using. If your driver is set to COM1 and you are using COM2 for the direct connect, you will not make a connection.* Symphony *Release 1.1/1.2's driver installation program asks if you want to use communications, and then the* Symphony *program allows you to choose which COM port you want to use on the Communications Settings sheet.*

SECTION
14

MACROS

Macro magic! The ability to automate repeated procedures, to create turnkey applications for other people, to use *1-2-3* and *Symphony* as a programming environment: all this and more are what make macros so exciting. Macros are a type of programming language, with some of the same capabilities of more formal languages. *1-2-3* and *Symphony* macros combine the simplicity of a BASIC-like language with the power of an integrated worksheet product. Because they can be approached on the most introductory level as well as on the most sophisticated, *1-2-3* and *Symphony* macros are one of the most widely used programming languages in the world today. In fact, for many people, macros are the only programming language they'll ever need to know.

Of course, like all programming languages, macros have their idiosyncrasies and limitations. But these are more than offset by their ease of use. One of the special macro features that *Symphony* offers, and that is also found in the Learn Add-in for *1-2-3* Release 2/2.01, is the "learn" facility. In this mode, the program keeps track of each keystroke you make as you work through a particular procedure. You are then able to edit and "play back" the recording — instant macro. While this method is fine for simple macros and for learning the basics, it doesn't automatically incorporate the more sophisticated and powerful flow-of-control commands that make macros a form of programming language. These advanced commands must be inserted manually.

We have already published a complete book on macros, *The Macro Book*, that compiles most of *LOTUS* magazine's Macro, Macro Basics, and For Developers columns, along with key macro-oriented feature articles. However, macros are so rich a topic that one book could not possibly exhaust the store of good ideas, so we have included additional tips for creating more-efficient macros and for finding the bugs that will inevitably creep into your first-draft code.

1

More-Efficient Macros

MACRO NAME CONSISTENCY

When I began using *1-2-3*, I would name my first macro \a, my second \b, and so on. However, I could never remember which macro did what on which worksheet. Now I name my macros by function. For example, the macro named \s is always a macro to save the current worksheet, the macro named \p is for printing, and the macro named \a always takes me to the macro section of the worksheet. Each worksheet usually includes a "mega-macro" that does most of the heavy-duty work, and I call that macro \w.

Stephen O'Keefe
Seattle, Washington

HOW TO STOP A MACRO

Whenever I put two or more macros in a worksheet, they always run sequentially. I cannot get one macro to execute at a time. Once my macros start, I cannot stop them. What am I doing wrong?

Jeffrey Adams
Lawrence, Kansas

Lotus programs read macros cell by cell down a column. You probably entered your macros one on top of the other in the same column. If your first macro is in cell A1, your second macro is right below it in cell A2, the next one is in A3, and so on. The software cannot tell where one macro ends and the next begins. Therefore, each time you start a macro, all the macros beneath it also run.

You have two choices. You can either leave a blank cell between the end of one macro and the beginning of the next, or, in most cases, you can put a Quit command at the end of each macro. Use /XQ in 1-2-3 Release 1A and {QUIT} in 1-2-3 Release 2/2.01 and Symphony.

By the way, you can usually stop a macro by pressing the Break key (Control-Break on the IBM PC).

282

REPEATING MACRO KEYWORDS

Any macro keyword can contain arguments that control how many times *1-2-3* Release 2/2.01 or *Symphony* will repeat that command. For example, the {ESC} keyword, which causes the macro to press the Escape key once, can also be written as {ESC 2} which causes the macro to press that key twice. I discovered that the numeric argument (the 2 in the preceding example) can consist of not only a number but a cell address or the range name of a cell containing a number. For example, the command {UP 5} in a macro causes the cell pointer to move up five cells. If the value 5 is in a cell named CNT, the command {UP CNT} causes the cell pointer to move up 5 cells as well.

Kurt Henning
South Hartford, N.Y.

SUPPRESSING SCREEN FLICKER

My monitor screen keeps flickering when I run my macro. This slows everything down. What can I do?

William Cavallini
Baltimore, Maryland

Every time your macro makes a cell entry, moves the pointer off-screen, switches windows, or does other common tasks, the screen must redraw itself. You can stop this time-consuming process in 1-2-3 Release 2/2.01 and Symphony by placing a {WINDOWSOFF} command keyword in your macro. If you want your macro to update the screen at any point, insert the {WINDOWSON} command keyword in the macro.

You can suppress the flicker of menus in the control panel by using the {PANELOFF} and {PANELON} keywords in your macros.

SPEEDIER MACRO SCREEN REDRAW

A *Symphony* macro that requires a significant amount of screen redrawing, which typically occurs because of cursor movement or recalculation, can take a long time to run. However, you can dramatically speed up this process by reducing the size of the current window down to one cell. I have a macro that takes 2.5 minutes to execute with a full-screen window but only 30 seconds with the reduced window.

The {WINDOWSOFF} and {PANELOFF} commands don't seem to have a significant effect on this macro's execution speed.

Dave Gorby
New Haven, Indiana

INCREASING THE NUMBER OF MACROS IN ONE WORKSHEET

Although the *1-2-3* documentation says that you can have only 27 macros in a worksheet (\a through \z and \∅), I have found a way to have as many as I choose. Here is how.

I create my macros and give them descriptive names (like ERASE or SAVE). In a cell named \a, I enter the following macro: /XG{NAME}{?} ~

When I invoke this macro, a menu appears listing all the ranges containing the worksheet's macros. I simply select the desired macro.

Jim Direnki
Cincinnati, Ohio

When you run the macro named \a, all range names will appear — not just the ones that contain macro code — so be careful when selecting a name from the list. You might try prefacing all your macro range names with A so that they appear together at the beginning of the alphabetical list and are clearly identified as macros.

CREATING A SLIDE SHOW

Recently my company held an open house. I knew I couldn't be at my PC all the time, so I wrote an entertaining continuous-run macro in *Symphony*. I "drew" a picture containing information about the company in a SHEET window and copied the picture by selecting the entire screen and paging down to specify the destination range. I changed the second picture a little and repeated the process, creating a series of screens. Then I created a separate window for each picture and wrote a macro that called each window in turn and displayed it for a little while (I used the {WAIT} statement to get the delay). By the time I had finished the macro, I had a self-running slide show advertising the company. It was easy and effective.

Kris Ellingson
Tempe, Ariz.

You can simulate this technique in 1-2-3 by using {GOTO} statements to move the cursor down a screen to get to the next "picture." With Release 1A, you can cause a delay between screens by setting up a loop in the macro that processes several hundred or a thousand times before passing control to the next {GOTO} command. With Release 2/2.01 of 1-2-3, as in Symphony, you can use the {WAIT} command to cause a delay.

2

Menus and Documentations

MACRO REMINDER FILE

I have created a large and complex system of worksheets that I use only occasionally. I find that after I've been away for an extended period and attempt to add a new function to the system, I must relearn and redebug some of the macros. To help me remember what the more complex macros do, I have set up a special file that lists and explains some of the programming routines. This cuts down on the time needed to get back up to speed.

W. J. Mechlenburg
Hylube, Inc.
Pauline, S.C.

Good internal documentation also helps. In the cell to the right of each cell that contains macro code, enter a short explanation of the function of that code.

SAFER MACRO PAUSE

If you want your menu-driven application to pause and require the user to press a key before continuing, but you don't want the user to be able to work on the spreadsheet during the pause, create a single-option menu. If you construct it properly, nothing happens unless the user presses Return or the first letter of the menu choice — in this case, the letter *P*. Even pressing Escape doesn't provide a way out. For example, the following code could be part of a longer *1-2-3* macro:

```
         A              B                           '
37              precedingcode...
38   start    /XMoption~
39            /XGstart~
40   next     followingcode...
41
42   option  Pause
43            Press Return to continue
44            /XGnext~
```

Gavin H. Livingstone
Berlin, Mass.

In Symphony *and* 1-2-3 *Release 2/2.01, the macro would be:*

```
        A               B
37              precedingcode...
38  start       {MENUBRANCH option}
39              {BRANCH start}
40  next        followingcode...
41
42  option Pause
43              Press Return to continue
44              {BRANCH next}
```

1-2-3 *Release 2/2.01, and* Symphony *users have a second option. They can use the* {MENUBRANCH location} *or* {MENUCALL location} *statements instead of the* /XM *command. However, the menu system would be constructed in the same way.*

There are several other commands you can also use to achieve this effect. For example, the {GET} *command causes a macro to pause until someone presses any key. With* Symphony *and* 1-2-3 *Release 2/2.01, you can lock users in even more effectively by using the* {BREAKOFF} *statement to disable the Control-Break key.*

3

Bugs and Debugging

AVOID MACRO BUGS

When creating macros, it is a good idea, particularly if your code contains subroutine calls and also inserts or deletes rows or columns, to place the macro code above the affected row or to the left of the affected column.

Paul D. Rice
North Fork, Calif.

FORBIDDEN MACRO SUBROUTINE RANGE NAMES

Including a range name in {braces} in a *Symphony* or *1-2-3* Release 2/2.01 macro causes the "flow of control" to shift to the top cell of that range. As always, it is best to use descriptive range names in macros and other applications. However, be careful not to use names that are also keywords for keys or macro commands.

When *Symphony* reads a {braced} word in a macro, it checks its table of range names. If the name is there, control passes to the cell in the top-left corner of that range, overriding the normal meaning of the keyword.

For example, if you include the statement {TYPE} in a *Symphony* macro, *Symphony* presses the TYPE key only if there is not a range with that name on the worksheet.

In *1-2-3*, macro key names take precedence. A subroutine named *down* will never process, because *1-2-3* always interprets {DOWN} or {down} to mean "Press the DownArrow key."

DEBUG MACROS WITH {INDICATE}

When I'm having problems with a *1-2-3* Release 2/2.01 macro, I use the {INDICATE} command to pinpoint which portion of the macro is at fault. The {INDICATE} command lets me display as many as five characters in the mode indicator at the top-right corner of the screen.

I use the {INDICATE} command to change the mode indicator both when I change routines within a macro and when I pass control to a new section of macro code. I either display the name of the macro routine in use or, if that name exceeds five characters, use a five-letter abbreviation of it. If the macro fails, the mode indicator shows the name of the offending routine, enabling me to identify where the problem occurred even if I leave my PC while the macro is running.

Donald Cornell
Mobil Chemical Co.
Pittsford, N.Y.

In Symphony *the {INDICATE} command will display as many as seven characters in the mode indicator.*

When a macro ends, the indicator set by the macro will remain until a new {INDICATE} command changes it or until you save and retrieve the file (which resets the indicator). Processing the {INDICATE} command with no argument returns the Ready mode indicator in 1-2-3 *or the window-type indicator in* Symphony. *The command {INDICATE ""} erases the mode indicator entirely.*

PAUSING MACROS

I've discovered that a macro pauses when I hold down the Control key and press the Numberlock key. I can restart the macro by pressing any key. This is a handy feature when I'm debugging macros. I've done this with *1-2-3* Release 1A, but I don't know if it works with other releases of *1-2-3* or *Symphony*.

Kirk Rowland
Garden City, Kan.

This feature extends to 1-2-3 *Release 2/2.01 and to* Symphony *Release 1.1/1.2. However, the increased macro-processing rates in these two programs make it more difficult to press the Pause key precisely where you want to examine or edit the macro. Another effective way to observe a macro while it processes is to press the Step key then start your macro. Now hold down any key to watch the macro run. Where you see a problem, release the key to make the macro pause. Press Control-Break to stop the macro altogether. Now you can edit the macro.*

TESTING MACROS

You can take advantage of the Window command in *1-2-3* and *Symphony* when you build your macros. Create an unsynchronized horizontal window by selecting /Worksheet Window Horizontal and /Worksheet Window Unsynchronized (SER-VICES Window Pane Horizontal in *Symphony*). Position the windows to view both the active worksheet and macro areas simultaneously. Be sure to make the top window current when you run the macro. This approach lets you view the macro commands as the macro runs. You may also put *1-2-3* or *Symphony* in the Step mode while you have two windows on the screen.

Kathy Sachs
Southfield, Mich.

USING THE INSERT KEY

In edit mode, when you press the Insert key, *1-2-3* Release 2/2.01 displays the *Ovr* indicator in the lower-right corner of the screen and allows you to overstrike characters. You can use that feature from within a macro by including the undocumented macro keyword {INSERT} in your macro.

Gaynard O. Nelson
Tempe, Ariz.

In Symphony, *you can activate overstrike mode only from within a DOC window.*

SECTION
15

MEMORY AND SECURITY

Memory may be getting cheaper, but it still isn't free. And many computers still being used don't have enormous amounts of RAM. So making the most efficient use of your computer's existing memory is of vital importance, especially if you're using *1-2-3* Release 1A or if your computer does not have any extended memory boards. Even later releases of *1-2-3* and *Symphony* can leave you memory-bound if you don't pay attention to the way you lay out your worksheet data. The new LIM 4.0 specification should solve many of these problems, but the rest of us need to use every memory trick available. If memory is a problem for you, the first few ideas in this section might make an enormous difference.

But once you've got your data in the worksheet, what then? What if you don't want anyone else to alter or even see it? Just as there is no foolproof lock, there is no unbreakable worksheet security system. Ultimately, the only safe method of data storage is to download everything to a floppy disk, tape drive, or Bernoulli box and then carry it around with you. But if you combine some or all of the methods presented in this section — from changing the file name extension to using passwords — you'll minimize the possibility of unauthorized access.

1

Memory

MEMORY USE PATTERNS IN 1-2-3 AND SYMPHONY

1-2-3 Release 1A and *Symphony* Release 1 can use up to 640K of conventional memory. With either program loaded into your computer, your RAM is structured like this:

Heap
Cell pointer array (CPA)
Add-ins (if any)
Symphony or *1-2-3* (and drivers)
DOS

DOS is located at the lowest memory position. The CPA contains one 4-byte pointer to the address of each cell in the active area of the worksheet. The active area is the rectangle whose upper-left corner is cell A1 and whose lower-right corner is the intersection of the rightmost column and lowest row containing cells that have, or in the current session have had, entries, formats, or protection. Finally, the Heap includes cell contents, window descriptors, settings, range names, and so on.

1-2-3 Release 2.0/2.01 and *Symphony* Release 1.1/1.2 support up to 640K of conventional memory plus an expanded memory board of up to 4 megabytes. With these programs loaded, RAM has this structure:

640K Conventional Memory	Expanded Memory Board
Heap	Cell contents (labels,
Cell array area (CAA)	formulas, floating
Add-ins (if any)	point numbers)
Symphony or *1-2-3* and drivers	
DOS	

292

Cell contents and certain other information are now stored in the expanded memory area and, when that is full, in any unused portions of the Heap. Up to 4 megabytes of information can be stored in the optional expanded memory board.

The CAA is similar to the CPA. It still contains pointers for every cell in the active area. However, the active area is structured differently. Each column of the worksheet is divided into four-cell segments — for example, cells A1..A4.

The CAA looks down every column and allocates memory beginning with the first four-cell segment that contains an active cell and ending with the last four-cell segment that contains an active cell. Because it allocates 4 bytes per cell in each segment, the CAA grows by 16 bytes for every four-cell segment within this active range.

In the example below, an X indicates active cells. The row numbers are arranged to emphasize the concept of the four-cell segments within each column. Assume there is nothing below row 13. The numbers at the bottom of each column represent the number of bytes the CAA uses to store the contents of that column.

	A	B	C	D	E
1		X			
2	X				
3	X				
4					

	A	B	C	D	E
5				X	
6				X	
7				X	
8				X	

	A	B	C	D	E
9					
10				X	
11		X			
12				X	

	A	B	C	D	E
13				X	X

Total CAA = 16 + 48 + 48 + 16 = 128 bytes

Columns B and D each require 48 bytes because their active ranges each contain three segments. In column B the active range begins with the first segment and ends with the third. In column D it goes from the second to the fourth. If columns A through D had no active cells, the total CAA required for this sheet would be only the 16 bytes needed for the segment in column E that contains an active cell.

Note that the CAA memory-allocation system improves memory use efficiency whether or not your computer has an expanded memory board. However, since the CAA must reside in conventional memory, the number of active cells in the worksheet is still limited by the amount of conventional memory available. Suppose that you have 640K of contiguous RAM and that 320,000 bytes are left after allowing for DOS, *Symphony* 1.1, and several windows. Given the CAA's need to use 4 bytes for each active cell, the worksheet could have an actual maximum of 80,000 cells (320,000 divided by 4). With 1 megabyte of expanded memory, the contents of these 80,000 cells could average 12.5 bytes each. With the full load of 4 megabytes of expanded memory, the average rises to 50 bytes per cell.

On the other hand, if you want to have an average of 100 bytes per cell, the full 4 megabytes of expanded memory still would allow you to use a little over 40,000 cells. As cell entries get larger, the limiting factor becomes the amount of expanded memory rather than the availability of conventional memory for the CAA.

DON'T FORMAT EMPTY CELLS

If you've ever found the MEM indicator blinking before you've entered very much data, you should press End then Home to go to the bottom-right corner of the worksheet's active area. The active area is the rectangle in which the upper-left corner is cell A1 and the lower-right is defined by the lowest row and rightmost column in which an activity occurred during the current session. The activities that extend the active area include formatting, protecting, and entering contents into a cell. The size of your worksheet's active area determines how much RAM Release 1A of *1-2-3* and Release 1 of *Symphony* use. Therefore, formatting large areas of the worksheet will use up memory even if you haven't yet entered much data.

To reduce the size of your active area, structure your worksheet in a compact rectangle as close as possible to cell A1. While creating a worksheet, you should occasionally press End-Home. If you find blank rows or columns between the last visible data and the bottom-right corner of the active area, try to discover the cause. Merely deleting the empty rows or columns, however, will not recover the allocated memory. You must also save and then retrieve the file. If this doesn't work, select /File Xtract to pull the part of the worksheet you wish to save into a separate file and then retrieve the file.

SAVE MEMORY, DON'T USE ACCESS

There is an easy way to shorten your startup time and save conventional memory space for larger worksheets. Change to the drive or directory that you start *1-2-3* or *Symphony* from, but instead of typing *lotus* at the DOS prompt, which will get you to the *1-2-3* Access system, simply type in *123*. Likewise for *Symphony*, instead of typing *access*, type in *symphony* at the DOS prompt.

If your computer automatically takes you to the Access sytem when you turn it on, you probably have a file, called AUTOEXEC.BAT, that executes commands to do this. To go directly in to *1-2-3* or *Symphony*, use an editor to change the commands from *lotus* (or *access*) to *123* (or *symphony*). Now every time you start your computer, you will go directly into *1-2-3* or *Symphony*.

DON'T LOSE ACCESS

I read the "Save Memory, Don't Use Access" tip and decided to try it. After following your advice, I wanted to exit to the Utility Disk but could not because Access was not available. Neither was PrintGraph!

John Schiraga
Gloucester, Massachusetts.

To use the Utility or PrintGraph disk, you must leave 1-2-3 *or* Symphony. *The DOS A> or C> prompt should be visible. Now insert the desired disk. If you are using* 1-2-3, *enter* lotus; *if you are using* Symphony, *enter* access. *The Access menu will appear. You can even run PrintGraph without going through Access; type* pgraph *at the DOS prompt. Be sure to have the PrintGraph disk in the specified drive.*

FILE LIST COMMAND FEATURES

Is it possible to discover the available disk space with the File List command? On page 97 of the *1-2-3* Release 2 manual, it states that the File List command displays the space, in bytes, still available on that disk, but I can't find the information on the screen.

W.A. Seedorff Jr.
Mas Minerals Associates
Cupertino, Calif.

You're right, the manuals for 1-2-3 *Release 2/2.01 incorrectly state that the File List command displays the amount of space available on the disk. The File List command in* 1-2-3 *Release 2/2.01 displays the names of Worksheet, Print, Graph, or other files (the menu choice Other displays the name, date, time, and file size of all files in the current directory).* 1-2-3 *Release 1A displays Worksheet, Print and Graph files, as well as available disk space (in bytes).*

To determine the amount of available disk space in 1-2-3 *Release 2/2.01, exit to DOS (or invoke the DOS Command Interpreter by selecting /System) and enter the DOS DIR command. After listing all the file names, bytes, dates and times, the DIR command displays the number of files and the number of bytes free. The number of bytes free equals the amount of available disk space. In all versions of* Symphony, *selecting SERVICES File Bytes displays the amount of available disk space.*

2

Security, Locking, Protection, Hiding, and Restrict Ranges

HIDDEN VALUES

I often need to include a value in a worksheet strictly for reference in calculations, but I don't want it to appear on the screen or in my printout. Assuming that I don't want to place the data or formulas in an out-of-the-way part of the worksheet, one solution is to narrow a column to one character wide. Any value or formula placed in a cell of this column appears and therefore prints as a single asterisk. By reserving an entire column for intermediary calculations, it appears as a border of asterisks separating two adjacent columns.

Tony W. Humphrey
Orange, Tex.

Both Symphony *and* 1-2-3 *Release 2/2.01, permit you to use the Hidden format, which removes cell contents from the screen display, although the empty cells still take up space on the screen.* 1-2-3 *Release 2/2.01, and* Symphony *Release 1.1/1.2, take you one step further. You can use* 1-2-3's /Worksheet Column Hide *command or* Symphony's *MENU Width Hide command to remove entire columns from the display. It's as if you've folded a piece of paper in thirds, then brought the left and right thirds together with the middle third hidden in a loop behind the displayed surface.*

1-2-3 Release 1A is unable to hide a column. However, you may be able to specify one range of your worksheet as your Print Border and another range of your worksheet as your Print range to avoid printing a middle range.

UNPROTECT TO INSERT

After creating an inventory worksheet in *1-2-3*, I selected /Worksheet Global Protection Enable (in *Symphony*, SERVICES Settings Global-Protection Yes) to protect myself against accidental changes. However, when I tried to expand my input area by inserting a row, I got a Protected Cell error message and the command was canceled.I've tried using Range Unprotect (in *Symphony*, MENU Range Protect Allow Changes) on the insertion row, but that doesn't work either.

Bryan S. Bloom
State University Retirement System
Champaign, Illinois

You have to disable protection temporarily to insert new rows or columns. Select /Worksheet Global Protection Disable in 1-2-3. *In* Symphony, *select SERVICES Settings Global-Protection No.*

WORKSHEET SECURITY — I

If you have a confidential file stored on a hard disk or floppy disk, the following *1-2-3* macro reduces the chance of unauthorized viewing: /WEY

I named the macro \0, so it automatically runs when the file is retrieved and immediately erases the worksheet from memory. To gain access, you must press Control-Break as soon as you see the worksheet appear. It's primitive, but it does discourage casual intrusions.

Walter M. Zengen
Salt Point, New York

The comparable Symphony *macro would be {SERVICES}NY. To make it an autoexecuting macro, select SERVICES Settings Auto-Execute, and point to the cell containing the code. However,* Symphony *users could also format confidential data as hidden, globally protect the worksheet, and lock it with a password.*

WORKSHEET SECURITY — II

You can protect *1-2-3* and *Symphony* files from unauthorized retrieval by renaming or eliminating the WKS, WK1, WRK, or WR1 file-name extension. Assuming your data disk is in drive B and you wish to eliminate the extension, save the file, exit to DOS, and enter:

    rename b:filename.wks b:filename

Replace *filename* with the actual name of your file, and replace *wks* with the appropriate extension for your Lotus product.

When you delete or change the file-name extension, the file will not appear on the File Retrieve menu, and because it isn't an ASCII file, it cannot be read with the DOS Type command. To regain access, simply rename it with the appropriate extension, for example:

    rename b:filename b:filename.wks

Patrick Yuen
Pier 39 Partnership
San Francisco, Calif.

Both 1-2-3 Release 2/2.01 and Symphony *let you select File Retrieve and then enter* * * *to provide access to all files. This avoids the need to replace the file-name* *extension. On the other hand, both 1-2-3 Release 2/2.01 and Symphony Release 1.1/1.2 also let you save files with a password to make unauthorized retrieval even more difficult.*

PASSWORD PROTECTION

Is there a way to protect a Lotus worksheet with a password?

Ida Calero
Hewlett-Packard
Aquadilla, Puerto Rico

You can password-protect 1-2-3 Release 2/2.01 and Symphony Release 1.1/1.2 worksheets. Start by selecting /File Save (1-2-3) or SERVICES File Save (Symphony). When the program prompts you for a file name, type the file name, press the Spacebar once, type P, and press Return. The program will then ask you for a password but will not display the password on the screen. Instead, a small box will appear for every character of your password. Your password can be up to 15 characters long. You will then be asked to verify your password. Type it in again.

Passwords are case-sensitive, which means that you must remember whether you typed the password in uppercase or lowercase letters or a combination of the two. Don't forget the password — you won't be able to get into the file without it! Also, don't use a space as the first character of the password. If you do, you won't be able to retrieve your file again. To remove password protection from a file, begin the File Save procedure, and when you are prompted for the password, press Escape and Return to save the file.

CASE-SENSITIVE SECURITY

You can protect files in *1-2-3* Release 2/2.01 using passwords. The manual says, "If you forget the password, however, you cannot retrieve the file." The manual does not tell you, however, that *1-2-3* is case-sensitive when checking passwords. So when you get the error message *Incorrect password*, don't assume your memory is failing and the file is lost. Try entering the password in both uppercase and lowercase letters before you give up hope.

C. Pockney
Palo Alto, Calif.

When checking passwords, 1-2-3 Release 2.01 and Symphony Releases 1.1 and 1.2 are also case-sensitive. 1-2-3 Release 1A does not have the password-security feature.

UNLOCKING WORKSHEET WITH FORGOTTEN PASSWORD

For those of you who have locked a worksheet (SERVICES Settings Security Lock) and then forgotten your password, I've found a way to unlock the worksheet without the password. The technique works in *Symphony* Releases 1.01/1.1. It requires only that global protection is off or, if global protection is on, that there is at least one unprotected cell in the worksheet. Here's how to do it:

First, create a blank worksheet and save it. Then retrieve your locked file. With your cell pointer on an unprotected cell, combine the blank worksheet by selecting SERVICES File Combine Copy Entire-File Ignore Formulas and entering the name of the blank file. Your worksheet is now unlocked.

P.S. Banks
West Midlands, England

PROTECT DATA WITH RESTRICT RANGES

Establishing window Restrict ranges is a good way to protect your data in a multiple-window *Symphony* worksheet. This reduces the chance of your unintentionally altering the contents of one *Symphony* window while working in another window. No matter how many windows you create in a *Symphony* file, they all look at different parts of the same worksheet. Therefore, any operations you do in one window may affect data contained in other windows. Inserting or deleting rows and columns in one SHEET window may have unintended results elsewhere. In addition, many DOC window operations, such as pressing Return or erasing lines, have the same effect upon the worksheet as inserting and deleting rows of a spreadsheet.

You can select the restrict option when you create a new window or when you select SERVICES Window Settings in an existing window. Highlight a Restrict range large enough to contain all the data you wish to enter but small enough not to overlap with the Restrict ranges of other windows that you wish to keep totally separate.

The Restrict range of a window can be as small as one cell or as large as the entire worksheet. Windows can have totally separate Restrict ranges, or their Restrict ranges can overlap in part or whole.

A window Restrict range limits the area of the worksheet accessible through the window while simultaneously limiting the effect of Insert, Delete, and related DOC commands. These commands will only affect the portion of the worksheet within the current window's Restrict range. Other windows will be affected only in the areas where their Restrict ranges overlap the current window's. However, you can insert or delete across the entire worksheet regardless of window Restrict ranges by selecting MENU Insert Global or MENU Delete Global, and then Columns or Rows.

When creating new windows, remember that they inherit the settings of their "parent" window, including Restrict range settings. The parent window is the window that you were in when you created the new one. You must separately assign Restrict ranges to both "parent" and "child" windows.

INDEX